THE SLOW
MEN

Other books by David Frith

Runs in the Family (with John Edrich)
'My Dear Victorious Stod'
The Archie Jackson Story
Great Moments in Cricket (as 'Andrew Thomas', with Norman Harris)
Cricket Gallery
The Fast Men
The Ashes '77 (with Greg Chappell)
England versus Australia: A Pictorial History of the Test Matches since 1877
The Golden Age of Cricket 1890-1914
The Ashes '79
Thommo (with Jeff Thomson)
Rothmans Presents 100 Years England v Australia (with Doug Ibbotson and Ralph Dellor)

THE SLOW MEN

MEN
DAVID FRITH

London
GEORGE ALLEN & UNWIN
Boston   Sydney

George Allen & Unwin (Publishers) Ltd
40 Museum Street, London WC1A 1LU, UK

George Allen & Unwin (Publishers) Ltd
Park Lane, Hemel Hempstead, Herts HP2 4TE, UK

Allen & Unwin Inc
9 Winchester Terrace, Winchester, Mass 01890, USA

George Allen & Unwin Australia Pty Ltd
8 Napier Street, North Sydney, NSW 2060, Australia

First published in 1984

ISBN 0 04 796069 8

Printed in Hong Kong

Contents

Illustrations

Main Sources

Arlott, John *John Arlott's Cricket Journal 2* (Heinemann)

Bassano, Brian *South Africa in International Cricket 1888-1970* (Chameleon)

Beldam, George W. & Fry, Charles B. *Great Bowlers and Fielders: Their Methods at a Glance* (Macmillan)

Berry, Scyld *Cricket Wallah* (Hodder & Stoughton)

Brittenden, R.T. *New Zealand Cricketers* (A.H. & A.W Reed)

Chappell, Ian, Robertson, Austin & Rigby, Paul *Chappelli Laughs Again* (Lansdowne)

Cozier, Tony *Benson & Hedges West Indies Cricket Annual* (Caribbean Communications)

Foot, David *From Grace to Botham* (Redcliffe)

Frindall, Bill *The Wisden Book of Cricket Records* (Queen Anne)

Gavaskar, Sunil *Sunny Days: An Autobiography* (Rupa)

Hordern, H.V. *Googlies* (Angus & Robertson)

Laker, Jim *A Spell from Laker* (Hamlyn)

Laker, Jim *Spinning Round the World* (Muller)

Lock, Tony *For Surrey and England* (Hodder & Stoughton)

Mailey, Arthur *10 for 66 and All That* (Phoenix)

Marriott, C.S. *The Complete Leg-Break Bowler* (Eyre & Spottiswoode)

Marshall, John *Sussex Cricket* (Heinemann)

McCool, Colin *Cricket is a Game* (Stanley Paul)

McGlew, Jackie *Cricket for South Africa* (Howard Timmins)

Mukherjee, Sujit *Playing for India* (Orient Longman)

Parkin, Cecil *Parkin on Cricket* (Hodder & Stoughton)

Payne, Francis *Rothmans New Zealand First-Class Cricket*

Peebles, Ian *Spinner's Yarn* (Collins)

Pollard, Jack *Australian Cricket: The Game and the Players* (Hodder & Stoughton)

Reddick, Tom *Never a Cross Bat* (Nelson)

Thomas, Peter *Yorkshire Cricketers 1839-1939* (Hodgson)

Underwood, Derek *Beating the Bat: An Autobiography* (Stanley Paul)

Whitington, R.S. *Time of the Tiger: The Bill O'Reilly Story* (Stanley Paul)

Wynne-Thomas, Peter *Nottinghamshire Cricketers 1821-1914* and *1919-1939*

Wisden Cricketers' Almanack

Cricket Scores & Biographies

Cricket: A Weekly Record of the Game

Various publications by the Association of Cricket Statisticians

In every branch of sport you'll find a man with talent rare,
Who plays for fun and shuns the solemn game;
And with sturdy independence, and superb, outrageous flair,
Finds an everlasting place in world acclaim.

With gnarled and leathery face, expression bland, and hazel eyes,
At any kind of joke he never smiled;
His technique was to convince men that he would not bowl them lies,
And the trusting souls were lost, perplexed, beguiled.

Descending from the stratosphere, a full-toss he'd produce,
On a vicious, spinning, dipping change of course;
Or an evil, bounding long-hop that so often would reduce
A mighty blow to wasted, mistimed force.

His fame is not in bowling deeds, but how he lived and played;
You'll find that many men have passed his score;
But no-one will eclipse the carefree impact that he made,
For they don't make them like Mailey any more.

Les Bailey

1. Smiling Villains

It would take a panel of learned sociologists and psychologists to establish why slow, spin bowling has gone out of favour — and only then if they understood cricket in all its subtleties. The game has always trotted obediently behind society as it has altered in mood and attitude. Perhaps only once, when Bosanquet and his disciples horrified the purists with the deception of the googly ball, viewed by some in those Edwardian days as cheating, did cricket's moral history move ahead of that of the world at large. Such a development belonged more typically to the modern age, when arch-professionalism is excused on the grounds that money is as oxygen, and success secures it — by fair means or 'professional foul'.

Even in the Caribbean territories, where Ramadhin and Valentine — folk heroes but actually the top pair out of thousands of similar practitioners of spin bowling — once were the beloved cynosure, now the fast bowlers, file upon file of them, are the heroes. The lad in the dusty street in Bridgetown or on the beach in Trinidad who wishes to bowl slowly is regarded as having a mental problem akin to retardation.

'One may smile, and smile, and be a villain,' quoth Hamlet; and this, rather than an incurable fascination over Iverson's mystery spin bowling, should have absorbed a lad's attention in the schoolroom in 1951. Shakespeare had something here, even though the cunning of the slow bowler may not have been much in evidence in English meadows in the 16th Century. 'At least I'm sure it may be so in Denmark,' the immortal blond-haired prince goes on to expound. The art of spin bowling, with the bland smile of the 'villain' that goes with it, was taken wherever the British flag was planted, and came back to haunt those who designed it. By 1982 there was barely a wrist-spinner to be seen in English first-class cricket. The West Indies Test team had crushed all opposition with its panzer division of fast bowlers, and on the 1981 tour of England, Australia used their sole spinner, Ray Bright, as a relief bowler while the fast men rested. Grim-faced, keen to back their physical assault with verbal jibes, the muscular men who bowled at 85 to 100 m.p.h. ruled world cricket by means of denial and brutality, while the crafty schemers with the tantalising loops and range of smiles — rueful when hit for six, smug and gently sinister when successful in their evil plans — were verging on extinction.

The game was the loser. Both the spectator and the batsman were deprived of a richness, for much more cricket is crammed into an afternoon of spin bowling: and with it a delicious variety. Skilled batsmen will punish loose bowling — all the harder if it is slow. The gradation of a day's cricket, begun with new-ball thrills as athletic fast bowlers operate and continued as the slow men take over, knows no parallel in terms of entertainment value. For those who can remember and for those who are too young ever to have known it, it is hoped that the cavalcade of personalities which follows will illustrate what an atrophied spectacle cricket threatens to become if the march towards extinction continues.

Fathers, schoolteachers, coaches, selectors and captains share an incalculable responsibility. Every young spinner turned into a colourless medium-pacer constitutes a crime against a beautiful game. Do the perpetrators not realise that a finely-tuned spinner, in regular practice, is unlikely to be significantly more expensive than a fast-medium bowler on a good pitch? Or that one wicket for seven or eight runs is, most times, more valuable than a maiden over?

A blind lament for a resurgence of spin bowling *per se* deserves to be stillborn. The cry is for a restoration of *balance* and *variety*. The sociologists may point to the world at large: global war, if it comes, will be waged by push-buttons and nuclear bombs. War as our grandfathers knew it was made by infantry, artillery and cavalry, augmented by off-shore bombardment and relatively light air combat. All the fun of the fair.

Trueman, Statham, Laker and Lock. . .or Gregory, McDonald, Mailey and Macartney. . .or McCarthy, Chubb, Rowan and Mann. . .or King, Worrell, Ramadhin and Valentine. Scowls and smiles; pace like fire and curling flight; the mixture is potent, the afterglow incomparable.

2. New Tricks

Lamborn — Tom Walker — William Lambert —
'Old Clarke' — William Lillywhite and
the roundarm revolution

It is as natural to bowl leg-spin underarm as it is to bowl off-spin overarm. Thus, in the early days of cricket as a popular pastime, it was not uncommon to see a bowler striving not merely for pace on those rough surfaces, but also for deviation from leg to off. In Hambledon days, so known because of the game's prominence around that Hampshire village in the 18th Century, bowlers chose the stretch of turf upon which the match would be played. Lumpy Stevens demonstrated the injustice of beating a batsman repeatedly only to see the ball shoot through the two stumps; so the middle stump was introduced soon after 1775. Scores were low by modern standards, so many factors being in favour of the bowler. The batsman wore hardly any protection. He was considered 'shabby' if he got his legs in the way of the ball. And the problem of hitting any great distance with the unsprung, hockey-type bats must have been daunting. There was little need for bowlers to try anything beyond hurling the projectile straight at the wicket, though 'bias' was often noted, almost certainly the product of a ball's indirect course when rolled along the ground.

Skilled batsmen, on the better pitches, would have been confident against slower bowling, even if it had a twist from leg. (Tom Boxall was probably the first exponent of respectable underarm leg-spin.) The earliest leg-breaks, if closely-observed, would have been innocent, since they were the only variant from the straight-up-and-down delivery. Imagine, then, the alarm created by the pioneer of underarm off-spin.

His name was Lamborn, and time has cheated us of his forename. Born in 1761, he enjoyed a brief fame, bowling for Hambledon between 1777 and 1781. He was, John Nyren wrote in his much-blessed chronicle of the times, 'a plain-spoken little bumpkin', and he developed his skill by hours of practice against a hurdle while tending his father's sheep. 'Very civil and inoffensive', he became known as 'the Little Farmer', and when Nyren senior started coaching him, pointing out what perhaps was patently obvious, he moved his line from leg stump to off stump, and began to trouble even the best of batsmen.

'Ah, it was tedious near you, sir!' has become a famous line of script. It was Lamborn's irreverent but understandable exclamation when an off-spinner deceived the Duke of Dorset and whizzed past the leg stump. His familiarity and broad Hampshire accent, far from shocking all within earshot into apprehensive silence, sent the gathering into gleeful laughter.

When Lamborn's father died he had to take over the running of the farm at Selsey. Like another cricketer in the years ahead, he was compelled to put livelihood before recreation. The work did him no harm. He lived to be 85.

One comment of Nyren's leaves a flashing question-mark over Lamborn's technique: 'I have never seen but one bowler who delivered his balls in the same way as our Little Farmer; with the jerkers the practice is not uncommon.' Were the 'jerkers' really off-spinners, already making their presence felt? And was Lambom, therefore, as a 'mystery man', the first bowler of the 'googly' or 'wrong'un'?

'Egad!' wrote Nyren of the Little Farmer's bowling, 'this new trick of his so bothered the Kent and Surrey men that they tumbled out one after another, as if they had been picked off by a rifle corps.'

A hundred and twenty-three years later, 'Plum' Warner, writing of Bosanquet, exuded a similar kind of pride: 'He can bowl as badly as anyone in the world, but, when he gets a length, those slow ''googlies'', as the Australian papers call them, are apt to paralyse the greatest players.'

Slowly the game matured as bowling became more varied and batsmen met the challenge, encouraged by coaches such as Harry Hall, the Farnham gingerbread baker, who believed passionately in the 'left-elbow-up' edict. There had been little point in batting defensively. On rough pitches and with a wicket two feet wide and a foot high to protect, life was short. Fennex and Beldham showed what quick and intelligent use of the feet could achieve in countering the better-length ball, but great store was held in the ball which rose swiftly from the turf — a rare achievement from an underarm bowler. David Harris, the champion fast-medium bowler, could do it; and so could the Reverend Lord Frederick Beauclerk, an autocratic gentleman, descendant of Charles II and Nell Gwynn, who bowled slows with much success — though his nerves were not improved by a cannonball straight-drive from John Hammond, a Sussex left-hander who believed in advancing to the pitch of the ball — so long as it wasn't a daisycutter!

Another irony in the career of the irascible and corruptible Beauclerk occurred in a three-a-side match at Lord's in 1806. His Lordship had introduced sawdust as a preferable drying agent to coaldust on wet grounds, and when this particular match seemed won — and with it a useful side-wager — he suddenly found himself bowled by a ball from 'Silver Billy' Beldham which turned the proverbial mile. The deviation, though, owed not so much to Beldham's prowess as a spinner as to the blob of mud and sawdust the bowler had squeezed against one side of the ball.

The assessment of all bowlers about this time depends upon the written word rather than upon figures, for only the fielders and wicketkeepers were credited with dismissals, the bowler's name appearing only when his victim was bowled. Again, Nyren's opinion is invaluable. Of Tom Walker, one of the earliest 'stonewall' batsmen and forerunner of the revolutionary roundarm bowlers, he wrote that he was 'one of the most fox-headed fellows I ever saw' — this when the tall Tom, 'Old Everlasting', had switched to slow lob bowling. One of a famous brotherhood from Thursley, near Hindhead, Tom made Beldham feel ashamed of his 'baby bowling'. It worked for a time, though, as such tactics to this day are liable to work against batsmen of less than top quality.

Two other batsmen of renown also had marked success as slow bowlers, though their characters were in contrast. William Ward, the upright gentleman, director of the Bank of England, Member of Parliament, and holder of the record score at Lord's (278) from 1820 to 1925, bowled as a banker might be expected to bowl. He once achieved 17 successive maiden overs. He also rendered cricket's eternal indebtedness by saving Lord's with an injection of money just as it was about to be sold off for development. William Lambert, on the other hand, from being the finest batsman in England, fell from grace when smeared by allegations that he sold a match at Lord's.

Lambert, a Surrey man, was the first to score two centuries in a match, and at 5ft 10ins and 15 stone, he batted with an intimidating effect such as might bear comparison with Ian Botham's aggression in our own time. As a bowler during those Napoleonic years, Lambert was one of those who preferred to raise the arm some distance from the side, so that, while not one of the rising roundarm brigade, nor was he strictly an underarm bowler. He turned from leg, the ball helped on its crooked way by one of the largest hands in the business.

Another hand which cast a spell over countless batsmen in the last quarter of the 18th Century was that of Robert Clifford, of Kent. The two smaller fingers of his right hand were pressed into the palm by a childhood accident. As we shall see, there were others in more recent times whose spinning ability was improved by digital handicap.

A claimant for the title 'best slow bowler in England' (not his own claim) was John Sparks, another to bowl closer to roundarm than underarm, a purveyor of leg-spin, with 'something peculiar' in his delivery. A small man, originally a gamekeeper, he coached at Cambridge and later at the Lansdown Club, Bath before taking up a coaching position at the Grange Club, Edinburgh, where he was to 'do everything' for £20 a summer, paying his own fare to and from Scotland. By now he was 57, but his skills were legendary, and only when he was into his seventies was he replaced at the nets by a Catapulta bowling machine.

The giant figure among scheming bowlers had by now chiselled his name into history. William Clarke, born in Bunker's Hill, Nottingham on Christmas Eve, 1798, played cricket as a youth, but had to wait until he was in his forties before national recognition came his way. Here was one of the most acute cricketing brains. Allied to what Haygarth called a 'cruelly deceptive' slow ball, which, launched from near the armpit, might turn from leg after an interesting flight and which bounced disconcertingly, was an analytical mind in the Illingworth-Benaud-Brearley class. 'Old Clarke' used to walk around the practice nets on the morning of a match, hands tucked under coat-flaps, observing the opposition planning, counting his wickets in advance, 'psyching' some of them, much as Fred Trueman enjoyed doing. He reckoned to be able to work out the 'exact pitch' fatal to any batsman, dropping the ball on the 'blind spot' he believed every player to have, irrespective of style and reach. Pycroft wrote that Clarke delivered the ball from the hip, 'with a little chuck or fling from the hand'. He also recalled that he preferred bowling from the pavilion end at Lord's so that the slope would arrest some of his sharp leg-spin.

The placing of his field was awesomely shrewd. He was the first in the line which was taken from his century, the 19th, into the 20th by Wilfred Rhodes, master of the art of trapping the unsuspecting. The prime belief of this school was that many batsmen can be got out by overplaying their strength in certain strokes: their execution came as a penalty for their inability to pick the subtle change in delivery. This ball looked the same as the last, which was hit to the boundary but. . .

Clarke, who learned most of his craft from William Lambert, was a solidly-built fellow, invariably bedecked in a tall hat, and favoured with sight only in one eye since an accident while playing fives when a young man. The damage caused when the ball hit his right eye was irreparable. Still, though the roundarm bowling fashion spread rapidly after its legalisation, Clarke continued to trundle, his great days still ahead of him when most cricketers would have been thinking of retirement. A widower, he had married widow Chapman, and, having already forsaken bricklaying for the life of a publican, he took over the running of his wife's pub, the Trent Bridge Inn, and laid out the cricket field at the back to a high standard of groundsmanship. Big matches began to be staged there — the locals had to get used to paying an admission fee — and eventually it became the county club's home ground, and the stage for many a Test match.

Within a few years, however, Clarke, having taken a benefit match in 1843, had moved down to London, taking up a position, at the age of 47, of practice bowler for the MCC at Lord's. There may have been an ulterior motive, though, for at the end of his first season in London, 1846, he advertised his first England XI match. Having gathered together the most prominent players of the day, he now embarked on gospel-spreading and money-making tours of the country. Here was the prototype for Mr Packer 130 years later.

Cricket was carried to the furthest corners of the land as Clarke's All-England XI, rich in talent and replete with famous names, played local teams of 22, 18, 16 or 14. Whatever the number, the villagers were invariably outplayed and overawed. Clarke bowled almost non-stop — he seemed never to know when to take himself off — and took 2385 wickets in the seven seasons 1849 to 1855, with 426 in the 1854 season his best. Just as impressive was the sum of money he made each year, the profit from which displeased some of his players, many of whom found the going hard. Arduous and seemingly interminable travel by rail and coach and poor after-care following a heavy cold led to the death of one, William Dorrinton, from Kent, at the age of 39. Payment of £4 to £6 per match was insufficient to prevent some of Clarke's men from joining John Wisden's breakaway group in 1852.

Clarke's vision and business acumen led, in a way, to the expansion of the game overseas, for it was his successor at the head of the All-England XI, George Parr, who took the first English team abroad, to North America in 1859, and another to Australia in 1863.

Clarke played for Nottinghamshire for the last time in 1855, when he was in his 57th year. His first game for the county had been played 39 years earlier, when he was only 17. His last match of all, a year later, found him with typical wilfulness taking a wicket with his final ball. He died that August in London, and was buried at Norwood, where there is no tombstone to mark the final resting place of one of cricket's major figures.

Older by a few years, and at least equally important in bowling's development was F. W. (William) Lillywhite, who, although a slow bowler, owed his inclusion in *The Fast Men* to his part in the revolution from underarm to roundarm bowling. Earlier a bricklayer, like 'Old Clarke', he was born near Chichester in 1792 and moved to Brighton at the age of thirty. Back in 1807, John Willes, inspired by the bowling of his sister, Christina, which came awkwardly at the bat after the roundarm delivery forced upon her by the voluminous crinolines, decided to use this method in a 'first-class' match. His raised bowling hand caused outrage — and serious thought. This, surely, was the answer to the growing skills of batsmen, the best of whom were often able to toy with what was now beginning to seem 'namby-pamby' underarm. Others emulated Willes; not that it did him much good. He was ostracised and eventually hounded from the game.

Thus, the roundarm movement, which had been hinted at by Tom Walker before he resigned himself to bowling slows, and which had been given a fateful shove by Willes, now needed finishing off, and the opinionated, determined Lillywhite was the man to complete the job. With Sussex colleague Jem Broadbridge, a bachelor farmer from Duncton who bowled fast-medium, Lillywhite, known as 'The Nonpareil', all five-foot-four of him, set up a three-match series of experimental matches, Sussex v All-England, to prove that legalising roundarm bowling would be the best thing that could happen.

After defeats at Sheffield and Lord's, the England team were choking with indignation. They refused to play the final match at Brighton unless the Sussex pair bowled 'fair — i.e. abstain from throwing'.

A team was got up, all the same, and Lillywhite should not have been displeased when Sussex lost this one, for it showed that the 'new' bowling was not insuperable. The cause was taken up by G. T. Knight in a series of persuasive letters to the *Sporting Magazine*, and though resistance came from such as John Nyren, William Ward, Thomas Lord and player-journalist William Denison, MCC modified Rule 10 in the spring of 1828. Henceforth the bowler's hand could be raised as high as elbow-level, with the back of the hand uppermost if required. This dispensation, interpreted strictly, forbade bowling of the Lillywhite-Broadbridge type because they wheeled their arms through horizontally. But umpires allowed it, perhaps sensing that MCC had been timid and that fully roundarm bowling was inevitable. Nyren feared that the change would mean that 'the elegant and scientific game of cricket will degenerate into a mere exhibition of rough, coarse horseplay!' Was he looking down from Heaven when progress was reversed at Melbourne on February 1, 1981 as Trevor Chappell won his Australian team copious prizemoney by bowling underarm to shocked and helpless New Zealander Brian McKechnie?

Bowling still had a long way to go, of course; and yet the next step was soon taken. MCC, then as now custodians of the laws of cricket, legalised roundarm, i.e. up to the level of the shoulder, bowling in 1835. There followed more liberties on the part of bowlers, many of whom blatantly bowled from a higher level still. In 1845 came the final freedom. The ball could be bowled in such a way that the bowler could practically brush his knee at one extreme of variation or his ear at the other — always provided that he informed the umpire of a change of action. Overarm bowling had arrived.

Through these transitions, few bowlers changed their styles. Once a roundarm bowler, it seemed, always a roundarm bowler. Even in relatively modern cricket there have been international bowlers who raised their arms barely above the horizontal. A dipping of the left shoulder created a compensatory elevation, so that not only the likes of Grimmett and Illingworth, but a fast bowler like Andy Roberts could obtain bounce.

Lillywhite, though, was the truculent little 'giant' who gave evolution its momentum. By 1837, the historic roundarm amendment now firmly written into the statute book, he had taken over the Royal Sovereign pub in Brighton and become proprietor of a cricket ground; but by 1844 he was in financial trouble; so, aged 52, he took an engagement as a groundstaff bowler at Lord's, still doubtless claiming that 'I bowls the best ball in England, and I suppose if I was to think every ball, they'd never get a run!' His skill stayed with him. Bowling averages were being more carefully kept, and though much of his early achievement was lost in vague recording, it was established that in one rich three-year period he took 685 wickets with his 'peculiars', which included the hypnotic delivery, the 'tice', a dropping ball; and in 1841 he had the satisfaction of taking nine wickets in an innings for Slow Bowlers v Fast Bowlers at Lord's. So much cricket did he continue to play that at the age of 60 he had 275 innings.

He could bat, but didn't bother. His professed genius was for bowling (which he pronounced to rhyme with 'howling'). 'Look here, sir,' he once addressed an argumentative captain, 'when I've bowled the ball, I've done with hur, and I leaves hur to my field!' Slow to praise others, like many a 'star', Lillywhite did concede that Charles Harenc of Kent, who changed his pace cleverly, was second only to himself.

So skilful was he that not a dozen wides floated from his hand in 27 seasons of cricket. This is something to be considered, for roundarm bowling is the hardest of all to control. Tom Emmett's wides were a perennial joke, just as those flung down by the mighty Alfred Mynn were a source of much relief to the trembling batsman.

Roundarm bowlers very often operated from around the wicket so as to avoid striking the umpire with the low arm. This, alongside the propensity to bowl wides, was seen by some as a disadvantage, and it was thought that many a young player who took up roundarm bowling, because it was in vogue, might have been better off bowling underarm. The game unquestionably lost disenchanted players through this, but it was all part of the price of evolution. For the time being and all through the 1840s and 1850s, fast bowling remained the pre-eminent practice.

A further question beckons. Why were so many of the leading bowlers — Clarke and Lillywhite paramount — middle-aged when they dominated the game? The answer surely was that the most important organ in slow bowling — as in sex, or so we are told by modern counsellors — is the brain. A fast bowler cannot get along with this alone, and indeed, on the evidence of some, can prosper with less than a moderate supply. But the slow bowler? Cunning...pure cunning. Plus accuracy.

'Three balls out of four straight is what we calls mediogrity,' said Lillywhite, who hammered home his point when someone boasted that he could land the ball on a piece of paper: 'Yes, but *I* could shift the paper and still hit it!'

To cunning and accuracy must be added confidence, and Old Clarke, like 'Nonpareil' Lillywhite, had much of this. Clarke knew, as did most *aficionados*, that Fuller Pilch was the finest batsman in England. He knew, too, that no-one played his bowling as well as did Pilch. And, he claimed, with the scoresheets to back him, Pilch never mastered him. The talented Surrey and England cricketer William Caffyn may best have assessed Clarke's strength when he suggested that the slower balls were simple enough, but the threat of the well-disguised fast ball played on batsmen's minds.

Perhaps part of Clarke's secret was diet. At lunch he would partake of soda-water and a cigar: 'most satisfying, with no after-effects of indigestion'. The cigar once came in useful to put a railway porter in his place. As the official called to the stationmaster for assistance in persuading Clarke to extinguish the cigar in a non-smoking compartment, he stubbed it out on the back of the porter's hand.

In the evening, when he usually dined alone, he often demolished a complete duck — perhaps in commemoration of the batting performances of a cluster of his opponents that afternoon.

Many a likeness of Clarke hangs still in drawing-rooms, static lithographs which must produce many a condescending smile — similarly for the picture of the obviously short Lillywhite, in his top-hat and cotton braces, and with his beer-drinker's waistline. But those who had to bat against them never laughed, not with sincerity. 'There will be a terrible accident,' the Nonpareil used to mutter as he watched indiscretions at the batting end (those with a greater bent for caricature would put an 'h' on 'accident'); and so often he was right. Consider Lillywhite's cold analysis of his trade, as expressed in a handbook published in 1844: 'By holding the ball slightly askew, with the thumb well across the seam, you will find by working the wrist as the ball leaves the hand, it will assist to cut and rick at the wicket, such balls are very troublesome to stop, to get rid of.'

Consider, too, the arrogant pride in his art implicit in the contempt Clarke expressed for a schoolmaster who wanted his public school pupils all to be fast bowlers: distraught at seeing so many promising cricketers steered into a 'wild style of bowling', he described it as nothing short of 'cruelty to animals'. Nor was he famed for passing on tips. Asked by a venerable grocer how he should set out to become a good bowler, Clarke replied: 'Get your fingernails cut.'

A further measure of his stature is that Nicholas Wanostrocht ('Felix') wrote a booklet, *How to Play Clarke*. Not even Jim Laker has received that kind of accolade.

Back to Lillywhite, though, for the supreme example of pride: 'Have me to bowl, Box to keep wicket, and Pilch to hit, and then you'll see cricket!' That combination (Box, of course, without pads or gloves) is portrayed in W. H. Mason's large and popular drawing Cricket Match between Sussex and Kent at Brighton. To the casual eye the threat to the masterly batsman Pilch from the diminutive, innocuous-looking Lillywhite seems slight. Contemporaries knew otherwise.

William Lillywhite's grave, unlike Clarke's, was marked by a noble obelisk paid for from public subscription, at Highgate Cemetery, and a glimpse of the shop bearing the family name, near Piccadilly Circus, seldom fails to send across the brain a flashing subliminal vision of 'Old Lilly', the man who helped substantially to put Sussex cricket on the map and to make slow bowling the art we know.

3. A Flea in a Bed

James Cobbett — V.E. Walker — R.C. Tinley —
lob bowlers

Champions provide inspiration, and slow bowling began to spread under the influence of the master performers, Clarke and Lillywhite. The classifications could be discerned: the canny, thinking bowlers, scheming, mean; the extravagant spinners, caring little for accuracy but much for prodigious turn, happy to beat wicketkeeper as well as batsman in demonstration of their power of wrist.

James Cobbett spun the ball 'like a top'. Born in Frimley, Surrey in 1804, he was a 'practice bowler' at Lord's for many years, playing in many important matches and reaping rewards with a method described colourfully in Pycroft's *The Cricket Field*: 'Cobbett gave the ball as much spin as possible: his fingers appeared wrapped round the ball: his wrist became horizontal: his hand thrown back at the delivery, and his fingers seemingly unglued joint by joint, till the ball quitted the tips of them last.' The delivery 'designed a spin, and the ball at the pitch had new life in it. No bowling so fair, and with so little rough play or violence, ever proved more effective than Cobbett's.'

It takes little imagination to visualise the sort of panic such bowling could induce in batting of less than the first order. Here was the Jack Walsh of his day, making the ball buzz, and conceivably turning more than one way. Poor Cobbett was dead at 38. Not for him the middle-aged triumphs such as befell Clarke and Lillywhite. He died in his bat shop in Lisson Grove, and was one of the earliest cricketers to have the sport recognised on his gravestone. At Kensal Green cemetery some fellow players saw to it that his virtues were extolled: 'Now mouldering here is one that was a man, whose name shone brilliant as through life he ran...'

Then there was John Bayley, who served MCC and Mitcham, and played in many an important match. A big man, he approached the crease in a 'shuffle', neither run nor walk, which Alfred D. Taylor compared with that of a tired waiter in a cheap restaurant. In keeping with the growing tradition, he gained his greatest successes from his late thirties onwards. A tailor by trade, he played for over 30 years before turning to umpiring.

A would-be historymaker was William Mathews, born in Guildford in 1793, who claimed to be the first to bowl high, slow roundarm. He was said to be very graceful, a tall man, strongly-built, 'very respectful and cheerful when in the field', his action 'like a well-regulated piece of machinery' — for one always looking for comparisons, perhaps an early Emburey.

An early example of exasperation in a batsman as he tried to deal with slow bowling of distinct cunning came from the autocratic Harrovian, the Honourable Robert Grimston, who, with his peculiar grip, the backs of both hands facing away from the bowler, bellowed at the Reverend John Frederick Fagge of Kent: 'I wish that Fred Fagge was dead!' 'What a bloodthirsty expression!' someone observed. 'Well,' said Grimston on second thoughts, 'I don't wish him *dead*, but I wish they would make him a bishop, so that we should see him no more.' Many a batsman since, embarrassed and strangulated by the precise curling menace of slow bowling, will have had related thoughts.

Many of the leading batsmen of the early Victorian age dabbled at bowling, the formalities of cricket as played then being less rigid. Charles G. Taylor, whose brilliant batsmanship was likened to that of Ranjitsinhji 40 or so years later, bowled a ball which Pilch declared hopped 'like a flea in a bed'. Like Pilch, he was once dismissed 'hat knocked on wicket' when his elegant white silk hat toppled from his noble head. An all-round sportsman of great repute, he could, it was said, match anyone at billiards, and could beat anyone at tennis, 'with a bottle for a racquet if necessary'. What was spinning a cricket ball after all that?

A genuine all-rounder, though, and probably the best in the world by 1860, was Vyell Edward Walker, one of seven brothers whose exploits and organisational capacities put Middlesex cricket on the map. V.E., known as Teddy, was the fifth son of a country squire, and was born in 1837. The Arnos Grove estate at Southgate, north of London, became a key venue, many important matches being staged there, with the Walker brothers prominent as players and hosts.

Teddy started his schooling at Stanmore, where a master attracted him by example to slow bowling. At Harrow he bowled roundarm, but when success was slow in coming, he changed to fastish underhand. Soon he was experimenting with slow lobs, interspersed with a fast ball each over (warning his slip fielder with a tug of his cap, the slip then sliding off to longstop). He preferred bowling round the wicket as he was apt to scrape his knuckles on the stumps.

He had a stooped run to the wicket, and put on just enough break — either way — to beat the bat. Nor was he afraid to toss up an absurdly high ball whose parabolic flight tested all but the coolest batsman. At the age of only 22 he made his first major impression on the record books.

Teddy Walker, large-eyed, wide of mouth, with sidewhiskers and a centre parting, brought off a then-unique feat at The Oval in July 1859. Captaining England against the strong Surrey XI, he took all 10 wickets in the first innings for 74 runs — and had the not-out batsman, Julius Caesar, dropped! Having scored 20 not out, he then made a chanceless 108 in the second innings and finished off his opponents with 4 for 17. Only three men

— E. M. Grace, W. G. Grace and the Australian, Frank Tarrant — have since scored a century and taken all 10 wickets in an innings in one and the same match.

Walker took another all-10 six years later, against Lancashire at Old Trafford, having taken all 10 Gentlemen of Kent wickets at Maidstone the previous season in a match denied first-class status. There was more to his skills than perplexing flight and variations: he was one of the most athletic — and brave — fielders to his own bowling, often racing up the pitch in pursuit of a caught-and-bowled, and occasionally hanging on to fierce drives headed for his face or other cherished parts. Once he took a catch off his own bowling at backward short leg, and another astonishing manoeuvre saw him running out the non-striking batsman with a reverse throw between his legs after he had gathered a driven ball.

V. E. Walker was a complete cricketer in that he excelled in all departments, including captaincy. A shrewd tactician, he was invariably philosophical about dropped catches, a quality which must have helped erring fieldsmen to face the next chance with better levels of confidence than if they had received an earful of censure.

Comparisons were naturally made between Walker and the great Clarke of the previous generation, and naturally most oldtimers voted for Clarke. But one of the changes that had overtaken batting between the years of Clarke and of Walker was that batsmen (with the exception of Caesar and a few others) were earlier reluctant to run forward to slow bowling — either on moral grounds or because of technical doubts — whereas the method was accepted by the 1870s. Walker thus had more adept and inventive batsmanship to overcome, more initiative. On that count he had some support as the finest slow bowler the game had seen to that point. He was modest towards his talents all his days, and, much respected, became MCC president in 1891. He died in 1906, aged 68.

In 1860, Middlesex cricket-lovers and others had much pride in the Walkers, V.E. chief among them, and belief that he was the best of cricketers. Further north, however, there were strong claims laid for Robert Crispin Tinley, a small Nottinghamshire man, born in 1830, and firstly a bowler of real speed. His career began before he was 17, and by the time he was 26, he was dispensing his slow underhand deliveries — and making runs with a powerful straight bat — for the All-England XI. With the terrifying express bowler John Jackson bowling opposite Cris Tinley, the attack, it was said, consisted of 'a corkscrew at one end and a thunderbolt at the other'.

Tinley took enough wickets, especially against the local teams of odds, to satisfy even the greediest ego, and kept up his rate when he toured Australia with George Parr in 1863-64: in 33 innings he collected over 250 wickets of bush batsmen at less than five apiece.

Richard Daft described Tinley as being 'like Ulysses, full of wiles'; he was 'quick and active as a kitten to field his own bowling'; and could almost make the ball talk on a helpful wicket. His attitude was doubtless similar to that of his illustrious Nottingham predecessor, William Clarke, who replied to the enquiry as to how he would get a certain batsman out with: 'Nothing easier, sir: I bowl him three balls to make him proud of his forward play, and then with the fourth I pitch shorter, twist, and catch him at the slip.' He would have used the width of the crease, too, which in those days was only three feet, and was one of the earliest recorded exploiters of the ruse whereby the ball was bowled from a yard or so behind the crease, often producing catches from premature forward strokes.

Tinley, one of the talented band of Notts professionals, looks serenely out of an 1862 group photograph, handsome in a rural way, neat in bow-tie, with spotted shirt and black ankle-boots (he later sported an Abe Lincoln beard). A ball rests on both index fingers, the tool of his trade, displayed like a navigator's sextant or a doctor's stethoscope. 'The Spider', George Parr called him, and almost 400 'flies' were trapped in his web in major matches.

Around this time, Henry Arkwright, a gentleman cricketer who became aide-de-camp to three Lord Lieutenants of Ireland, was confusing batsmen with slow, curving roundarm deliveries. After some dazzling performances for Cambridge, MCC, the Gentlemen and I Zingari, he might have played for England had he not been killed, at 28, by an avalanche while climbing Mont Blanc.

Most of the eminent lob-bowlers were, like V. E. Walker, amateurs, and two of them, W. B. Money and E. T. Drake, became ministers of the church, their ordination taking them from the first-class game since it was not thought fitting for a man of the cloth. Drake took too much punishment too often to rank with the top names, but Money performed a hat-trick for Harrow against Eton at Lord's in 1866, and was Cambridge captain in 1870 when the thrilling 'Cobden's match' was won by two runs. With Oxford needing three to win with three wickets in hand, F. C. Cobden dismissed the last three batsmen in as many balls and was carried round the ground in triumph. The match was of a similarly sensational nature to the Test match at Headingley in 1981, when Botham, Dilley, Old and Willis turned almost certain defeat into victory. In 1870, at Lord's, the Cambridge batting heroes had been J. W. Dale (67) and William Yardley (100), who had helped their side to a lead of 178 after the fifth wicket had fallen when they were only 12 ahead. Dale almost messed things up in the fourth innings when he missed an easy catch from Tylecote. 'Sorry, Walter,' he called to Money, his captain, 'I was looking at a lady getting out of a drag!' Money would have been as amused as Brearley might have been if Dilley had missed Marsh on the long-leg boundary because he was 'eyeing some bird'.

Money's bowling left him mid-career (though not before he had returned figures of all 10 for 66 against the United South of England XI at Godalming — shades of Arthur Mailey 54 years later) and he developed as a batsman. Another of the leading lob-bowlers, though, A. W. 'Jammy' Ridley, an Eton man, like Money, had a full career, and was thought unlucky not to have gained selection for England in some of the early Test matches. His greatest moment with the ball came in 1875 when, as Oxford's captain, he spun Cambridge to defeat by six runs by bravely bringing himself on in the tense closing stage and taking two of the last three wickets. The humiliation felt by A. F. Smith, last out, bowled by a childish-looking lob, must have been considerable.

Ridley was the last of the famous amateur lob-bowlers until Jephson and Simpson-Hayward gave the system a brief 'gentleman's' comeback at the end of the Century and into Edwardian times. Slow bowling was developing in other directions, the arm higher, the fingers and wrist exploring other possibilities. The days of underhand deception, when a bowler such as W. M. Rose might take all 19 wickets which fell to English bowling in an innings of 22 of Montreal (1872), were slipping into the vale of ancient curiosities, to be taken less than seriously by scoffing 'moderns'.

Even in 1871, the *Daily News* was echoing a restless mood when it proclaimed: 'Bowling has but kept pace with the age; we travel faster, make love faster, gain and lose money faster, and exhaust our vitality faster than did our forefathers. As slow bowling would unquestionably be out of keeping with all our other "signs of the times", we must reluctantly admit that its supersession by the catapult method is required by the eternal fitness of things, and make up our minds to long scores and mutilation.'

And Bradman, Lillee and Croft were a long way yet from being born!

4. Wonderful Drinking Men

Tour pioneers — James Southerton — David Buchanan —
the Graces — Tom Kendall — Frank Allan —
George Giffen — Hugh Trumble

The early English touring teams which visited North America and
Australasia overran their largely unschooled opposition by means of
unfamiliar pace bowling and teasing spin, though there were observers
even then who predicted that the curse would be returned as the game
strengthened — albeit with the assistance of English coaches — on those
far-flung fields.

H. H. Stephenson, the Surrey all-rounder who led the first English side
to Australia in 1861-62, remarked during the course of one of his numerous
speeches that many Australian bowlers were good, but needed more
'science' in their game. There was not enough 'twist' about them. They
lacked suppleness of wrist. 'In this respect,' he warned, 'the mother is
ahead of the daughter, and the latter must be content to learn.'

Roger Iddison, the Yorkshireman, had other observations to make on his
colonial opponents: 'Well, I doan't think mooch of their play, but they're a
woonderful lot of drinking men!'

Charlie Lawrence, an itinerant professional who bowled 'slow
underhand twisters', stayed on after the tour to coach for the Albert club in
Sydney. It was he who led the Aboriginal team to England in 1868, topping
the bowling with 250 wickets at 12 apiece — though Johnny Mullagh took
245 at 10, and Cuzens's 114 cost only 11.3. The Aborigines themselves
understandably were confused by slow bowling wherever they encountered
it.

Another leading English cricketer, William Caffyn of Surrey and All-
England, went with the first and second (1863-64) teams to Australia, and
stayed on for seven years after the latter trip, coaching at the Melbourne
club and subsequently carrying on his trade as a barber (in partnership
with his hairdresser wife) in George Street, Sydney. In this city he coached
at the Warwick club, and found his charges not only eager to learn, but
capable of doing so with some rapidity: 'one was able to perceive the germs
from which the present perfect Australian bowling has sprung' — this
written in 1899. Four children were born to the Caffyns in Australia, but
two of the boys died there, and with his wife finding the climate oppressive,
they returned to Surrey in 1871, six years before the first of all Test

matches was staged in Melbourne, when Caffyn's best pupil, Charles Bannerman, scored 165 retired hurt for Australia.

Before looking at the peculiar part slow bowling played in that first Test, mention should be made of a Kentish slow bowler, George 'Farmer' Bennett, who went with H. H. Stephenson on the pioneering tour in 1861. An all-rounder, he bowled very slow high-tossed roundarm stuff, and was cool and clever enough to return some extraordinary analyses, including 8 for 25 for South v North at Lord's in 1866. He also had the rare distinction of taking a wicket without releasing the ball. For Kent against Sussex at Gravesend in 1866, he stepped forward to bowl to George 'Tiny' Wells, a midget of a man who took guard only inches from the stumps, rather as Alan Knott did when facing Lillee and Thomson. Wells lifted his bat, broke his wicket, and the umpire gave him out 'hit wicket', as he was in the act of playing.

Bennett, who had served a jail sentence for burglary in his younger days, had two utterly memorable overs, one in 1863, the other a year later. In the first, for England against Surrey at The Oval, four eminent batsmen — Stephenson, Caffyn (run out), Dowson and Griffith — fell to consecutive balls in the four-ball over. In 1864 his fortunes were reversed as George Griffith, a mighty left-hand hitter, smote all four balls of the over clean out of the ground at Hastings for six, each hit travelling over 100 yards over long-on.

But for apparently innocuous slow bowling, few episodes could match that concerning Tom Armitage, the bulky Yorkshireman, who added colour to the first Test match, at Melbourne in 1877. With Bannerman and his partners proving obstinate, James Lillywhite called up Armitage in an endeavour to confuse the Australians with his underhand lobs. Bannerman enjoyed them to the tune of 10 runs from the opening over. In the two overs following, Armitage tossed the ball so high, hoping to score a direct hit on the bails, that 'wide' was called. One was so far above the batsman's head that it was considered that nothing shorter than a clothes-prop would have touched it. Armitage then tried a 'grubber' all along the ground — Trevor Chappell wasn't the first — and Lillywhite took him off.

Armitage was not unpractised at this caddish ploy, known as a 'sneak'. In the previous English season he had foiled Middlesex batsman A. J. Webbe, who had been lashing his wide-turning lobs, by rolling the ball along the ground and having him lbw as he swung across the line. The crowd, since it was at Bramall Lane, Sheffield, laughed uproariously.

Despite all this, Armitage was not devoid of chivalry. When the English cricketers were in New Zealand just before sailing to Melbourne for the first Test, their horse-drawn coaches had to cross the Otira Gorge one wild night. When the horses pulling the second coach dropped with exhaustion, the players had to wade across in waist-high water, and Armitage was the one to volunteer to carry the sole lady passenger on his back.

England had another, and more dependable, slow bowler in the side for that historic first Test match. James Southerton, who, at 49 years 119 days, remains the oldest player to make a Test debut (and is likely to remain so forever), was to die only three years later. His years in big cricket came late. Born in Petworth, Sussex, but taken, when a baby, to Mitcham (where he later became landlord of the celebrated Cricketers pub), he became known as 'the man of many counties', starting with Surrey, withdrawing through 'over-exertion' after a few matches for Sussex, with Hampshire, and Sussex, and eventually settling with Surrey in 1873, when the first county qualifications were introduced. Playing for all three counties in one season gave him as odd an entry in the annals as his antiquity on Test debut.

A slow roundarm bowler, steady in length (and wides were an extreme rarity for him), with a good deal of turn, at the age of 44 Southerton took 340 wickets in all matches in 1872, two years after he had made his first appearance in the important Gentlemen v Players match. He was considered Alfred Shaw's closest rival though the rotund little Nottingham-shire man, who sent down the first ball in the first Test, was more of a medium-pacer, mercilessly accurate, and was in the ascendant as Southerton's powers gradually waned.

Jimmy Southerton's nerve also showed signs of shredding in later seasons. It was said that he would lie awake at night before playing against C. I. Thornton — who was often referred to in his day as the greatest hitter the world had seen — wondering what he should do if one of those bullet-like straight-drives came back at him. Perhaps he had good cause: in 1871 Thornton hit him over the pavilion, the scorebox and the racquets court — exits from three different sides of The Oval!

Only 5½ feet tall, known sometimes as 'The Debonair', Southerton six times took eight wickets in an innings for Surrey — and yet is better remembered for one further curiosity. His sense of honour expressed itself immortally when he refused to take any notice of the umpires, who declared him 'not out'. His dismissal thus was entered: 'J. Southerton, retired, thinking he was caught, 0'.

Fred Gale wrote that Southerton's action was higher and more wristy than 'Old Lillywhite's', but that 'the break of the ball is just like the old man's used to be'. Southerton himself compared bowling with fishing, the fieldsmen being the landing nets. In the 1873 *Lillywhite's Annual* he wrote of how a straight ball had claimed many an esteemed wicket, including that of W. G. Grace, who could not conceal his disgust.

Southerton died at his post, in a manner of speaking. Appointed superintendent of the groundstaff bowlers at the Surrey nets, he was conscientious to a fault, and a chill caught needlessly proved fatal. His younger son was editor of *Wisden Cricketers' Almanack* from 1934 until his death in 1935.

A mainstay of the Surrey bowling as Southerton's powers waned was Ted Barratt, born in Stockton-on-Tees, who was 'spotted' by W. G. Grace. He was a slow left-arm bowler, roundarm in style, who could impart such spin that on certain pitches he was regarded as 'unplayable'.

The greatest of his many fine achievements was when bowling at The Oval not for Surrey but for the Players against the earliest Australian touring team, in 1878. A dispute over fees (a number of Notts and Yorkshire players withdrew beforehand when the Australians would not meet their demand of £20 per man) was temporarily forgotten when Barratt took all 10 wickets on the first day, for 43 runs off 29 four-ball overs — and not one was bowled. The touring team made 77 (Charles Bannerman 51), but went on to win a low-scoring match. The English players received their £20 after all, and Barratt was presented by the Australian manager with the mounted ball and an extra £5 — useful remuneration for a plumber and part-time professional cricketer.

If all slow bowlers have a breaking point, Barratt revealed his when a herculean hitter was shaping to smash a loose delivery: 'Don't hit her, sir! *I'll give you four!*' he called out. There was less hitting to leg in those far-off days, and any batsman of repute would drive frequently and with unedifying force. That was how Southerton came to lose sleep, and Barratt his composure. Not everyone could be a Teddy Walker, fearlessly clinging to rocketing caught-and-bowleds halfway down the pitch.

Barratt, described by *Scores and Biographies* as one of the earliest of Surrey's 'foreigners or mercenaries', took 790 wickets in first-class cricket, against Southerton's 1681, and at three runs per wicket more. But his value to a developing county was real, and he was mourned widely when he died from the then-hopeless ailment, consumption, in 1891, at the age of 46.

Another slow man who came to full fame relatively late in life — and who also felt the raging fury of C. I. Thornton's stupendous bat — was David Buchanan, a left-arm bowler, short, stout and bearded, Scottish-born. After two decades of bowling fast, one fateful afternoon at Old Trafford, when the batting was well on top, he turned to slows and had some success. He never looked back. For over 20 years he prospered as a somewhat profligate spinner, succeeding where it mattered in the 1860s and 1870s: the Gentlemen v Players matches. In 19 innings in these showpieces at Lord's and The Oval, he took 87 wickets at less than 15 apiece.

'He bowled to be hit,' said *Wisden* whimsically. 'Mr Buchanan set little store on what is known as a good length.' He depended for his wickets, we are told, on pitched-up balls with plenty of spin on them. Writing at the time of his death, in 1900, the 'bible' questioned whether he would have troubled the top professional batsmen of now, though it was a fact that Daft, Jupp and others found him a handful in those ultra-serious Gentlemen v Players contests.

'Plum' Warner, himself an Old Rugbeian, observed that Buchanan (who was one of the founders of Warwickshire County Cricket Club) could bowl out any side around Rugby when he lived there in later years — playing much Free Foresters cricket — with the noted exception of the boys of the school, who were familiar with his bowling from facing him hours on end in the nets.

C. I. Thornton, brutal scourge of slow bowlers, hit Buchanan for 6, 4, 4,

6 off a four-ball over at Cambridge in 1871. Yet even the clever V. E. Walker was liable to be swept up by the Thornton whirlwind, as two years previously, when all four balls of one of his overs disappeared from the St Lawrence ground, Canterbury.

Buchanan did well enough in other encounters with 'Buns' Thornton to finish with an even book. He was still good enough at 48 to be invited by Lord Harris to tour Australia, but family considerations persuaded him to decline. He left behind one of the most thoughtful (and sought-after) instruction booklets, *Hints to Bowlers*, which, almost as much as slow bowler Boxall's 1801 publication, is practically impossible to obtain. Students who read any of the early manuals will be struck by the soundness — and simplicity — of the advice offered by any of these major practitioners.

The doughty little Buchanan sprang from north of the border, but slow bowlers from the north of England were some time in making a mark. One of the best during the mid-1800s was Ikey Hodgson, though his fame was earned in an unusual way. He used to attach himself to numerous regional teams of 22 in their battles with the touring All-England XI, and but for his useless batting and fielding, might have risen to even greater heights *with* Clarke's feared band. As it was, his slow left-arm roundarm bowling brought him an astonishing aggregate of 475 of All-England's wickets in the six seasons from 1860.

With his friend, Billy Slinn, a fast bowler, he joined all manner of sides as 'given men', bowling in a style, according to Richard Daft, similar to that of Wilfred Rhodes, though perhaps a trifle faster. Hodgson stands in history as the first of a famous line, therefore, as for over a century Yorkshire boasted a slow left-arm bowler of world class: Peate, Peel, Rhodes, Verity, Wardle, Wilson.

One of his finest hours was at Glasgow, when the All-England XI needed only 49 to win. After rain, Hodgson knew the batsmen would be expecting him to push the ball through. Instead, warning his fieldsmen to anticipate a few catches, he tossed the ball up, and finished with 7 for 8. England all out 20. Daft, Caesar, Hayward, Clarke junior, Anderson, Parr and H. H. Stephenson were all subjected to his wide grin as they left the crease.

Hodgson played for Yorkshire — a county side known as 'a team of ale-cans' until Lord Hawke introduced some discipline — but he was a consumptive, and, like so many in his time, failed to see 40. Saul Wade, a purveyor of very slow off-spin, at least lived till 73, even if his career with Yorkshire was brief. He survived the embarrassment of being hit for 22 off the last over when the Australians of 1886 wanted 19, and went on to return some startling figures in county matches, including 7 for 10 against Leicestershire.

The 1880s, with county cricket growing in organisation and strength, and Test matches augmenting it as a major public attraction, saw the emergence of many overarm and roundarm slow bowlers of skill, and as pitches improved — the crowd at Lord's had fewer instances of kept-out shooters to applaud — so ordinary medium-pace prospered less. The need was for true speed or measured flight and spin. This situation was emphasised even more greatly for decades in Australia, where pitches tended to be hard and fast.

Naturally the innocuous bowler, given good support in the field, could still reap a harvest of wickets — especially if he had such an overwhelming stature and reputation as Dr W. G. Grace.

His elder brother, E. M. Grace, had done it all before him, making huge scores and taking bags of wickets with a talkative expertise, bowling cunning underhands, sometimes dropping from the sky, and — essential, this — taking extremely long tenancies of the bowling crease, which has always been a help to slow men: more easily accomplished when one is one's own captain. E.M. — 'The Coroner' — emulated V. E. Walker in 1862 when he scored a century and took ten wickets in an innings. For MCC against a mediocre Gentlemen of Kent XII (batting one short), at Canterbury, he took 5 for 77 and 10 for 69, and made 192 not out, carrying his bat. And he was not even a member of MCC!

From having taken 13 wickets in a grown-ups' match when aged only nine, E. M. Grace took 655 wickets for the Thornbury club when in his 64th and 65th years, many of which must have been 'suicides'. Nor was he the kind of cricketer to blind himself to the advantages of cajoling or even bullying the umpire into supporting his endeavours.

W.G. carried on the family trait, though with more of a dash of good humour than history is inclined to accredit him. He was, of course, the colossus among cricketers, remembered with almost as much reverence today as at the time of his death in 1915. Tall, strong, bearded, he played first-class cricket from 1865, when he was 16, until 1908, leaving over 54,000 runs in the record book, with 126 (or 124 by amended calculations) centuries.

He also took almost 3000 wickets, a high proportion of which came from batsmanship which, for want of a more technical word, could only be described as 'silly'. His obituary in *The Times* gave a clear impression of his approach:

> WG's bowling was unique. No-one else placed his field as he did. To the spectator nobody looked an uglier or a much worse bowler, but to the batsman he was very difficult. He was slow, with a most ungainly action, but he could bowl on either side of the wicket, did not object to being hit, and he soon found out the weak points of an opponent. What made his bowling difficult was his length and direction. The ball dropped down from a great height and frequently looked like a half-volley till the batsman tried to hit it, then it was found to be a good length. He had a long arm and often bowled round the wicket, so that his ball looked to the batsman a beauty to hit to leg; the batsman tried to do so, but misjudged the length and missed it and was astonished to find himself given out leg-before-wicket. He used to have a deep square-leg field and many a time used he to get batsmen out by bowling for catches.

The newspaper was too polite to remind readers that he more than once got a wicket by innocently directing a batsman's gaze towards a flock of birds (real or imaginary) flying across a dazzling sun.

D. L. A. Jephson, a noted lob-bowler, recalled W.G.'s approach as a few short, shuffling strides, with a 'curious rotary action before delivery, *and the wonderful length.*' Further: 'The hand is large and the ball well-concealed', and the ball 'seems to leave by the back door, as it were, that is, over the knuckle of the little finger.'

Jephson noted the seeming innocence of W.G.'s bowling, but knew it to be subtly varied, with an occasional ball 'with a bit of top on it' which went straight through past an ambitious bat for an lbw. He was particularly successful against batsmen unfamiliar with his bowling. Jephson never wrote a truer phrase than when he concluded: 'He stands alone'.

W.G. often exploited leg-theory — without the speed and violence to the thigh and lower abdomen of left-armers Hirst and Frank Foster, of course. In contrast, one of his Gloucestershire colleagues, R. F. Miles, a banker by profession, bowled his left-arm slows so wide of the off stump that in 1878, when someone happened to be counting, he actually bowled 48 wides. He nevertheless made a worthy contribution to the county's successes through-out the 1870s, though his best figures came while still at Oxford: 6 for 65 against the All-England XI — always a mark of true credit.

The first high-class spinner Australia played against England was Tom Kendall, Bedford-born, who spun his adopted country to 45-run victory in the first-ever Test with 7 for 55 in the second innings at Melbourne. A slow left-arm bowler with a high action, he broke either way, and would have walked into any representative side had he lived in England, according to Southerton. Kendall had the distinction of dismissing W. G. Grace on both the Champion's tours of Australia — 18 years apart!

As the years passed, Kendall put on a lot of weight, and 'lost his energy and elasticity'. A.G. Steel, though, still saw him as being as good a bowler as the much-feared J.C. Shaw of Notts. Kendall came no closer to touring England than embarking upon the 1878 tour — and leaving the ship before it steamed out into the Pacific.

One who stayed aboard was Frank Allan, a Victorian six-footer who was known as 'the bowler of a century' — meaning once in a hundred years, not by reference to any bowling analysis. He was the first bowler to be 'hyped' with intensive advance propaganda by the Australians. He was said to have developed his strong and precise wristwork by hunting possum with the Aborigines, flicking a waddy (a short thick stick) up at the tree branches.

Allan, a left-hander, spun the ball a lot and made it curl in the air before hopping towards first slip, and though he could not be bothered playing in the first Test, in 1877, and managed only 4 for 80 in his only Test two years later, he took a fat hoard of wickets in intercolonial matches. In the inclement weather of 1878, he sent 106 English batsmen packing during the tour, though the grind of daily exertion wore him down.

The two spin bowlers who did succeed on the first and subsequent tours of Britain were Tom Garrett and Harry Boyle. The tall and gaunt Garrett remains Australia's youngest player against England at 18 years 232 days, and lived longer than any of the other players in that inaugural Test. He took almost 150 wickets in all matches on the 1878 tour, bowling with unusual coolness when under attack, and holding a steady line on and outside off stump, breaking back or going with the arm. Boyle, on the other hand, was faster through the air and moved the ball both ways, after a sometimes deceptive flight, proving the perfect foil for the 'Demon' Spofforth. English cricket took a long time to recover from this pair's demolition of a strong MCC side at Lord's in 1878, when the premier club were shot out for 33 and 19 (Spofforth 6 for 4, including the hat-trick, and 4 for 16; Boyle 3 for 14 and 6 for 3) and lost by nine wickets inside a day.

Boyle, with his spade beard, was referred to as 'the very devil', and, between overs, his presence at silly mid-on, a position he pioneered, did nothing to ease the Englishmen's acute discomfort. Boyle had been the first Australian to bowl W. G. Grace, a deed which had the entire audience of the Theatre Royal, Melbourne rising and cheering for five minutes when he entered. He had watched Grace at the practice nets and announced he would get a ball through a gap to his leg stump.

Boyle took almost 200 wickets in all matches on that tour, and toured three further times, taking 250 wickets in 1880, when he was 32. This was the tour that introduced English crowds to George Eugene Palmer, then only 20, whose portrait conjures up visions of a Wild West marshal — or even one of the smoother outlaws. 'Joey' Palmer had already made a deep impression against the 1878-79 English touring team, when, at 18, he was a last-minute replacement for Frank Allan. Closer to medium-pace than slow, with a chest-on action, he could be lethal on a helpful wicket, and, even more valuably, he bowled well on hard, dry pitches, sending down a fastish leg-break which eventually proved his undoing. He used it not so much as a surprise ball — that was his lightning-fast yorker — but as a stock-in-trade. Yet his record of 78 Test wickets at 21 each gives him exalted rank. A figure to ponder upon is his 533 wickets in Australia, England and America during the full course of the 1880 tour, when his success was all the more welcome in view of Spofforth's lesser performance because of injury. His form deserted him after a crippling knee injury in 1886, but he then developed his batting.

These, then, were the bowlers who, with the batsmanship of Murdoch, Horan, the Bannermans, McDonnell, Bonnor and Massie, put Australia on the cricket map. There might have been another, for Edwin Evans, a clever 'flight' bowler, tall, bearded and bronzed as any bushman, was the best all-rounder in Australia just before the birth of Test cricket. The big international contests came just too late for him, though his analyses in NSW's matches against Victoria make startling reading. Nevertheless, he would have derived much pleasure from the success of his nephew, Bill Howell, who took 49 wickets in 18 Tests, spinning his off-breaks vigorously

— they buzzed through the air — and taking England by storm from his very first delivery. That accounted for Surrey's Bobby Abel at the start of the 1899 tour, and Howell finished with all 10 Surrey wickets for 28. To this day there has never been such a staggering tour debut. Howell, a bee-keeper, toured England twice again, although the 1902 tour was ruined for him when news came through during the Yorkshire match (when the county bowled out the Australians for 23) that his mother had died; two days later a further message told of his father's death.

A cricketer emerged during the 1880s, however, who was to carry Australian cricket on his square shoulders well into the 1890s. This was George Giffen of South Australia, the 'W.G. of Australia'. Giffen got his early inspiration, like so many of the Australians, from a visiting English player, in his case the immaculate Alfred Shaw. Not for him the extravagant spin. When Giffen went out to the net after Shaw had had a long practice bowl at Adelaide he found a worn patch no bigger than a saucer, a small one at that, as Giffen later wrote. In time Giffen developed into a tireless and often over-willing bowler of slow to medium off-breaks with subtle variations; accuracy was the keynote; and so many large scores did he make with batting no less businesslike than his bowling that Australian cricket was built around him for 10 years or more.

On his earlier tours of England he suspected he was used only on the better batting wickets, the opening bowlers having their fill on softer, trickier pitches. This was remedied when he became captain. Indeed, as captain of South Australia, it sometimes seemed the only time he didn't have the ball in his hand was during the alternate overs.

Prematurely grey, solidly built, he gave nothing away in his run up to the wicket to bowl. Albert Knight, the God-fearing Leicestershire batsman, wrote that the first time one played against Giffen 'the ball seemed to come out of the back of his neck'. With his initial movements 'much resembling those of a kangaroo looked at from the side', the final action revealed as much of his back as of his face — in contrast to Palmer's square-on delivery. 'To a spectator,' wrote Knight, 'his action was distinctly amusing; to the batsman an undoubted and added difficulty.' 'Giff' is one of a large company of cricket 'greats' of whom moving film does not exist, more's the frustration.

After W. G. Grace, he was the first man to score a century and take a hat-trick in the same game: against Lancashire in 1884. Only a few months previously he had become the first to take the whimsically admirable 'William the Conqueror' analysis of 10 for 66, for Australia against The Rest, the first instance of all-10 in first-class cricket outside England. In all, he toured England five times, achieving the double of 1000 runs and 100 wickets in 1886, 1893 and 1896, truly remarkable cricket. In 1886 he took 40 wickets in five consecutive innings against Derbyshire, Cambridge and Lancashire, a feat without equal; if the six against the Gentlemen in the preceding innings is taken into account, he has another world record — 46 in six innings — equalled only by 'Tich' Freeman of Kent.

To Giffen, of all bowlers, is attributed most strongly the tedious retort, 'A change of bowling? Ah, yes, I'll change ends.' But with him it paid dividends, even if he had to bowl 87 six-ball overs to take 5 for 309 for his State against Stoddart's 1894-95 English team.

He was a fairly emotional chap as slowish bowlers go, though he was probably entitled to feel petulant about losing seniority in the Postal Department because of absences to play all this cricket. The Australian public did have a chance to show their appreciation with a sizeable testimonial. One who would hardly have chosen to contribute to it was the mighty Middlesex and England medium-pacer J. T. Hearne, who was deprived of an all-10 against the Australians for MCC in 1896 when Giffen found some excuse not to bat — leaving Hearne with all nine. That was the match in which the Australians were humbled as never before or since in their first innings: 18 all out, Hearne 4 for 4 and the Leicestershire off-spinner, tall, jug-eared 'Dick' Pougher, 5 for 0 from a series of deliveries that hardly turned but kept low. (Bobby Abel thought Pougher the most difficult bowler he faced in a long career.)

Giffen's giant's position in Test cricket is confirmed by his double of 1238 runs and 103 wickets in 31 Tests against England, with one century, a monumental 161 at Sydney in 1894-95, when he also took eight wickets, but finished on the losing side, England winning by 10 runs after following-on. Memories of the match were revived in 1981 when England similarly pulled a match back from the dead at Headingley.

Giffen rolled his sophisticated arm over not just from noon till sunset, but from youth till middle age, and many were the admiring glances at Adelaide in 1903 when, a few days before his 44th birthday, and having made a special effort to stay fit, he took 15 wickets for 185 off 76 overs and scored 81 and 97 not out. Such was his recurring misfortune that this match too was lost; but he finished first in the bowling and second in the batting in that season's Sheffield Shield averages.

How many who take their seats in the stand bearing his name at Adelaide Oval realise what a stupendous cricketer he was?

Of the other eminent Australian slow bowlers of the period, W. H. Cooper was, despite his glowing reputation at home, a 'near miss' as far as English audiences were concerned. He bowled monstrous leg-breaks. So far did they spin that to most British spectators he was quite original. Unfortunately for him and the 1884 touring team, he damaged his right hand on the voyage and was a failure in England. He managed to take only six wickets in five matches, and though he bowled around the wicket, wide of the leg stump, with fair spin, and with only two men on the off side, he lacked the advantage of the glaring light which had assisted him in taking nine wickets in the first Test at Melbourne in 1881-82. This Maidstone-born man, who had taken up bowling at 27 for the exercise after medical advice, retired ten years later, seldom to be recalled to mind until the 1960s, when his great-grandson, Paul Sheahan, earned 31 caps for Australia.

Another wide spinner of the ball was Harry Trott, elder brother of Albert, whose disappointment at missing the 1896 tour led to his counter-emigration and a career with Middlesex, for whom he hit many robust runs and took hundreds of wickets with every known variety of delivery — a precursor of Keith Miller and Ian Botham. There is a story that on one of his visits to England, big brother Harry met Albert in the street — and they exchanged a nod to each other. Harry, bothered later by bouts of mental instability, toured England four times, leading his country in 1896. He started as a junior on Melbourne's concrete pitches, learning to spin the leg-break accurately enough to be invited to play senior club cricket at 19. He announced himself with seven wickets in each innings.

He was more successful as a batsman than as a bowler in Test cricket, and his brave 143 in the Lord's Test of '96 ranks among the finest of innings. In the next Test, though, at Old Trafford, he did something which perhaps ought to be tried more often today — if only there were the spinners to be thus employed: he put himself on immediately when England went in against Australia's 412 and had Grace and Stoddart, two of the world's greatest, both stumped within a few overs.

Harry Trott was an incidental bowler. One who earned his reputation at it — and eventually a dubious reputation at that — was Tom McKibbin, born near Bathurst, NSW in 1870, who had a peculiar hop in his run, and, at a briskish pace, turned the ball either way. He was accurate, and broke even on the hardest pitch — without giving a clue as to which way the deviation would be. It is even supposed that he might have bowled the googly before that particular ball was recognised. (Reference in those pre-Bosanquet days was made, however, to 'googlies' as balls which were 'slow and dropping'.) Giffen recalled with obvious admiration how McKibbin had taken 7 for 51 and 8 for 74 on a hard wicket at Adelaide, a notorious batsman's paradise. He also regarded some of the attempts of batsmen to play him in England as 'ludicrous'. But the shadow of legal dubiousness in his action hung over him. He was never no-balled, but the editor of *Wisden* spoke for many when he wrote that 'there can be little doubt that he continually threw when putting on his off-break'. S. H. Pardon then cited Australian wicketkeeper Jack Blackham's earlier opinion that McKibbin would be no-balled if he ever toured England. The other suspect in the party, express bowler Ernie Jones, was 'radically unfair', according to Pardon, and a year later was indeed no-balled for throwing.

McKibbin had the last laugh on the 1896 tour, with figures of 7 for 73 against Yorkshire, 7 for 80 against Surrey, 6 for 48 (W.G. stumped) against Gloucestershire, and an hysterical 6 for 27 and 7 for 11 against Lancashire at Liverpool. An inoffensive fellow — until he got a cricket ball in his capable fingers.

The giant among Australian bowlers through all these years, and into the 20th Century — in size as well as performance — was, however, Hugh Trumble, the genial Melbourne cricketer with the oriental eyes, drooping moustache, and cool bowling brain which accounted for 141 English Test wickets in 31 matches between 1890 and 1904. He took only 17 wickets in his first eight Tests; but then he came into his own. Twelve in the Oval Test of 1896, 19 in the 1897-98 series, 15 in the 1899 series, 28 in the 1901-02 series, 26 in only three Tests in 1902 (his 12 at The Oval, when he bowled unchanged throughout from the pavilion end, forgotten in the wake of Jessop's glorious match-winning century), and 24 in his last four Tests, in the fascinating 1903-04 series, when he finished with 7 for 28 at Melbourne, including his second hat-trick. He remains the only bowler — apart from Jimmy Matthews — to take two Test hat-tricks, the first having come on the same ground two years before.

What sort of bowler was he? This was the question heard in 1981 when his record of 141 wickets in Ashes Tests was overtaken at last by Dennis Lillee. With a high arm and deadly accuracy, Trumble, son of an Irishman, turned mainly from the off, and knew the value of a straight ball. His club cricket was played for Melbourne, where he was to finish up as club secretary after a career in banking. The bowler at the other end was usually the mature Spofforth, which naturally helped the advancement of a cricketer keen to expand his intelligence. By 1900, when the Melbourne club toured New Zealand, he was billed as 'the greatest bowler in the world'.

There was little that was dramatic about his bowling to the eye of the distant observer, but he made the ball bounce from his great height, and his shrewdness manifested itself in the swiftness with which he found a batsman's weaknesses, often with the assistance of wicketkeeper Blackham. He also often let a player get himself out by over-exuberance on a strength, setting traps in the field and using all manner of dodges to unbalance the batsman's equilibrium — without, of course, resorting to the modern ploy of verbal abuse. When Trumble opened his lips it was invariably to utter a compliment or a dry witticism or an appeal.

With his little finger doubled up beneath the ball, he approached off a moderate run, and his right shoulder was held back as his arm came up, only to loosen suddenly in the act of delivery. The descent of the ball was steep, as it is from the hand of West Indian fast bowler Joel Garner, and judging the length was the first problem besetting the batsman. Many a 'full toss' simply was not so. In Trumble's wisdom he saw that a couple of inches of turn would be likely to do more damage than six inches, and in an era when the ball had to pitch between wicket and wicket to gain an lbw, he often bowled round the wicket. He shunned the use of a surprise leg-break. Recollections of 'Joey' Palmer's latter-day wild persistence with the fast leg-break saddened him.

'Little Eva', they called Trumble, and those long arms pulled in countless slip catches. He was a very useful batsman too, though he got his head down only when runs were urgently needed. One of those occasions was at Melbourne in 1897-98, when he and Clem Hill added 165 for the seventh wicket, a record for Australia against England which is older than all others bar one.

He preferred bowling in England, where the wickets gave more help. So masterful was he that Jessop, for one, considered him his *bete noire*, getting away with his characteristic liberties only on that famous afternoon in 1902. Archie MacLaren, one of so many 'Golden Age' batsmen tormented by him, proclaimed that 'the team without Trumble was something like codfish without oyster sauce'. When in his 70th year, Hugh Trumble was still fit enough to remove his stetson and coat and turn his off-breaks on a length at the Melbourne nets.

Watching NSW all-rounder Graeme Beard bowling at the nets at Lord's in 1981 prompted the imagining that he could well be in the Trumble mould: tall, with a high delivery, and movement from the off. But the only reference to Trumble during that eventful series was when Lillee broke his record. The Victorian giant would have been the first to shake the fast bowler's sweaty hand.

5. The Smashed Toilet-Seat

Billy Bates — Edmund Peate — amateur dearth —
tragic Briggs and boozy Peel

That there was no shortage of spin bowlers in Australia's ranks in the last two decades of Queen Victoria's reign is apparent. Nor did English county cricket lack slow men, several of whom went on to national fame in the home Test matches and during the arduous tours of Australia, when long coach journeys and tossing voyages on coastal steamers frequently left the players exhausted as a new match commenced.

One of the great triers was Billy Bates of Yorkshire, who toured Australia five times in the 1880s, becoming the first Englishman to take a Test hat-trick, and the first of the few to take 14 wickets in a Test. As he also scored 55 in England's innings victory in this Melbourne encounter in January 1883, the Test could truly be said to have been 'Bates's match'.

It was a most distinguished hat-trick, achieved in the best of scheming traditions. Bates, bowling slow roundarm off-breaks, had bowled the aggressive Percy McDonnell, caught-and-bowled Giffen next ball, and then intimidated the gigantic George Bonnor by placing Walter Read at silly mid-on, a move demanding courage on the part of the fielder. Bonnor obligingly prodded nervously forward to a faster ball, and Bates had made history. His material rewards included a silver miniature top-hat and a collection for £31, while the victory enabled England to go on to win the first-ever Ashes series. True immortality came Bates's way when his name appeared centrally on the little urn itself, viewed (the replica, that is) by thousands each year in its showcase at Lord's.

Bates was known as 'The Duke' for his smart dressing, and no happier cricketer ever toured, even though his 15 Tests were all played in Australia, suggesting that his face perhaps did not fit in certain home circles. His singing voice was so good that King Kalakaua of the Sandwich Islands had him in his cabin each morning to sing *The Bonny Yorkshire Lass* during the 1881 voyage to Australia. But disaster befell 'The Duke' during the 1887-88 tour.

Four days before Christmas, the Englishmen were practising at the Melbourne nets when a fierce drive from a neighbouring net cannoned against Bates's right cheekbone. The injury was stitched, and a month later he sailed for England, leaving the team to continue their tour. So melancholic did the usually jolly Bates become during the sea journey that he attempted suicide. By the spring, with his wife seriously ill and his son fighting off complications of the throat and chest, Bates was writing to a friend that, having been able to see only 20 yards when he reached England, he could now see a mile and a half. Alas, there was to be no more big cricket for him. In 1891 his wife died, and, having been Haslingden's professional, he was living off the interest on a sum collected for him and his son. The son grew up to play for Yorkshire and Glamorgan. Billy Bates died in January 1900, aged 44, A. W. Pullin writing of him: 'He had his failings — who has not? — but he had also trials that fall to the lot of few men. He was a great cricketer, and a most kindly soul.'

For Yorkshire he took 660 wickets at 16.70, and for England 50 wickets at a fraction less. As for his batsmanship, Lord Hawke considered that until Jack Hobbs came along, Bates was 'the most engaging of all professional rungetters'.

A fellow-Yorkshireman of the period, Edmund Peate, could never have aspired to such a description. He was one of those who went in at number 11 only if there wasn't a number 12. But his bowling, slow left-arm, won him a high position in the ranks of the slow men. Like so many others, he began as a fastish bowler. His career was colourful. At 19 he joined Treloar's Clown Cricketers, travelling the country with seven others in a troupe who performed alongside acrobats and clowns. The tour finished in Sheffield, where the grinders 'mobbed and sodded' the joking cricketers. They wanted only the serious stuff. What reception might they have given the 1981 10-overs-a-side night 'cricket'?

Peate felt the lure of slow bowling while he practised in a shed during his winter work for Myers as a warp-twister. He bowled at the bales of 'mungo' which was to be made into red shawls for export to China, and though he was later thought to be a bowler of persistent length and big spin, he ridiculed this, saying he spun little and bowled a varying length to make things accordingly difficult for the batsman.

He took wickets from the start once Yorkshire had recruited him, and was taken to Australia via America in 1881-82, when he took 8 for 57 at Sydney in the third Test. Against Victoria he took four wickets without conceding a run, Bates helping him to reduce them to six down for seven. Often opening the attack, Peate found most of the batsmen in minor matches in Australia totally helpless against his innocent-looking but sinister deliveries, and finished well ahead of his team-mates with 264 wickets in all matches at 5.84 apiece. The men at the other end of the pitch were the clowns now.

In the English season which followed, 1882, he 'upset the House of Lords and knocked out Home Rule in three balls' in the match against Kent at Sheffield. What he meant was that he dismissed Lord Harris, Lord Throwley and O'Shaughnessy, an Irishman, to complete a hat-trick, which brought him some talent money and a presentation silver walking-stick handle.

His most famous match, however, came six weeks later, when he took 4 for 31 and 4 for 40 in the Test match at The Oval. These figures are forgotten in the general hysteria surrounding the finish of the match. England needed ten to win when Peate went in, last man, to join C. T. Studd, who had already made two centuries against the tourists that summer. Making no attempt to hand over the strike to his senior, Peate had a slog at Boyle and was bowled, giving Australia their historic seven-run Ashes triumph. 'Ah couldn't troost Maister Stood,' Peate replied when challenged later.

Bowling at times with as many as eight fieldsmen on the off side, Peate played until 1887, when Lord Hawke dispensed with his services because he didn't altogether approve of his style of living. He was not a morbid drunk, but ale increased his weight considerably. He went on returning barely credible figures in club cricket in Yorkshire, and could look back on such analyses as 8 for 5 against Surrey in 1883 in his hometown of Holbeck, a satisfying 12 wickets for 40 for the North in their match against the 1886 Australians, and 9 for 21 against Sussex the same season.

One further tale will serve to show what a mesmeric effect he had on opponents with his smooth and beautiful low-slung action. Bonnor, the Australian, was fast developing a complex about him, and to boost his nerve he began playing strokes in the dressing-room, saying as he did so, 'That's the way to play you, Peate!' and 'Not this time, Peate, my boy!' Launching into a vicious leg shot, he cried 'How do you like that, Peate?' This time his bat caught the toilet seat, smashing it to pieces.

The warm-up was to no avail. Peate got him again cheaply.

And lest it be thought that Peate had no mind of his own, when spectators formed an ugly protest mob at The Oval in a match against the Australians which was held up by damp turf, he answered the Surrey secretary's plea that he should address the crowd with 'No thank you. I came here to play cricket, not to quell a riot!'

Peate died in 1900, a few weeks after Billy Bates.

Of the relatively few amateurs who excelled as slow bowlers at this time, Allan Gibson Steel, a fine, adaptive batsman from Lancashire, was prominent. His two Test centuries, at Sydney and Lord's, remain among the best in Ashes history, and if his bowling was less than telling in Test cricket, it brought him 238 wickets at only 13 for his county.

Giffen thought his bowling, which could turn either way, was often extremely puzzling, though 'Buns' Thornton must have felt otherwise the day he smacked him over a four-storey building, out of the Scarborough ground and into Trafalgar Square, an incident which gave rise to the naive response from a lady at a tea party: 'Oh, really? Where were you playing, Mr Steel, Lord's or The Oval?'

Steel, a small man with intense eyes and flaring nostrils, was disturbed at the fact that so few amateur slow bowlers of note were playing in the 1890s. He acknowledged E. A. Nepean of Oxford and Middlesex, who earned undying fame by bowling the usually unshiftable Shrewsbury round his legs with a wide leg-break, and C. M. Wells, the eminent Classics student at Cambridge, who went on to some sterling all-round deeds for Surrey and Middlesex. Wells would toss the ball from left hand to right as he came in to bowl, and with an action rather resembling the classic medium-pacer Lohmann's, favoured off-breaks, with high-tossed leg-breaks which turned little but earned him many lbws. Unusually, like Mailey and Benaud, he hardly employed his thumb when spinning the leg-break. Wisely, though, he trained himself for some smart reflex fielding off his own bowling — a necessity for anyone who believes in following through well down the pitch against strong hitters. A 10-yard catch from Billy Barnes's crashing straight-drive off a slow full-toss was talked about for years. The alternative would probably have been an early obituary for Wells.

A. G. Steel saw a reason — without identifying the undeniable snobbery surrounding batting — for there being so few amateur slow bowlers, and this was the profusion of professional cricketers coaching at the public schools. This caused the boys to bat and do little else at practice. They rarely needed to bowl at each other, and when they did, it was seen as time to have fun: 'I'll give you some of Spofforth's patents!' they would cry, hurling erratically; or 'Would you like some of W.G.'s?' — tossing the ball 'lifeless up in the air'. All this was a waste of time. Not that Steel lacked respect for the genuine W. G. Grace. He knew why the Old Man had such success with young batsmen: if he sees 'an enormous man rushing up to the wickets, with both elbows out, great black beard blowing on each side of him, and a huge yellow cap on the top of a dark swarthy face', he naturally expects more than the gentle lobbed-up ball that comes.

Steel himself advocated a wide leg-side ball to a new batsman, delivered in the hope that he would hole out at square leg. The advice, if taken seriously today, would need a rider or two, for the new batsman might have the hooking power of a Norman O'Neill or a Viv Richards.

Had there been a *pair* of highly-skilled amateur slow bowlers in England during the ten years from 1885, they would have had to be good to have found places in the national team against the competition of two Northerners who were masters of the art of slow left-arm bowling: Bobby Peel of Yorkshire and Johnny Briggs of Lancashire (though born in Sutton-in-Ashfield, Notts), the same Briggs whom a child thought to be W. G. Grace's 'baby' when he saw them entering the field together. For he was a chubby midget-like man, a 'funny little object', as one of the last surviving witnesses of Briggs on the cricket field recalled.

Peel and Briggs. English names, with a down-to-earth sound about them. Peel had a harder kind of humour about him, and drank too much. The weakness led to a grand story concerning a famous Test victory at Sydney; it led to his premature dismissal by Yorkshire; and it made him less than a considerate husband. But he lived to 84, having reclaimed some of the 'quiet civil ways' in his dotage that were observed in his early days, when he was a bits-and-pieces player for Yorkshire, waiting for the big chance. His batting was very useful, even though he did register three 'pairs' in Test matches. His 210 not out in an innings total of 887 at Edgbaston in 1896 was thought at the time to have been the finest innings ever by a left-hand batsman. But it was when Peate fell from grace that the chunky Peel assumed the honoured post of Yorkshire's slow left-armer.

Johnny Briggs had started earlier, his first match for Lancashire being in 1879, when he was only 16. Another slow left-armer, George Nash, also joined the county that year, but he was a thrower — like the other Lancashire bowlers, Watson and Crossland — though, probably because of his less dramatic pace, he was not no-balled for an illegal action.

From the start Briggs was much loved. His very nature endeared him to all who came into his presence — even opponents. Cardus remembered him as a Grimaldi among cricketers, a joker, prankster, always ready to laugh, but with sad, bulbous eyes, and a thread of tragedy running through him.

Peel and Briggs shared their Test debut, at Adelaide in December 1884, when Peel took eight wickets while Briggs could not get a bowl. In fact, Shrewsbury gave him only eight overs in the entire five-match series. Briefly, in 1886, Briggs gained preference, but soon they were to be seen bowling together for England, and in many a Players v Gentlemen match.

It may seem strange that two such similar bowlers should be chosen, but they were among the best of all species in England — or the world — and cricket was by no means dominated by fast bowling as we know it today. Their records help establish their true worth: Briggs took 97 Australian wickets (plus 21 in two fiasco Tests in South Africa), Peel 102 (at 16.81) in 20 Australian Tests, the first Englishman to take a century of wickets against Australia.

Archie MacLaren, Briggs's Lancashire captain, wrote picturesquely of both bowlers in the rare 1914 magazine *The World of Cricket*. Peel, he recalled, used to position his left arm behind his back with the suspicion of a flourish, and then 'fairly whip the ball down'. He was 'like a terrier on a rat' as soon as he spotted a batsman's weakness. 'The highest in the land had to confess themselves nonplussed by the Yorkshireman's many wiles.' He varied his speed, trajectory and spin according to the nature of the pitch and the ability of the batsman. MacLaren knew many an occasion, in both countries, when Peel would get up at five to watch a gallop on the race-course before going down to the ground to reduce some poor batting side to helplessness. 'At shooting,' MacLaren wrote, 'he is distinctly interesting. He generally claims everything that falls.' But he disgusted Ranjitsinhji and his keeper when, having blasted eight barrels at a hare, taking off a few legs and an ear or so, he chased the wretched thing into the forbidden territory of a neighbouring property, vaulting a stile, ignoring the protests of the keeper, and 'proceeded to entertain us with a combination of hunting and shooting, the ultimate outcome of which was luckily the death of the poor puss.'

On the voyage out in 1894 Peel brought a fellow professional down from his privileged hammock with a nocturnal slash across the ropes with a carving-knife, while the same chap next found himself locked in a boiler-room, with the heat at Hell's level, before MacLaren let him out just in time. It would have meant more than the end of Peel's playing days, had the door remained shut a further few minutes.

As for Briggs, 'the sun seemed always shining when Johnny was with us'. Floating the ball up more invitingly than Peel, he would say to his captain after being hit a few times, wiping his global forehead with his handkerchief, 'It's a fine day, Mr MacLaren.' Always willing, he bowled 630 balls (taking 4 for 306) in Lancashire's match against Sussex at Old Trafford in 1897 — still a Championship record.

Johnny Briggs was an epileptic, and it was consciousness of the nearness of a record — his 100 wickets against Australia — which triggered off his crucial breakdown. MacLaren, aware of the six wickets needed, and, of course, of Briggs's continuing good form, urged his inclusion in the England team for the third Test of 1899, at Headingley — Leeds' first Test match. Briggs got Kelly, Darling and Laver on the opening day, but 'the excitement proved too much for him and sent him off his head'. He had a seizure and was taken from the field. Later he had a further fit while watching a variety show at the Empire, Leeds, and was admitted to Cheadle Asylum. He returned for a successful season in 1900 (taking 10 for 55 against Worcestershire) but a relapse ended his career, and he died on January 11, 1902, at the age of 39, leaving his beloved wife and twin sons to face the future.

All his life he had been accident-prone. As a young man, he broke his right arm while warming up for the Widnes v Sale rugby match; he badly sprained his right leg while trying to avoid a run-out in a Roses match; his right eyebrow was cut to the bone while playing hockey; he damaged a thumb when his bicycle crashed into a tram near Old Trafford; a sizzling straight-drive from Tom Hayward thudded against his heart, causing him to groan 'This will kill me', and an X-ray showed a rib pressing against a heart-valve; in Australia he was thrown from a bucking horse and had the stem of his pipe rammed through his gum into the roof of his mouth; another horse kicked him almost over the edge of a high precipice; but the main factor was held to be the sunstroke he suffered in South Africa, on which tour he took 7 for 17 and 8 for 11 (all bowled) in a match at Cape Town which was granted Test status. Then again, at Colombo he went for a swim with William Gunn in a harbour which they later found to be infested with sharks.

Briggs lived dangerously, even when he bowled. In a Lancashire-Yorkshire match, with six runs needed for victory, he threw up an alluring high delivery to the feared hitter, Ulyett. Not for him the spoiling ball at the pads. Ulyett smote it high and handsome — and Ward caught it against the rails.

Twelve times he took 100 or more wickets in a season, and when he died his tally of 2221 wickets was second only to Grace's. Scrupulously fair in his appealing, his conscience never had to cope with a batsman cheated out off his bowling. He was also one of the great cover fielders, and his batting, reduced in opportunity by the vast amount of bowling expected of him, brought him ten centuries, the highest 186 against Surrey at Liverpool, when he and Dick Pilling, the wicketkeeper, put on 173 in 100 minutes for the tenth wicket, a record. On that July day in 1885 Briggs had been a married man for no more than 24 hours.

D. L. A. Jephson described Briggs' bowling graphically: 'The ball left his hand with a finger flick that you could hear in the pavilion, and here was every known variety of flight...the ball was at you, spinning like a top; first a balloon of a ball that would drop much farther off than you thought, a lower one just on the same spot, both breaking away like smoke; then another, with nothing on, straight at the sticks...'

With these ploys, plus the fast yorker and even the ball which flew full-pitch to the batsman's shoulder, Briggs, all 5ft 5ins of him, bowled his way round Australia six times, making, he said, no more money in all than an Australian cricketer would pick up on just one tour of Britain. But Australian spectators remembered him with just as much affection. He scored a fast century in a Melbourne Test, took a Test hat-trick at Sydney, and had his best return — 12 for 136 — in an Ashes Test at Adelaide. At Lord's he took 11 for 74 in 1886, when no other England bowler could do much with the ball, and seven years later, at The Oval, he captured 10 Australians for 148 to help regain the Ashes. After these performances his pleasant singing voice would have been much in evidence in the dressing-room — if he was not being inspired to recite from *Macbeth*.

Bobby Peel, only an inch taller than Briggs, had not the same kind of bubbly innocence of nature. But he had plenty of determination, even when under the weather. At Sydney in December 1894, England, having followed-on, managed to set Australia 177 to win. By evening they had crawled to 113 for the loss of only two wickets, and it seemed all over. But it rained during the night, and the sixth morning broke to brilliant sunshine: a sure formula for a sticky pitch. England had the bowlers to use it... except that Peel had got drunk the night before, supposing the match to be all but lost. He had also had five teeth extracted just before the match, so when he arrived late at the ground, with Lockwood, who had also overslept, he must have felt confused at the prospect of England's sudden victory chance as well as embarrassed by Blackham's generosity in permitting a late start with England two short. The delay only worsened the glutinosity of the wicket, and after Drewy Stoddart, the English captain, had hurriedly put Peel under a cold shower to sober him up, the Yorkshireman exclaimed, 'Give me t'ball, Mr Stoddart, and I'll get t'boogers out before lunch!'

Two minutes before lunch it was all over. Peel, after being hit clean over the fence by left-hander Joe Darling, had him caught in front of the two-and-sixpenny seats, and when little snubnosed Briggs took over from big Tom Richardson, the procession began. The two slow men made the ball spin and jump, and on the treacherous turf Australia dissolved for 166, giving England victory by 10 runs, Peel 6 for 67, Briggs 3 for 25. Christmas was especially joyful for the travelling cricketers so far from home.

This was the last of Peel's four Australian tours. Before the next began, he was in disgrace. The story may have been coloured up over the years. Certainly his sobriety was sufficiently in doubt for Lord Hawke, who had seen it all before, to banish him. His friend, the yeoman all-rounder George Hirst, had tried to cover for him, telling His Lordship that Peel was ill and would not be down to the ground for some time. As the team, with substitute, took the field, a swaying Robert Peel appeared, red-faced, cap askew. To impress his captain of his fitness, he grabbed the ball and bowled it. He thought he was bowling at the stumps; the ball actually careered off and thudded against the sightscreen. The final disaster, which may or may not be accepted as fact, was Peel's decision to pass water on the pitch. His bladder may well have reached the point of painfully emphatic discomfort, which condition may have been coupled with a desire to recreate the awkward batting conditions at Sydney two or three years before. Lord Hawke understandably had had enough. At the age of 40 Peel was redundant, and had to find employment in league cricket.

Granted a long life, nevertheless he had more accomplishment than most with which to warm himself. For a man of his batting skill it was surprising that he did the double only once, in 1896; but he scored over 11,000 runs for Yorkshire, average 21, and still shared the county's eighth-wicket record at the time of his death. Nine times he took 100 wickets, and his best figures were 9 for 22 against Somerset in 1895. For England he had three outstanding sets of figures apart from the 6 for 67 at Sydney. In 1887-88, at that ground, he took 5 for 18 and 5 for 40. At Old Trafford a few months later he bamboozled Australia with 7 for 31 and 4 for 37, the match finishing before lunch on the second day. And at The Oval in 1896, in his final Test appearance, he took 6 for 23 as he and Hearne devastated the tourists for 44. To these may be added the special glory of having been in at the kill, as batsman or bowler, in all three English victories in Australia in 1894-95. What a man to have in the side. These rather than the humiliating personal anecdotes are the data which will endure in the record books. Peel was a man who not only succumbed frequently to temptation and probably had his head turned a degree or two by his success, but he did go about his cricket in a most manly style, barely blinking if he was hit to the boundary or dismissed cheaply. In spite of his occasional high scores, he had enough experience of failure, making three 'pairs' in his last four Test matches! If there was a perversity in his character it was shown, as Hawke said, 'when at his deadliest and congratulated afterwards one could detect no gleam of pleasure on his countenance.' Unlike Briggs, who would have grinned from ear to ear.

6. Edwardian Days

Edwin Tyler — Charlie Townsend — Ted Wainwright —
Walter Mead — Jephson, Simpson-Hayward and
Humphreys — Len Braund — 'Razor' Smith

Cricket was played with such gay abandon during the 1890s and in the
Edwardian years, thanks in the main to the stream of adventurous
amateurs who entered county cricket from the public schools and
universities, that bowlers such as Edwin Tyler could commit the ball to a
steepling flight-path in the knowledge that the challenge would be accepted,
with all the risk that went with it. It was honourable — not a matter of
shame — to be caught out in the country off a bold hit...in general terms
at least.

Tyler, with batsmen Palairet and Hewett and devil-may-care all-rounder
Sammy Woods, helped obtain first-class status for Somerset in 1891, and it
was not until 1900 that Tyler, for long under suspicion, was no-balled for
throwing. 'He was too slow to hurt anybody,' said *Wisden*, 'and so his
action, though often talked about, passed muster for many years.'

During those years he took all ten for 49 against Surrey, 9 for 33 against
Notts, both at Taunton, and six times took eight wickets in an innings.
Mighty Yorkshire found themselves worn away by his persistence to the
tune of 14 for 247 at Taunton in 1895. His action resembled that of a shot-
putter, and the finger-spun ball, which bounced steeply and quickly at
times, was a long time reaching a batsman, which disturbed many of them.
So slow was he that, like J. M. Barrie, the playwright, had he not been
satisfied with the flight he might almost have run after the ball and brought
it back. He was hit into the churchyard at Taunton often, of course, but he
was cheerful and disconcertingly generous in his applause of a good shot.
Like Bedi in the 1970s, he did nothing for an intelligent batsman's
confidence by clapping a six off his bowling. Tyler's next tempter would as
likely as not be held by Palairet or Daniell against the pavilion rails, or by
the brave Woods at short mid-off.

On the hard, spinning pitches of the West Country, a long line of
succession developed, the short-lived Beaumont Cranfield and Surrey exile
Braund linking the periods of Tyler and J. C. White for Somerset, while
Gloucestershire were well served by Woof, Paish, Townsend, Dennett and
Parker up to the 1930s.

Charlie Townsend was a remarkable cricketer, even as a teenager. A tall, gangling 16-year-old, he made his county debut while still at Clifton College, backing up vast leg-breaks with vigorous left-hand batting which was to bring him 21 centuries in the summers ahead, when his activities as a solicitor cut severely into his time. In 1895, while still only 18, he ranked as the finest amateur slow bowler since A. G. Steel, spinning out 16 Notts batsmen at Trent Bridge and 13 at Cheltenham, 15 Yorkshiremen, and a dozen each of Sussex, Surrey and Somerset, and having a gluttonous meal of 47 wickets in seven innings. Three years later he bettered this with 50 in seven innings. Back in 1893, his opening season, he had put an entry in the book which is unique to this day: a hat-trick of stumpings, tailenders Newton, Nichols and Tyler being beaten back to their crease by W. H. Brain's glovework at Cheltenham. Deservedly was Townsend — whose father, two brothers, and son played county cricket — one of the most talked-about players in a golden epoch.

Twice, in 1898 and 1899, he completed watchable 'doubles', defying the fears of those who felt his long, bony frame would not stand the exertion of constant play. On damp pitches he sometimes switched from leg-breaks to steadier off-breaks, his shambling approach and big delivery stride changing hardly at all. Gradually his batting gained preference altogether over his bowling. He achieved little in his two Test matches, but he was unquestionably one of cricket's phenomena, the more emphatically so in view of his tender years.

Arthur Paish, who took 354 wickets in his five seasons with Gloucestershire around the turn of the century, bowled slow left-arm on and outside off stump, a tempter in method. In 1948, when 74, he recalled, in a recording with John Arlott to mark the centenary of W. G. Grace's birth, just how sympathetic a captain old W.G. was, telling, in his lovely light Gloucester voice, how his huge skipper put his arm round his shoulder before his first county match and said, 'Now, my boy, you're not afraid to bowl to a man who's just made 300, are you?' He referred to Frank Sugg, of Lancashire, but, as with many an aged cricketer, Paish's memory was betraying him. Sugg made a mere 169 in the preceding match against Somerset.

Paish, who as a youngster had assisted Billy Woof at the Cheltenham College nets, died only weeks after the recording. It would have been fascinating to have heard his views on the catastrophe which befell him in his final season, 1903, when he was no-balled for throwing in consecutive matches at Bristol. Like Tyler and most of the successful left-arm slows, he tortured batsmen by somehow holding the ball back in the air. C. B. Fry, one of the game's most penetrative thinkers, was certain that left-arm bowlers imparted an altogether different kind of flight to that of right-armers, and for no apparent reason. He supported his theory with the claim that left-hand batsmen he had consulted also felt this was true. If so, it would help explain why Arthur Conan Doyle felt so strongly that they should be banned by law.

Among the other purveyors of mystical bowling late in the 19th Century was Harry Baldwin, who, in a well-known photograph, is shown hitching up his capacious flannels around a body shaped like a rugby ball. He played for Hampshire for nearly 20 years, before they were any sort of power in the land, bowling from his 5ft 6ins with a fastish arm action, and letting the ball occasionally go early, producing a provocative slow one. At times batsmen capitulated to him like lemmings.

In the north, Ted Wainwright established himself as one of the most successful all-rounders Yorkshire has ever had, with a highest score of 228 against Surrey in 1899. As a bowler, he spun a deadly off-break on a helpful wicket, as at Dewsbury in 1894, where he took 6 for 18 and 7 for 20 against a helpless Sussex, bowling throughout both innings with Peel. Wainwright finished the match by taking five wickets in seven balls. 'Slow in its flight,' Jephson described his bowling, 'yet on touching the mud it would rush at you — I had almost said bite you.'

Tall and good-humoured, with the ears and features of a pugilist, Wainwright was a popular player; but a failure in Australia with Stoddart's second team. Neville Cardus got to know him in 1913 when he was coach at Shrewsbury School, and Cardus a slightly bewildered assistant. 'Every night,' wrote Cardus, 'he got drunk as a matter of course, quietly and masterfully.' Perhaps he was trying to forget the Australian tour, when he finished 11th in the team's bowling and was played in four Tests, none too successfully, as a batsman. Perhaps apocryphally, but believably, he was said to have fallen to his knees and kissed the ground when he returned and saw his first green English cricket square in the spring of 1898.

Cardus tells of a county match in which Wainwright bowled out ten men. 'Where were their legs?' he was asked, for in those days one could not be lbw if the ball pitched outside off stump. It was explained that padding the ball away would have been considered contrary to aesthetic morality. Such attitudes never bothered the great Shrewsbury. Wainwright said, 'Ah once bowled all day at him on a Trent Bridge beauty, and Ah never gets a glimpse of 'is stumps; and gettin' on for half-past six Ah asks 'im, "Has t'a gotten noa wickets behind thi at yon end?"'

Around the Home Counties, Kent had Alec Hearne, and Essex had Walter Mead and F. G. Bull. To look at Hearne first: he was a member of a prolific cricketing family whose more famous members would need a chapter to themselves as well as a genealogical diagram. Alec, 5ft 6ins, which would seem to be the average height for leg-spinners and slow left-armers, was a fine defensive batsman, and still shares Kent's oldest partnership record: 321 for the third wicket, with J. R. Mason, against Notts in 1899. As a bowler, he sent down leg-spinners and occasional off-breaks at a brisk pace, and had the skill to make one of the major batsmen of his day play back, then forward, then half-cock before being clean bowled, still ignorant of what the ball did and how he might have countered it. Hearne's field, as shown in a photograph in C. B. Fry's *Book of Cricket*, included a first slip very deep, a second slip deeper still, and a gully, which suggests bowling of the more pacy S. F. Barnes variety, well-nigh impossible to repel on its day. With the caution often wrought by maturity, Alec Hearne switched almost entirely to off-spin as the years passed, and worked his way up the batting order from the tailend to opener. He was hardheadedly professional enough to run out Tyler at Taunton when he left the non-striker's crease before the ball was bowled.

Diminutive Walter Mead was known as 'The Essex Treasure', though whether the affection inherent in the nickname was upheld in 1903, when he offended the committee by pressing obstinately for more winter pay, is a matter of conjecture. Here was one of the big wicket-takers in a struggling county where such talent was sorely required. He took 1916 wickets in a long career, and would have passed 2000 but for the two years he was missing from the Essex XI, Bert Tremlin filling his place. The cloth-caps of Leyton were glad to see him back, lugubrious of countenance though he was, and though his 'long, strong sinuous' forefinger was not to bring him quite such sensational returns as before, he remained a valuable player until 1913, by which time he was 44.

Mead was one of the genuine spin bowlers; no specialisation, but with mastery of the off-break and the leg-break — Fry said the off-break often came from a leg-spinner's action, which prompts the question yet again: was he bowling googlies before Bosanquet? He used the leg-break sparingly, aware of its tendency to be wayward, and that the change in action was not exactly a secret. 'Muffling' the ball in his stomach as he ran up, with the ball cupped by thumb and second finger, he bowled with a high arm and dipping left shoulder, with a circular arm-swing and springy followthrough. Unlike fellow Essex bowler Bill Reeves, later so famous as one of the drollest of witty umpires, Mead gave the ball air, causing his leg-break to leave the ground with a 'curious upward curl'. He was often too much for even the strongest side, taking 9 for 136 and 8 for 69 against the 1893 Australians, and three times taking nine wickets in an innings of a county match (having taken eight in the first innings of Hampshire in 1895). Yet only once did he play for England. At Lord's in 1899 he took only one for 91 as young Trumper and Hill made wondrous centuries. Had he had the fortune to bowl on a helpful wicket a few seasons earlier, his Test career might have been longer, and his reputation guaranteed through posterity. As it is, he stands behind only three others in Essex's all-time wicket-takers' list.

Frederick George Bull had a lot of success for Essex — and the Gentlemen — in the late 1890s before taking up a series of league professional appointments in the north. P. F. Warner regarded him as the best slow bowler in England in 1897, when, aged only 21, he took 120 wickets. Like Mead, he turned the ball either way, and was thought of as foremost among 'thinking' bowlers. Assistant secretary for Essex, he was the most successful bowler on Warner's American tour in 1897, a year in which he was in the news not only for his 9 for 93 against Surrey, 13 for 156 in the Derbyshire match, and 14 for 176 against Lancashire, but for trying to avoid a Lancashire follow-on in the face of a compulsory follow-on rule.

He attempted to give the opposition runs by bowling wides, but Arthur Mold, awake to the ruse, knocked his own stumps over. Lancashire thus batted again, but Essex eventually won.

Bull's end was a grim one. Weighting his pockets with stones and placing a 7lb rock in a large handkerchief around his neck, he drowned himself in the sea off St Annes. He was 34.

Of bowlers in the Hearne/Mead mould, Willis Cuttell of Lancashire was a heavy wicket-taker as well as a centurymaker. On a 'billiard-table' pitch he could bowl tight, and once conceded only three runs in a spell of 75 minutes against Surrey. A league professional before his belated county debut (after a couple of appearances for Yorkshire) at the age of 31, he was the first Lancashire player to do the double. He played twice for England during Lord Hawke's tour of South Africa in 1898-99, holding the batsmen down at Johannesburg with 24 maidens in his 32 overs as South Africa managed only 99, losing by 32 runs. Albert Trott took 5 for 49 in that innings, and so 'superlative' was the English team's reputation, according to their leader, that 'it was even said that the smoke from Trott's cigarette broke in from leg'.

Surrey seemed to have found themselves a top left-arm slow bowler in F. E. Smith, who gave the mighty pace pair, Richardson and Lockwood, the perfect support during the Championship years of 1894 and 1895. In the former season they took 414 wickets between them, no-one else managing more than 14. Frank Smith came from Suffolk, but hopes of a long career were shattered by a loss of form, and he spent later years coaching in South Africa and at Sedbergh School, Yorkshire. Surrey, unlike Yorkshire, have lacked a long line of slow left-arm bowlers.

They did, though, have a highly successful lob bowler in D. L. A. Jephson, a tall-scoring all-rounder who began as a fast roundarm bowler. He developed the lob when it was already becoming a quaint memory, and bowled it well enough to take 6 for 21 in the Gentlemen-Players match at Lord's in 1899. He also diddled out three Middlesex batsmen for a hat-trick at The Oval five years later, and twice took all ten in club cricket. He aimed usually to leg, with two short legs, two mid-ons, a long leg, long-on and straight-hit fieldsman in the country. Sunday League cricket in the 1970s has forced batsmen to step back and clout leg-side bowling through the covers — none did it better than Barry Richards — but in Jephson's time this would have been thought too revolutionary — even improper — though bold men such as Sir Timothy O'Brien of Middlesex were not averse to smashing bouncing lobs and suchlike straight at the wicketkeeper, whose strident protests would persuade the bowler to alter his line.

Jephson, who bore a striking resemblance to Prime Minister Harold Macmillan, was a man of humour and inventiveness. He often bowled a batsman with a sudden straight ball which kept low, or one which came in from the off. He also used a surprise full-pitch, as well as the teaser tossed high and dropping short of a length.

Jephson, the subject of the only *horizontal* 'Spy' cartoon ('The Lobster')

— because of his crouching action — believed that lobs, in a healthy team, should only be used 'medicinally', i.e. when the need arose and not as stock bowling. He wrote poetry, most of which is best forgotten, and stylish and instructional prose, much of which gives great insight into the game of 80 years ago and more. 'We, the solitary few who still strive to hold upright the tottering pillars in the ruined temple of lob bowling,' he wrote in the Country Life Library, 'unto whose shrine the bowlers of the olden time for ever flocked, today we are but of small account; there is scarcely a ground in England where derision is not our lot, or where laughter and jaunting jeers are not hurled broadcast at us.'

He goes on to pay tribute to G. H. T. Simpson-Hayward, the Worcestershire 'lobster', who flicked the ball 'as we have all seen many a wrathful billiard-player do when returning the white from a most unexpected pocket — it spins and spins and breaks sharply from the off, and it sometimes hits the wicket.' Like Lamborn over 100 years before him, George Simpson-Hayward had the field practically to himself, and the unfamiliarity of his bowling must have brought him much of his success. He gathered 510 wickets at 21.46 in the years leading up to the Great War, adding to his fame and popularity by taking 6 for 43 on the Johannesburg matting in the first of his five Test matches in 1909-10.

Taken by Leveson Gower to South Africa by way of experiment, Simpson-Hayward must have given his captain deep satisfaction at his ability to worry the likes of Sinclair and Zulch. He was the bowling success of the tour, with Jack Hobbs the batting revelation. South Africa, though, had the bowling trumps in Vogler and Faulkner, and won three-two. England's third-Test victory, however, owed much to Simpson-Hayward, who showed his liking for Johannesburg with a second-innings return of 5 for 69. He would have been a more effective bowler, said his skipper, if he had been a better fielder to his own bowling. Still, his rewards in South Africa might have inspired a new breed of lob bowlers. But they didn't. The only genuine lobster to play county cricket after the First World War was Trevor Molony, a Reptonian, who played just four times for Surrey in 1921, taking four wickets, including 3 for 11 at Trent Bridge. Since then — apart from the Chappell outrage at Melbourne in February 1981, and odd little protests, such as that by Reg Simpson, the Notts captain, who bowled an over of lobs against a go-slow Glamorgan in 1951 — this particular 'art form' awaits revival.

Digby Jephson, in his 1901 article, discussed the relative merits of contemporary bowlers of leg-spin, 'or *tosh*, as we were wont to call it', branding it a more effective way of getting rid of many a great batsman than faster, straighter bowling on firm wickets. The slowest, he felt, was the Reverend G. B. Raikes of Hampshire, with Fred Geeson of Leicestershire close in pace. Geeson turned to leg-breaks after the county captains had condemned his medium-pace bowling action at their December 1900 meeting. Immediately, Geeson embarked on a new technique, at which he must certainly have dabbled in past years, probably at the practice nets, and in 1901 he took an amazing tally of 125 wickets. But he was a one-season wonder. After half-a-dozen seasons in county cricket, his style-switch must have created much surprise among his adversaries. All the same, at the age of 38 it was a daring thing to do, and won for him at least an entry in the lists of curiosities, for Whiteside stumped the first four Essex batsmen off his bowling in one innings.

At the other end of the pace scale was Joe Vine. His leg-breaks were delivered at such a speed that, of all those mentioned, he alone needed a long-stop fieldsman. Bowling around the wicket, with a low arm, Vine differed from those who were expert in imparting leg-spin to genuinely fast balls — such as the supreme S. F. Barnes, jokey Billy Buttress, and the comical, gangling Notts bowler Tom Wass — only in his trajectory, which was lower, and in his field-placing, which was heavily accented to the leg side. On his day, Vine would aspire to that magical, mystical but only truly theoretical delivery: the 'unplayable'. The batsmen thus concerned were much inclined to rate him the best of the period. His career stretched from 1896 to 1922, by which time he was 47, and his value as a flexible, adaptable and unselfish all-rounder for Sussex came close to matching that of George Hirst, the model professional, for Yorkshire. Short and with the obligatory moustache of the period, Vine played only twice for England. He did not bowl, but batted his way into the record book with a seventh-wicket stand of 143 with Frank Woolley in the fifth Test of the 1911-12 series, at Sydney.

Only slightly behind Vine in speed through the air was Len Braund, who turned to Somerset after a few unspectacular seasons with Surrey. Renowned for his accuracy (C. B. Fry claimed that not even Grimmett was more accurate), he could keep the best of batsmen quiet on a hard wicket, and, even more unusually, he could get the best out of a damp wicket, when the off-spinner and slow left-armer are supposed to have conditions all to themselves. A clue to his accuracy is the fact that he bowled close to the stumps, cocked wrist whirling over them, with his front foot coming down near the batting blockhole. His strong finger-action and wristwork ensured pace from the pitch, and, with an alerting if easily-recognised fast ball mixed in, he wore away at the target, seldom switching to tempters outside leg. Almost alone, Braund would seem to have been a leg-spin bowler who would reap rich rewards in the tougher atmosphere prevailing in the 1980s. It is inconceivable that today's batsmen would have got out so frequently to catches on the leg side off wide deliveries; even those spinning in sharply would be repelled by pads, the safest weapons — or, if the 1980 ruling of lbw against a ball pitching outside leg (from a spinner operating over the wicket) rendered this dangerous, then a dab here and there would suffice. In any case, if the ghosts of those late-Victorian and Edwardian leg-spinners were herded to the front seats of the pavilion on the rare occasion when a spinner — especially an off-spinner — were in action today, they would ask in unison why there were so few fielders on the on side. The answer is in the files of the administrators.

Back to Len Braund. Here was another complete all-rounder: a very fine batsman, with 25 centuries to his name, three for England, and a glorious slip fieldsman, whose catch off a firm glance by Clem Hill at leg slip after darting across from slip was the talk of the nation for days. The setting was Edgbaston, and Australia slid to 36 all out. If there had been television in the home in 1902, how that event — and the most memorable of Braund's 547 catches — would have been played back again and again.

He played in 23 Tests, and paid 38.51 for his 47 wickets, conceding just under three runs per six-ball over and needing 80 balls to take each wicket. But 15 of those Tests were played during his three tours of Australia, where batsmen were well-versed in facing leg-spin, and were already using their feet to get to the pitch of the ball in such a fashion as to establish a reputation — shared by South Africans and West Indians — of advancing like cavalrymen to the arched ball rather than playing it cautiously from the crease. Even so, Braund had a field day at Melbourne in March 1904, when he took 8 for 81 after opening the bowling with Hirst. His left-hand caught-and-bowled to send Trumper on his way for 88 was a beauty, and he had a hand in a ninth wicket when he caught Hill at slip off Rhodes. Although England lost in the end, it was a memorable conclusion to the series for Braund, who had scored a century in the first Test match, adding 192 with R. E. Foster (287) for the fifth wicket.

He was a yeoman cricketer, always a trier, whose persistent line and length would have been an inspiration to any young wrist-spinner. There were days, naturally, when he was hit. Jessop, the most ferocious and consistent hitter in history, once smashed six boundaries, two of them out of the ground, in an over at Bristol, clumping him through the empty off side even though the direction was leg-side, to an appropriate field. Braund never panicked, though he would not have been human had he not felt a passing depression.

He went on to become an umpire, standing in Tests, and was a respected coach. During the Second World War the front windows of his house in Fulham were blown out several times by German bombing, and leg ailments led to the amputation of first one limb then the other. But through it all, to judge from surviving letters, he remained indomitable and cheerful, and when cricket was resumed he was glad to reminisce from his bathchair as he watched cricket at Lord's, where he had once made a century against South Africa.

Of the other leg-spinners around the turn of the century, A. O. Jones, the Nottinghamshire captain, bowled a wide break, a curling delivery from a lowish arm, though he used himself more as a change bowler; tiny Billy Quaife of Warwickshire, surviving an ominous county captains' report on his action, went on to take over 900 wickets by his retirement at the age of 56; and Worcestershire's Dick Pearson, a loyal utility player, who bowled fast-medium as well as 'leggers' with plenty of spin for a quarter of a century, carrying the attack with swing bowler Fred Root. There were also wicketkeepers who took an occasional turn with the ball: the rough-and-ready Bill Storer of Derbyshire was often effective, spinning the ball in the manner of Australia's Harry Trott; Dick Lilley of Warwickshire and England actually bowled in a Test match, having success (like Storer) when he had Trott caught behind by J. T. Brown (himself an occasional leg-spinner who once did the hat-trick). Lilley's joy was short-lived. W. G. Grace thanked him and told him to put the gloves back on. Earlier still, the Honourable Alfred Lyttelton had been called upon to break an obstinate Australian stand in the Oval Test of 1884. It is thought that the lanky future Colonial Secretary did not even bother removing his pads as he amused all bar the Australians by taking 4 for 19 with lobs. All eleven Englishmen bowled in Australia's innings of 551. And earlier still, Tom Lockyer, the Surrey and All-England wicketkeeper, sometimes bowled slow teasers to advantage. To this day, wicketkeepers can often be observed bowling fizzing, twisting deliveries at the nets; but the practice of using them as surprise weapons during a match has all but died.

An interesting leg-spinner of the pre-Great War years was prolific Essex rungetter Charlie McGahey, whose system was similar to that of the gargantuan Australian, Warwick Armstrong. Coming down from a good height, the ball turned only a little way; but his direction was reliable — and negative. It was not unknown for him to have every single fieldsman on the leg side. He was feared on a crumbling pitch, though on one occasion so sporting was his captain, A. P. Lucas, that he took the demon fast bowler Kortright off when he saw the rough marks he was making in his followthrough. McGahey could land on them as if manipulated by a computer, and such tactics offended the sense of decency then prevailing.

Of the other successful slow bowlers on view daily on the county grounds of England as Victoria's lengthy reign drew to a close, Walter Humphreys, one of the last of the lob bowlers, did his stuff for Sussex — and almost for England. Stoddart took him to Australia in 1894-95, but while the batsmen in the lesser matches found him too much for them, the senior players would have applied themselves patiently to his gentle underhand guile. There was no call for him in an England XI which boasted Richardson, Lockwood, Peel and Briggs, with a few all-rounders available to hold the fort while they recovered from their exertions in the heat. Humphreys was 45 by now; but he proved a good tourist, carving the roast beef and taking charge of celebrations during the Christmas break. Prematurely grey, Humphreys kept himself fit by riding a tricycle. 'Lob bowling takes it out of you,' he once stunningly remarked. The fatigue must have resulted from an unduly long run-up and extensive followthrough. He claimed it gave him a unique kind of excitement to run through after delivery, especially to a hard-hitter. An underhand bowler since boyhood, when he discovered he could spin the ball half a yard from the off, he liked fast wickets, where the ball would hurry through. Slow pitches gave the batsman time to adjust. George Giffen once reacted with strange logic after missing an off-break and running a bye: 'If I'd only known which way that ball was going to break I'd have given him Johnny up the orchard, I can tell you!' Many a lesser batsman has comforted himself with just such a stupid observation.

Humphreys, though a mild and cheerful man, sometimes upset opposing batsmen with the flapping of his loose shirtsleeve. It was not gamesmanship on his part; purely for convenience; and he always buttoned or rolled it up if a protest reached his ears. Nor was Sussex wicketkeeper Harry Phillips always at ease when taking his bowling. Humphreys had been playing for Sussex for nine years before he felt ready to put his studies of lob bowling into practice. A hat-trick against the 1880 Australians was an early stimulus, but his progress thereafter was very slow. . . until the Australians of 1884 provided him with another hat-trick. It was a high-class threesome too: McDonnell, Giffen and Scott. Murdoch, in the 1882 match, even when he was 200 not out, could not tell with confidence which way Humphreys would turn the ball, which suggests that he may have sent down an occasional underhand googly. He took almost 700 wickets for Sussex, with 148 in 1893 by far his best season's work, and several times he took eight wickets in an innings. In club cricket he often appeared as a smiling, crafty demon, once taking 8 for 0, and three times taking all ten wickets for Brighton Brunswick. If it does 'take it out of you', lob bowling — then at least — was often worth the sweat.

A most potent slow bowler, one of those 'near all-time greats but all but forgotten', was W. C. Smith, christened 'Razor' by Tom Richardson. He was born in Oxford in 1877, and was destined never to enjoy maximum health. He was frail of build and had a weak heart — in the physical sense — thus seldom playing a full season. For years he was used, rather like early Underwood, as a wet-wicket specialist. He spun a very sharp off-break and caused the ball to swerve out with the spin. In 1910, when he added a new variety to his repertoire, a fast, kicking leg-break, which produced many short-leg catches for the brave and skilful Bill Hitch, Smith bagged 247 wickets in all first-class matches at an average of 13.05. The next-highest wicket-taker was Blythe with 175.

The best figures of this sensational summer came against Northants at The Oval in July, when Smith took 6 for 16 and 8 for 13 as the visitors collapsed for 51 in each innings, and finished with a hat-trick denied him in the first innings by a dropped catch. During this season, in which it was almost a matter for comment if 'Razor' Smith did not take five or six wickets in an innings, P. F. Warner voiced disapproval at the nearness of Hitch at short leg. But the rugged all-rounder was favoured by Smith's immaculate length and his own smart reflexes — and helmets in the field were not even a dream.

'Razor' performed well against successive Australian touring teams, but none came in 1910, his *annus mirabilis*, when he must have gained a Test cap. As it remained, he went uncapped, his highest representative marks being two good analyses for the Players against the Gentlemen and an MCC tour to West Indies in 1912-13, some years before the islands had Test status. He took five wickets on the tour, average 53, and *Wisden's* pathetic comment was: 'W. C. Smith bowled to no purpose'.

Back in 1909 he had bowled to some purpose against reigning champions Yorkshire, whose all-out total of 26 on a treacherous Oval pitch was to be their lowest until 1965. Needing 113 to win in 80 minutes, they were all out with half an hour to spare, Tom Rushby 5 for 9, Smith 5 for 12.

Herbert Strudwick, Surrey's gentlemanly little wicketkeeper, was understandably a firm admirer of 'Razor', off whom he even took catches some feet up the pitch, so lively was he. He wrote once of 'Razor's' bad luck at Cheltenham. After three lbws, another plumb one was denied him. 'Why not?' demanded 'Razor'. 'Well,' replied the umpire, 'I've already given three out, and I can't give any more out just yet.'

In 1909 some of the Surrey players came close to being jailed at Chesterfield when a policeman found them indulging in nothing more harmful than kicking around the street (with a small horde of local boys) a large ball which 'Razor' had bought for one of his children. While 'Razor' and the Australian, Alan Marshal, were being interviewed by the constable, Strudwick and Walter Lees slipped off. Their 'loyal' team-mates saw to it, though, that their names were top of the list in the morning paper, in which the item was headed SURREY TEAM ARRESTED. 'Razor' Smith was not put off his game, taking seven Derbyshire wickets for 46 to set up an innings victory.

Smith died in 1946 from heart failure, in the office of Stuart Surridge, where he had worked for a number of years. He was 68, and regarded still as the finest Surrey slow bowler since Southerton. In that curious manner of sequence characteristic of cricket history, two days afterwards, a young off-spinner made his debut for the county against Combined Services. His name was Jim Laker.

7. 'Bosie'

B.J.T. Bosanquet's revolution — R.O. Schwarz

The 20th Century, the most eventful century in the history of man, ingeniously inventive at the same time as it has been criminally destructive, was quick to produce a technical phenomenon for cricket. It was christened the 'googly' (despite the existing and quite different meaning of the term); or the 'bosie' (acknowledging its chief practitioner); or, particularly in Australia, the 'wrong'un', a wry description of a piece of bowling which was meant to deceive. 'Wrong'un' was a term often applied to felons, divorcees and homosexuals (*cf* Lord Alfred Douglas, Oscar Wilde's favourite boyfriend, who also, curiously enough, was referred to as 'Bosey'). However it was called, it rapidly moved out of the joke class into a bowling weapon capable of winning a Test match, a Test series.

Bernard James Tindal Bosanquet was no more the inventor of the googly than Wilbur and Orville Wright, around the same time, were the inventors of propelled flying machines. Others had dabbled, though in the case of the googly ball the instances were undoubtedly accidental. What Bosanquet and the Wright brothers had in common was that they are acknowledged as the first to succeed 'in the field'. The flimsy-framed aircraft that stayed airborne for 12 seconds at Kitty Hawk, North Carolina on December 17, 1903 was the forerunner of Concorde; Bosanquet's little mischief was handed on to a school of clever, determined South Africans and on through a line of exponents whose pleasure at fooling batsmen of even the highest reputation has been deep and incomparable. Though a precious rarity today, especially in Test cricket, the googly has at least long outlived its original association with immorality. As with the early roundarm and then overarm deliveries, it was regarded by some as cheating — if not as clowning.

Bosanquet was born in Enfield, Middlesex, on October 13, 1877, and went from Eton to Oxford, where he was a fast-bowling batsman, also representing the University at hammer-throwing and billiards. Strangely, his batting was notably short of wristwork, and though he was good enough twice to score twin centuries in a match for Middlesex at Lord's, he did it with the power that came through strong forearms, with little freedom of swing: 'a quick stabbing lift, picking the ball up on the rise'.

The year 1897 found Bosanquet first fascinated by the ball which, he later wrote, is 'merely a ball with an ordinary break produced by an extraordinary method'. He was playing 'twisti-twosti', a pastime as daffy as its name suggests. The object is to spin a tennis-ball past your opponent, who is seated at the other end of a table. Bosanquet's over-the-wrist action sent the ball puzzlingly bouncing from his opponent's right side to his left. At the time, it seemed too much for the intellect to absorb. Within a couple of years Bosanquet had become the 'star turn' at the nets during intervals of matches at Oxford, demonstrating his reverse spin with a cricket ball, to his own vast amusement and the despair of a parade of eminent visiting batsmen.

After further experiment in minor matches, he eventually gathered the nerve to bowl a googly in a county game. The unfortunate batsman was left-handed Sam Coe of Leicestershire. He was rendered triply unfortunate by the facts that the ball bounced four times before the wicketkeeper took it and stumped him — and his score was 98. This also happened to be one of the matches in which Bosanquet himself scored two centuries, the second helping his side to make 304 for victory by five wickets. This convivial and good-humoured man's nature had sufficient of a dark side to it for him to pretend that this and further successes were all mysterious accidents, and he even persuaded his captain, P. F. Warner, not to put it about that the science of bowling was in the process of having a fresh chapter written.

Bosanquet acknowledged that bowlers previously had probably bowled this ball without quite realising what they had been doing. He cited William Attewell, the Nottinghamshire and England medium-pacer, and the eccentric E. R. Wilson of Rugby, Cambridge and Yorkshire. To their names might have been added A. G. Steel, 'Joey' Palmer the Australian, and H. V. Page of Oxford and Gloucestershire, who, according to K. J. Key in a letter to Jack Hobbs, bowled genuine googlies as long ago as 1885, though only at the fall of a wicket, never actually in a match. (Nonetheless, Page was known to bowl a ball with a leg-break action which curled from leg and broke from the off — a sure sign.)

Bosanquet knew what he was doing all right; having long grown tired of bowling fast on a flat pitch and under a sweltering sun, he preferred to 'walk slowly up to the wicket and gently propel the ball into the air'.

Recalling his pioneering days in an article in the 1925 *Wisden*, he wrote: 'It took any amount of perseverance, but for a year or two the results were more than worth it, for in addition to adding to the merriment of the cricketing world, I found that batsmen who used to grin at the sight of me and grasp their bat firmly by the long handle began to show a marked preference for the other end!' Sussex must have been among the first to experience this emotional switch when he took 9 for 31 (15 for 65) against them for Oxford in 1900.

One evening at Lord's in 1902 he sent his first Australian packing. Opening the bowling for Middlesex against makeshift opener, wicket-keeper Jim Kelly, he had him lbw; but had to be taken off after four overs as Trumper started to hit him about. Within the year he was making his most telling breakthrough, for at the end of Lord Hawke's tour of New Zealand, three matches were played in Australia. In the first, against Victoria, Bosanquet's bowling was again a bit on the wild side: Harry Graham had to skip out to point to hit one ball! But at the then modestly-developed Sydney Cricket Ground, against NSW, he bowled two leg-breaks to the immortal Trumper, who had made a swift 37, which were played with characteristic ease and beauty of movement into the covers. Then, 'with a silent prayer', the googly was dispatched. Trumper played forward again languidly, and his middle stump was tilted backwards. In subsequent Bosanquet-Trumper duels, according to A. E. Knight, the batsman often saw the googly coming, yet was barely able to cope. The extra pace and bounce induced by the top-spin — analogous to the 'following-up' stroke at billiards — gave the bowler a supremacy against any but the most watchful, skilled batsman.

The great Shrewsbury, being unable to decipher him, played everything as an off-break, mumbling darkly to his colleagues that the googly was 'unfair'. Some, like the Warwickshire and England wicketkeeper 'Dick' Lilley, who was behind the stumps in all of Bosanquet's seven Test matches announced rather too audibly that they could pick the wrong'un. The bowler, alerted to the news and faced with a fresh challenge, bowled Lilley two overs of standard leg-breaks, then altered his body and arm action while sending down an identical ball. Lilley played a delicate and confident leg-glance as he imagined the ball to turn towards his pads. . . and had his off stump flattened.

The mystique surrounding the revolutionary ball was hardly lessened by its being given a name. Indeed, the name of its first regular exploiter (pronounced Bo-san-kay) hinted at something foreign: and therefore not to be trusted! He was of Huguenot descent — as was one of his finest disciples half-a-century later, Richie Benaud — but we shall probably never know positively how the term 'googly' came about. As already discussed, the earlier 'googly' or 'googler' was no more than a high-tossed teasing delivery, and in Australia the ordinary leg-break was often referred to as such. Bosanquet's ball, suggested Tom Horan, writing as 'Felix' for *The Australasian*, was aptly named if one accepted that 'goo' was a sound associated with babyish matters, and when added to 'guile', made a complete and acceptable appellation. Less likely but more romantic is the suggestion that the word is of Maori origin, borrowed during the 1902-03 tour, when, embarrassing his captain if not himself, Bosanquet frequently let slip a three- or four-bouncer to a bemused New Zealand batsman.

The acid test came on the 1903-04 tour of Australia, the first to be conducted under the flag of MCC. The selection committee, which included A. G. Steel, chose three spin bowlers, Rhodes, all-rounder Braund, and Bosanquet, whose selection caused quite a furore, with accusations that 'Plum' Warner must have insisted on the inclusion of his Oxford and Middlesex 'pet'. Warner would have known, however, that if

Bosanquet's bowling failed, his batting would stand him in good stead.

So off they sailed in *Orontes*, 'Bosie' inevitably wondering some nights, as he lay his head on the pillow, just how he would fare, how steady his length would be, how alive to his ruses would Trumper, Hill, Duff, and Noble be. Little he did before the opening Test match, apart from innings of 79 against Victoria and 99 (run out) in a minor match, and a timely 4 for 60 against NSW, offered much encouragement. But he was chosen for the first international, rendered famous by R. E. Foster's 287 and Trumper's 185 not out, and took three important wickets for 152 in his Test debut, bowling Warwick Armstrong after a 2½-hour innings and hitting Syd Gregory's middle and leg stumps with googlies in the first innings. In the second, when he troubled Trumper, his luck was out, and his one wicket, Noble (stumped), cost 100 runs off 23 overs. England won one of the most talked-about Test matches by five wickets, but Bosanquet lost his place. Once more, though, cricket history throws up a neat line in continuity in that two of the great googly bowlers of the future had been watching and taking it all in — Herbert Hordern in the members' stand and poor boy Arthur Mailey on the Hill.

Bosanquet was back for the third Test, at Adelaide, and took 3 for 95 and 4 for 73; but centuries by Trumper and Gregory helped Australia to victory by 216 runs, making it two-one to England with two to play.

Fine attacking centuries against Tasmania and NSW (75 minutes) might not have been enough to secure his place for the fourth Test at Sydney, especially as he bowled 'abominably' in the Apple Isle; but here 'Dick' Lilley had a fateful hand in matters. He urged Warner to give Bosanquet another over on the last day against NSW, and then another; and he finished with 6 for 45, bowling Hopkins and the brilliant 'Sunny Jim' Mackay with googlies. He was in for the fourth Test at Sydney, and about to snatch some glory.

In the final innings of the match Australia needed 329 to win, which would have been easily the highest total of the match. Yet the pitch was in fair order, and quite fast. With McAlister, Duff and Trumper out for 59, Warner called up Bosanquet (called 'Elsie' by the occupants of the Hill in reaction to his colourful sweater) fifteen minutes before the tea interval. He instantly had Clem Hill stumped and Gregory lbw, and after the break he was indebted to Lilley for stumping Hopkins, catching Charlie McLeod, and stumping Trumble (for a 'pair') — at which stage Bosanquet had 5 for 12. Later he had Kelly caught by R. E. Foster at slip, and would have had Noble lbw if he had bothered to appeal. No such mistake would be made in Test cricket of the Space Age.

The muscular fast bowler 'Tibby' Cotter belted him for a few fours, spoiling his final figures, but his 15-1-51-6 was the eye-catching statistic that afternoon that England won back the Ashes, and suddenly all the ridicule must have seemed immaterial. Nobody smiled more broadly than skipper Warner.

The final Test followed immediately in Melbourne, and Bosanquet did nothing of note, his four overs costing 27 runs. Australia had a face-saving victory and Hugh Trumble a hat-trick and 7 for 28 in his ultimate Test match. But England had the Ashes, and it remained to be seen how the individual successes of the tour would fare in coming years.

B. J. T. Bosanquet fared well in 1904. He comfortably did the double for the only time, and at Sheffield made up for his five Yorkshire wickets with bowling of 'wretched' length by scoring 141 when Middlesex batted. Two matches, however, were of far-reaching significance. Frank Mitchell's South African side toured England in 1904, and had in their ranks R. O. Schwarz, an acquaintance of Bosanquet's. Handsome, modest, and, as *Wisden* made a point of stating, with 'a peculiarly attractive voice', Reggie Schwarz won three caps as a half-back for the England XV, and played cricket a few times for Middlesex before taking up a position as secretary to Sir Abe Bailey, a Transvaal financier.

Bosanquet showed his pleasure at meeting Schwarz again in the spring of 1904, in the opening match of the tour, MCC at Lord's, by taking 9 for 107. Schwarz was one of four Springboks to be stumped. Three weeks later the tourists met Middlesex, Bosanquet this time making a century and bowling Tancred and Sinclair, while Schwarz took 5 for 48 in the second innings. The match finished in a tie, but equally notable was the fact that there was now another reliable practitioner of the googly. Schwarz had thought about it, practised it, and tried it against Oxford University, taking 5 for 27. Now here he was, at the game's headquarters, skittling the county, Warner among his victims. Three further weeks on, he was back at Lord's, bowling nothing but googlies and top-spinners — here was something different again — and taking four wickets in each innings against an England XI, including Ranjitsinhji (lbw and stumped) and Jessop (bowled). When the South Africans next visited England, three years on, Schwarz and three others were to sweep like a spinning scourge across the land, having sounded a loud warning on their own matting wickets in 1905-06, when they beat England in four of the five Tests.

For Bosanquet, after his magnificent season of 1904, there remained one more summer of fulfilment. The 1905 Australians shaped well before the first Test match, at Trent Bridge, and were satisfied with a first-innings lead there. In England's second innings, though, MacLaren hit a century, Tyldesley 61, and F. S. Jackson, the captain, who could do no wrong that series, 82 not out before his declaration set Australia 402 for victory in under five hours, with Trumper's strained back preventing him from batting. The situation was ideal for the use of a bowler who might spray the ball everywhere — in between bowling the 'unplayable'.

'Bosie' was erratic at first, though this was little comfort to the Australian batsmen. It is easier to play a length ball than one which bounces twice. Jackson kept him on. After lunch the first wicket fell at 62: Duff c & b Bosanquet. At 75, Bosanquet began a spell in which he captured three more wickets in four overs: Noble stumped, Darling, the captain and a left-hander, bowled for 40, and Hill wonderfully caught-and-bowled one-handed up high, the bowler landing on his backside. When Armstrong was caught by Jackson at cover, Australia were 100 for 5, all the wickets belonging to Bosanquet.

Now he was hit around a bit by Cotter, whom Rhodes eventually bowled; and to Bosanquet went three more wickets as the light faded badly, one being Gregory (51), held by a juggling catch at mid-on as he tried to hit Bosanquet out of the attack; another being Frank Laver, who gave Lilley his best-ever stumping. The batsman, attempting a sweep, hid the ball from view with his burly body; suddenly the ball showed, Lilley snapped it up, and took off the bails before Laver could drop his bat.

One more sample of the chivalrous attitude of the time: Charlie McLeod felt that the match might be saved with an appeal against the light — there were no sightscreens — but wanted first to consult his captain. Darling came down to the fence and told him that England had earned her victory, and so to fight on. Bosanquet finished the match soon afterwards, trapping McLeod lbw. Trumper, in agony, was helped as far as the gate, but could not go on. Darling waved the players in. Australia all out 188, Bosanquet 8 for 107 (Jackson said only Duff and McLeod succumbed to the googly) off 32.4 overs — with two maidens that somehow crept in. It was Arthur Mailey who was to speak for slow bowlers everywhere when he stated that maiden overs were no use to him: there were two or three medium-pacers in the side who could bowl maiden overs. He was there to take wickets.

That was practically the end of Bosanquet as a wicket-taker — at least at Test level. He was not used in the rain-spoilt second Test at Lord's, and in the third Test, at Headingley, he managed only one wicket, Noble stumped, in 19 overs. He was dropped, never to return. 'Bosanquet was a complete disappointment,' said *Wisden* sadly.

And he knew it. By his own admission, some of the critical, 'ribald' Press items cut him, and with the incision died the googly as bowled by its father. Not that 1905 was all disappointment, for he had a stupendous match against Sussex at Lord's immediately before the first Test, scoring 103 in even time and 100 not out in 75 minutes, and taking 3 for 75 and 8 for 53. Yet from 1906 on, though he was to make plenty more runs for Middlesex, in that stiff, strong style of his (plus an astonishing 25-minute century for Uxbridge v MCC in 1908), the bowling was now left to others.

Traces of that open, slightly melancholy face could later be seen in his son Reginald, the toupeed television newsreader, who was but four when his father died in 1936 at Wykehurst Farm, Ewhurst, Surrey, a day before his 59th birthday. The family vault at Enfield Cemetery is imposing in its siting and proportions. Upon it ought to have been inscribed a quotation from an Australian newspaper: 'He is the worst length bowler in England and yet he is the only bowler the Australians fear.'

8.   The Costly Export

The South African googly quartet — H.V. Hordern

It is difficult to understand why, in the expansive free-and-easy mood prevailing in the Edwardian years, the googly did not spread around the counties. Apart from D. W. Carr, who played for England almost straight out of the ranks of club cricket, the counties were influenced hardly at all. Slow left-arm, fast and medium-pace bowling continued to hold sway, while, ironically, Bosanquet's discovery was pursued by overseas bowlers — Hordern, the Australian, and a quartet of South Africans — with startling results. It was, as someone else has since observed, English cricket's most costly (to itself) export.

The first stage of the South African revenge came in the shape of four victories in the five-Test series of 1905-06 — when South Africa fielded the same team each time — starting with a thrilling one-wicket win at Johannesburg and finishing with an innings victory at Cape Town. It was not by a long way the strongest England XI. When they were at full strength in 1907 they had considerably the better of a three-Test series. Yet whether a full-strength England in 1909-10 could have coped with the formidable googly battery on South Africa's matting pitches, where the ball sometimes bounced chest-high, is open to debate. South Africa won again, though not so comfortably, and against a slightly stronger English combination.

Pitch conditions varied from centre to centre. Johannesburg's mat was stretched over hard red dust; Cape Town's over turf, which made it appreciably slower. All the '05-06 Tests were played on these two grounds. In '09-10 two Tests each were played at the Old Wanderers ground, Johannesburg and Newlands, Cape Town, and one at Durban, where the matting was laid over superfine yellow-grey gravel-dust. On these three wickets, S. F. Barnes was to take 49 wickets in four Test matches in 1913-14, only Herby Taylor putting up any sort of show against the fast-medium spin.

To return to the initial impact of South Africa's spin quartet: Schwarz took 18 wickets in the 1905-06 series, Faulkner 14, Vogler nine, and White two in as many innings. Schwarz had started to spread the gospel, but further incantations lay ahead. By the time the team reached England in

1907, all four operators were ready to conquer. Fast bowlers used to hunt in pairs. The latter-day West Indians have taken to hunting in a pack of four. Spinners, too, have often worked well as duets. Twice, however, a country has based its attack on a squad of them: South Africa immediately post-Bosanquet, and India during the 1970s. For a time they swept all before them, and batsmen's dreams were not of death by violence but of slow torture, the intellectual challenge and the powers of physical response being stretched excruciatingly on the remorseless rack.

The popular 1907 South Africans were led by Percy Sherwell, whose wicketkeeping to the four googly bowlers was an important feature of the tour. He was one man who could not afford to guess. The achievements of his four googlers, off whom only four centuries (Braund, Hardstaff, Fry and Hayward) were hit all summer, were as follows: Schwarz 137 first-class wickets at 11.79 (top nationally); Vogler 119 at 15.62; Faulkner 64 at 15.82; White 56 at 14.73. Faulkner and White were key batsmen too. In the three Tests the returns were: Schwarz nine wickets at 21.33; Vogler 15 at 19.66; Faulkner 12 at 18.16; White four at 31.75. Opinion was divided as to whether Vogler or Faulkner was the best of them, though the South Africans themselves felt that White, who had made a lot of runs in the '05-06 Tests, could be the most difficult. Whatever the case, at least two of them seemed on song whenever the cream of English batting opposed them during the county matches. Twenty-one of their 31 matches were won.

Schwarz alone eschewed the leg-break, which he felt would interfere with his accuracy. He bowled googlies and top-spinners, with a wide-turning off-break for further variety. The other three had the leg-break as a stock ball with the hard-to-pick googly as a lethal wicket-taker. Their stories may now be taken up individually.

Reginald Oscar Schwarz, of Silesian descent, was born in Lee, Kent, on May 4, 1875, and was educated at St Paul's School before going up to Cambridge. His friendship with Bosanquet was the thread which led directly to the great South African googly attack, for not only did they see much of each other while Bosanquet was at Oxford and Schwarz playing for Oxfordshire and then Middlesex, but he toured the USA with Bosanquet's side in 1901. He was 27 when he took up his South African appointment. The 1904 tour, financed by his employer, Sir Abe Bailey, saw his blossoming, and he was to enjoy much success in the Test series to follow. He faded during the 1909-10 series against England, and did little in his final series, the ill-fated Triangular series in England in 1912; but, toiling away in Australia in 1910-11 — 'Faulkner's tour' — he did pick up 5 for 102 and a score of 61 in the opening Test at Sydney, 4 for 48 in the solitary victory at Adelaide (where Trumper made a glittering 214 not out), and a heartening 6 for 47 in the final contest at Sydney, when his bag included Trumper, Macartney, Hill, Armstrong and Ransford. This was his best Test performance. He had the satisfaction of finishing second to Llewellyn in the tour averages, taking most wickets, 61 at 25.90, while his Test performances put him at the head of South Africa's bowling with 25 wickets at 26.04. In minor matches he was still effective enough to take wickets almost at will. Altogether a wonderful performance on Australia's bone-hard pitches.

R. E. Foster, in a vivid article in the 1908 *Wisden*, wrote that Schwarz was slow through the air and fast off the pitch, coming in from the off anything from six to 18 inches — even a yard on a sticky wicket! Small wonder he found no use for the leg-break. Foster, one of the loveliest batsmen on view during the Golden Age, was England's captain during that 1907 series; but his highest score was only 51, and that innings at The Oval was something of an embarrassment — numerous snicks between pads and stumps or through slips. C. B. Fry managed to salvage England's reputation with a blemish-free century, no doubt relishing the challenge to his vast intellect.

Schwarz served in the Great War, firstly in German South-West Africa and then in France. He reached the rank of major and won the Military Cross, being twice wounded. He died a week after the Armistice, having contracted influenza. He was 43.

Alfred Edward Ernest Vogler was quite a different sort of man. Born in Swartwater, Cape Province on November 28, 1876, he spent his boyhood in Durban. After a few matches for Natal, he settled in Pretoria, and in 1905 decided to become a full-time professional. Although already 28 years of age, he was accepted on the MCC groundstaff, and in 1906 his bowling might have been penetrative enough for Middlesex to have offered him a contract had there not been strong opinion against yet another 'colonial' joining Albert Trott and Frank Tarrant in the county side. As it was, he played once for the county, against Cambridge.

Ernie Vogler had achieved little in his maiden Test series, at home against England in 1905-06; but in 1907 he proved his point at Lord's in the first Test by taking 7 for 128 off 47.2 overs, bowling a steady length and turning both ways. Braund made a century and Jessop belted 93 in an hour and a quarter, sometimes cutting the googlies off his middle stump. But Vogler's haul included him as well as Fry, Hayward, Tyldesley, Foster, Hirst and Lilley, every one a gem. Foster thought him the best bowler in the world at that time, and described his action thus: 'He has rather a hesitating run up to the wicket, but in the last few steps never gets out of his stride. The ball is well concealed from the batsman before delivery, and the flight and variation of pace are very deceptive indeed.'

Vogler used the new ball, swinging it and bowling off-breaks. When the shine was gone, he would settle into a leg-spin attack, with perhaps one 'wrong'un' every two overs. Some batsmen were reduced to the numbers game, playing him by guesswork. Certainly his wicketkeeper, Sherwell, found him the most difficult to pick. And Vogler could bowl for hours.

By watching his hand, hawklike, Foster could sometimes see the ball come over the top; but there was still no guarantee it would turn the three or four inches from the off. It could be the top-spinner, hastening straight through. He also bowled a slow, quivering yorker, which twice sent Fry on his way in the '07 series.

Strongly-built, with low-slung, protruding ears and eyes inclined to a twinkle, Vogler was another to find gainful employment with Sir Abe Bailey. There were problems, though, after the Australian tour of 1910-11, and a letter from Vogler to Australian captain Clem Hill tells of the googly bowler's plight: 'Just a line to ask you to do me a great favour. As you know I am out here under contract with Sir A. Bailey, and my agreement does not expire until Sept next, but since last March he has refused payment so I am taking it to court, as the amount is 475. I have already issued summons, and he is defending the case. His defence I believe is that I was drinking heavy in Australia. Now I would esteem it a great favour if you would give me a letter to show that this was not the case during any matches we played against you when I was playing and it would assist my case greatly if you could get some of the players who were playing for you to endorse what you say in your letter.'

He went on to say that he had been chosen for the 1912 tour of England, but could not be sure of going, with the case hanging over him. It is not known whether Hill replied. He probably did. Whether he gave Vogler the support he needed, and whether, if so, it was not at the risk of perjury, also remains unknown. He did not make the tour, though he played as a professional for various English, Scottish and Irish clubs.

Sir Abe Bailey, and all South Africans, would have been deeply disappointed at Vogler's form in Australia, where he took only four wickets and registered three ducks in his two Tests. It would have been better to have ended his international career a year earlier, when he was at the pinnacle: for then, in 1909-10, on his home pitches, he spun out 36 England batsmen in the five Tests at an average of 21.75. After Simpson-Hayward's lobs had brought him 6 for 43 at Johannesburg on the opening day, Vogler took 5 for 87 and 7 for 94, including Hobbs, Rhodes and Woolley in both innings. South Africa won by 19 runs. At Durban he took 5 for 83 and 2 for 93; at Johannesburg, 4 for 98 and 4 for 109 — collecting a handsome whip-round of £50 from spectators who thought their side were going to win (Hobbs' unbeaten 93 saw England to an exciting three-wicket victory); at Cape Town 2 for 28 and 5 for 72.

So, in common with many another cricketer, Vogler left a success story in the good book which not even time can rob, notwithstanding that his career ended sadly. His 36 wickets in the Test rubber was a world record for a year, and for many years his 62 not out at Cape Town in 1906 was the highest score by a number 11 batsman in a Test match. He was also the only one of the four googly merchants to take all 10 wickets in an innings, the first instance in South African first-class cricket. He took 6 for 12 and 10 for 26 for Eastern Province against Griqualand West at Johannesburg in 1906-07 — all in one day. The opposition may well have been below first-class in skill, yet this remains a Currie Cup record.

Ernie Vogler died at Pietermaritzburg on August 10, 1946, aged 69.

Gordon Charles White was born at Port St John's, in what is now Transkei, on February 5, 1882, and was a stylish batsman for Transvaal. A soccer international too, he made an important 81 in his first Test, the one-wicket thriller at Johannesburg in 1905-06, and in the third of the series he scored 147, an innings which sent P. F. Warner into raptures. Four years later he scored 118 in a Durban Test, also won. But as a bowler, perhaps because his batting and smart fielding took so much of his energy, he was very much the fourth member of the squad. His 56 wickets at 14.73 on the 1907 tour placed him second to Schwarz, but in 17 Tests altogether he was to take only nine wickets. Even so, on his best days White was hard to detect, bowling more top-spinners than the others and gaining lbws. Indeed, Hobbs thought him the hardest to pick, and the Kent batsmen in 1904 would not have been too sanguine either. His 5 for 46 included a hat-trick.

White missed the Australian tour of 1910-11 through business, but went to England with the 1912 side. The years were winding down for him, as for Schwarz. White enlisted, and almost made it through the war; but he died from wounds at Gaza, Palestine, on October 17, 1918, a month before Schwarz's death. Gordon White was only 36.

And so to the fourth and most illustrious member of the historic quartet, George Aubrey Faulkner. Born in Port Elizabeth on December 17, 1881, he ranks as an all-rounder in the highest division. His batting alone would have ensured his lasting fame, and as with Miller, Sobers, Botham and a number of others, he left the world wondering what he might have achieved had he specialised. His first major Test performance came in his second series, in England in 1907, when he took 6 for 17 at Headingley, breaking the ball great distances both ways. 'Dick' Lilley best summed up the typical Faulkner delivery by saying it was 'Briggs through the air, Richardson off the pitch'. His Headingley effort was wasted, for Blythe took 15 for 99 for England, and the South Africans in the fourth innings went one run worse than England's opening total of 76.

Faulkner's greatest achievements, however, came at home against England in 1909-10, and a year later in Australia — and a famous performance a couple of years after the Great War, when he was filling out at 40. His sustained Test match performances against England and then in Australia speak for themselves. Against a team which included Hobbs, Rhodes, Woolley, Denton, Buckenham, G. J. Thompson and lobster Simpson-Hayward he recorded: 78 and 123, 5 for 120 and 3 for 40 at Johannesburg; 47 and 9, 2 for 51 and 6 for 87 at Durban; 76 and 44, 4 for 89 and 2 for 75 at Johannesburg; 10 and 49 not out, 1 for 61 and 3 for 40 at Cape Town; 10 and 99, 3 for 72 at Cape Town. Against a team which included Trumper, Bardsley, Hill, Armstrong, Macartney, Ransford, Kelleway, Cotter, Whitty (a fast left-armer who took 37 wickets in the series), and googly bowler Hordern, he recorded: 62 and 43, 0 for 71 at Sydney; 204 and 8, 2 for 34 and 1 for 55 at Melbourne; 56 and 115, 1 for 59 and 2 for 56 at Adelaide; 20 and 80, 1 for 82 and 3 for 101 at Melbourne; 52 and 92, 0 for 38 and 0 for 18 at Sydney.

South Africa were drubbed four-one in that series, even though Faulkner scored 732 runs in his uncompromising style, with a 'two-eyed' stance. The price paid was a loss of penetration in his bowling: the explanation was a simple one: the right hand wearied from the hot hours of batting. Thus, the googly squad of three failed in its mission. Faulkner's stupendous batting streak tired him; Vogler's form had disappeared, possibly down the neck of a beer-bottle; and Schwarz, well as he bowled, could not carry the attack without support. This time it was the batsmen who ganged up.

There was support from other spinners in Charlie Llewellyn, left-arm, and tall, young Sid Pegler, orthodox leg- and off-spin, but the Australian batting line-up on such perfect pitches was formidable. 'Buck' Llewellyn, who may perhaps have had some coloured blood, was now 34, and had just finished a most successful career as an all-rounder for Hampshire, scoring many a century and taking 711 wickets with slow-medium spin, sometimes bowling that devilish ball, the left-hander's googly. Three times he had performed a season's double, and in 1902 he was actually in the England squad for the Edgbaston Test match, but was omitted.

Pegler's career, like so many of the South Africans', was erratic in that, after touring for the 1912 Triangular series (when he shocked England with 7 for 95 in the Lord's Test, and took 189 wickets on the full tour), he came back 12 years later to play in the 1924 Tests, having in the meantime sustained war wounds and spent his time somewhere in the jungle.

Thus, Aubrey Faulkner's batting efforts and unrewarded bowling in Australia were in vain. He made a mark on the 1912 Tests, scoring a century against Australia at Old Trafford and scattering England with 7 for 84 at The Oval. Then, after a 'good war' (DSO and Order of the Nile), he settled in England, having scored 2868 runs and taken 218 wickets one fabulous season in Nottingham club cricket. He reappeared for his country in one Test match in 1924.

In 1921 he turned in perhaps his most renowned match performance. The all-conquering Australians, led by Warwick Armstrong, faced a side specially got together by the 49-year-old Archie MacLaren. He knew he could do better than the England selectors, and sure enough, after a disastrous first day, MacLaren's side fought back, Hubert Ashton making 75 and Faulkner 153 in 3½ hours, withstanding the fury of McDonald. Needing 196, Armstrong's men were out for 167, Clem Gibson taking six wickets, and Faulkner, still with a lovely, wheeling action, 2 for 13 to complement his first-innings 4 for 50. Armstrong was not amused. MacLaren was quietly satisfied. Faulkner went back to his coaching.

For such a calculating theorist, it was natural that he should establish the first coaching centre. The Faulkner Cricket School in south London — in converted garages first in Richmond then Walham Green — welcomed through its doors numerous players who were destined for great things: Tom Killick, Duleepsinhji, Freddie Brown, R. W. V. Robins, Stan Squires, Maurice Turnbull, T. P. B. Smith, Doug Wright and Ian Peebles, who also worked as his secretary. Peebles, recalling Faulkner as a teetotaller, non-smoker and 'lusty and highly-sexed', also learned that, as a young man, he had once beaten up his father for assaulting his mother. He obviously worshipped Faulkner, despite his characteristic hard face. The Scotsman owed him much in his development and advancement.

Faulkner worked too hard at his school. When his right arm gave out, he would bowl to his pupils with his left, still finding a perfect length and turning the ball. Life finally became too much. Three weeks after writing in praise of Bradman and Jackson, the Australian youngsters, for their long and brave stand in the Oval Test of 1930, he committed suicide, gassing himself at the school, having left a note which said: 'I am off to another world via the bat room.'

South Africa, then, had taken Bosanquet's match-winning ball and given it a new meaning. Who could have predicted, though, that the googly would never again be a Springbok specialty, or, for that matter, a medium of international devastation at the hands of Bosanquet's own national descendants. Years ahead, Indians would take to it with an understandable and natural avidity. But, through the 1920s, 1930s and 1940s the science was to be upheld in all its potent splendour by a succession of Australians, the first of them being Dr Herbert Vivian Hordern.

The influence of Bosanquet was first seen on the Sheffield Shield circuit when Charlie Barnes, primarily a batsman, and Syd 'Mad Mick' Emery, both members of the Redfern club in Sydney, exploited the mystery ball to advantage. George Garnsey was then the best leg-spinner pure and simple in Australia, but Barnes, in a match at Sydney in January 1909 which produced a then-world record of 1911 runs for 34 wickets (NSW making 815), used the googly to take 6 for 59 and 5 for 147 against Victoria. Emery, a fine 'natural' spinner, fell away after a good start on the 1912 tour of England, though he did bowl Hobbs out at Lord's after he had made a century, as well as ending Warner's final Test innings with a huge full-toss. A few minutes earlier, when Spooner had had a close shave to a similar ball, Warner had called out to him: 'A simple full-toss, Reggie. You should have hit it for six!' Mailey — and for that matter Bradman — were later to take important wickets with full-tosses. What might this absurd delivery achieve today if used with discrimination?

Emery, 'strong as Hercules', was the joker who, when an appeal against the light was refused in a grade match in Sydney, asked the umpire for a match, lit it, and placed it on the bails. Another who was somewhat on the wild side, he responded to M. A. Noble's suggestion that he could be a great bowler with better control of that fast googly by saying: 'I'd be a great *man* if only I could control *myself*!' Like Rhodes, Phil Mead and Abel, Emery was afflicted by blindness in later years.

'Ranji' Hordern, so-named because of an imagined facial resemblance to the great Indian batsman, took part in only two Test series, but with dramatic effect. Called up for the fourth Test against the South Africans in the 1910-11 series, which was played in a most generous spirit, he beat them at their own game, taking 3 for 39 and 5 for 66 at Melbourne, and 4 for 73 and 2 for 117, besides scoring 50, at Sydney. A year later, against an England side which won the last four Tests, he went some way towards returning the 1903-04 compliment of Bosanquet by taking 32 wickets at 24.38. His 5 for 85 and 7 for 90 also went some way towards Australia's sole victory in the first Test (not until Bob Massie took 16 for 137 in 1972 did an Australian bowler take as many as 12 wickets in an Ashes Test debut) and in the fourth Test, at Melbourne, he indulged his considerable humour by being sent in to open the innings when Australia were inserted and going in last in the second innings. In between, as he stood unwillingly close at short mid-on to Frank Foster, a thunderous lifting drive crashed against his thigh and lodged in his left armpit. Hordern shook his fist at captain Hill as the crowd gave three loud cheers. A spin bowler's fingers are his most precious asset, and Hordern, who often massaged his fingers even as he walked down the street, had already had a finger smashed by Dave Nourse the season before.

With no Trumble or Noble in the ranks, fast bowler Cotter past his best, and the remainder uninspired, Hordern was Australia's one top-class bowler. The captains of both sides knew it, and as Hill gave way to the temptation to use him as a stock bowler, so the Englishmen did their best to wear him down. At Adelaide they did their best, too, to have Hordern and Kelleway disciplined for allegedly using powered resin on their bowling fingers. Hordern was such a sportsman that it seems unrealistic to attribute gamesmanship to him. His heroes were the gentlemen of the game, Trumper — and Hobbs, whose word of commiseration after he had been dropped off Hordern's bowling in the first Test touched the Australian deeply. He got Hobbs five times in the series, but never felt he had truly deceived him. Indeed, he told Rhodes: 'I like to bowl at your last six. The first five know a bit too much!'

Hordern, born in 1884, bowled leg-breaks at school, and was playing first grade for North Sydney at 15, almost all the club's players having represented the State or even Australia. He was, understandably, not an instant success; but when 111 wickets in 11 matches in lower grades got him back into the first XI when he was 21, he speedily rose to State honours, taking 8 for 81 against Queensland. This was the season, 1905-06, when he went to work on the googly, adding the top-spinner two years later.

He was from a well-to-do family, and in 1906 he enrolled at the University of Pennsylvania 'in search of knowledge'. Actually, he was to study dentistry, as had M. A. Noble. He qualified in 1910, though his years in Philadelphia were not packed with work alone. He played more cricket, and made more tours, than at any other stage of his life. Indeed, he became a legendary figure as he tore holes in all kinds of opposition with his spin variations. Almost all American bowlers, like West Indians of today, aimed to bowl fast in emulation of J. B. King. Only M. R. Cobb of New York had any sort of reputation as a slow bowler.

On tour in Jamaica, Hordern awoke one morning to find five black boys examining his hand, seeking an explanation for the magic (8 for 55 and 8 for 31) they had seen this creature from outer space dispense on the previous afternoons. In 1907, when MCC toured Philadelphia, there was an historic meeting between Hordern and Schwarz, the googly 'missionary'. Hordern was pleased with his 5 for 41, particularly when he bowled the MCC captain, E. G. Wynyard, whose bat was raised aloft helplessly as the ball spun back and bowled him: 'My heavens, a googly!' he roared. But Schwarz outdid him in figures (about which, advisedly, he never much cared): 8 for 55. The two of them had hours of intense discussion and practice together.

Hordern had a marvellously placid temperament, but even he could be worried by constant hitting. A large Jamaican was well on the way to belting every ball of an over for four — when the googly came to the rescue. The batsman could not believe his eyes, and for the rest of the tour, whenever Hordern opposed him, he had only to hold the ball up at him and gaze sternly, and the batsman was finished.

Two tours and much friendly club cricket showed Hordern to English audiences. In 1907, for the University, he took 110 wickets at 9.68 against many of the major English public schools in what was hardly a fair match, but a year later, although troubled by a serious leg injury sustained as he bowled a fast one to finish off the match against Worcestershire, he impressed with 70-odd wickets, even though he lamented: 'I had not proved myself an Ernest Vogler or a Reggie Schwarz.' He even opened the batting with W.G. for London County. He soon discovered that the Old Man 'ran occasionally for himself, and never for his partner.'

He tried to regard Test cricket as being no different from the stuff he had played at the Saffrons ground, Eastbourne and at Sutton, but he was not allowed to, especially by the Englishmen. Nevertheless, his record for the 1911-12 series is almost parallel with that of S. F. Barnes, even though it is less well remembered.

Hordern was closer to Bill O'Reilly in pace and method than any other Australian. His Test career was much shorter; but the noble line was established. 'Ranji' Hordern went off to war, came back and 'went walk-about' down the south coast, once actually playing against a short-trousered Don Bradman, whom the locals induced to show his promising leg-breaks and googlies to Hordern. In 1932, six years before his death, and when Australia was in need of a dose of gently humorous reminiscence, with the menace of Bodyline blotting out the sun, he committed himself to paper, publishing *Googlies*, a book such as the whimsical Arthur Mailey himself could have written. As may be seen in the foreword, Hordern simply 'bowled because he loved to do so.' You don't get many fast bowlers feeling that way.

9.   With the Left Arm

George Dennett — Charlie Macartney — Frank Tarrant —
Wilfred Rhodes — Blythe and Woolley

While the googly revolution bounced its tricky way into technical lore
during the summers leading up to the Kaiser's war, slow bowling prospered
generally in the strong fingers of the left-arm bowlers. Supreme among
Englishmen in this department were Rhodes of Yorkshire and Blythe of
Kent; but there were others whose skills would have won them regular
international honours had these two pursued something else for a living.

Sam Hargreave of Warwickshire took over 900 wickets in 10 years to
1909, his action elegant and his accuracy impeccable, as the helpless Surrey
batsmen discovered at The Oval in 1903 when, on a difficult wicket, he
took 6 for 41 and 9 for 35.

George Cox of Sussex, like Hargreave, specialised in the 'arm ball',
either curving in when new or describing a similar, slower arc when
undercut with finger-spin. Cox took over 1800 wickets in a long career,
finishing when he was 54. His greatest triumph came at Horsham in 1926,
when he had two seasons left. Seventeen Warwickshire batsmen fell to him
in the match, but by then he would have shelved all hope of representing his
country, even if Rhodes was called up a few weeks later for the Oval Test at
the age of 48. By now, Cox would have been starting to nurture ambitions
for his young son. George jnr, however, though he was to play hundreds of
high-class innings for Sussex, was also overlooked by the Test selectors.
This kind, gentle and humorous son claimed during many a cricket dinner
speech that he was sired during the tea interval of a match; but since his
birthday was August 23, the match would need to have been overseas.
Since father coached in South Africa and India, there may be truth in his
story. The same may not necessarily be said of another tale told by the
gleeful George jnr: when he lost his way between county matches, the
captain, booking into the hotel, announced to a startled receptionist that
'there are ten of us without Cox.'

Another slow left-armer who must have rued often the existence of
Rhodes and Blythe was George Dennett of Gloucestershire. Here was a
bowler of such poise and persistence that he took over 100 wickets in 12
seasons, once topping 200. Another to become a fixture in his county XI,
he played regularly from 1903 to 1925, starting with a pasting by

Middlesex, who piled up 502. Dennett's coolness under fire was noted, as was his rare ability to shrug off dropped catches, the source of so much moral destruction among bowlers. He played the major role in 1907, the year of his 201 wickets, in the dismissal of Northants for the equal-lowest total in first-class cricket: 12. His 8 for 9, including a hat-trick, formed part of a 15-wicket haul in the day. The previous season had seen him take all 10 Essex wickets for 40 at Bristol.

Not dissimilar to Schwarz facially, Dennett had a quick arm action, with a peculiar habit of watching the ball leaving his hand. Many of his wickets were taken by catches in the off-side field, the bounce making him deceptively difficult to drive. He served in both the Boer War and the First World War, and later coached at Cheltenham, succeeding another Gloucester slow left-arm bowler, Billy Woof. If one thing could be held against Dennett it was that he stunted the development of the great Charlie Parker, persuading him to bowl seamers during the overlap of their careers, obviously and understandably fearing an early displacement by the talented younger man.

S. G. Smith, a Trinidadian of British parentage, was one of the most able of all-rounders of the period, and joined Northants after the 1906 West Indians' tour. A fine batsman and short-leg fielder, he bowled slow left-arm with all the nuances, and did the double three times. After captaining the county, he moved to New Zealand in 1915, and gave great service to Auckland until well into his forties. A hat-trick against Leicestershire and four-in-four against Warwickshire were sample measures of his class.

James Hallows, a small Lancashire all-rounder, was another to reap consistent success with slow left-arm bowling, partly filling the gap left by S. F. Barnes in the county ranks, though he died young, at 36, one of cricket's few epileptics. A Lancashire contemporary of similar method was J. S. Heap, who suffered the terrible irony of knowing that damp weather would produce ideal wickets for him at the same time as it convulsed him with rheumatism and lumbago. Still, he left an imperishable mark with 11 wickets twice in matches against the hated Yorkshire, and a return of 9 for 43 against the perennially hapless Northants. MacLaren at slip could never nod off when Heap was bowling. There was also around this time a fine Lancashire off-spinner in Bill Huddleston, who, though also coming into his own only when rain set up the conditions for him, did enough to earn a regular contract. Clearly, so many of these matchwinners of old would find no place in the modern game, with its covered pitches.

Australia, too, produced some slow left-arm bowlers of high quality in the Edwardian years. Charlie Macartney was a considerable force before he earned recognition in the 1920s as one of the game's batting geniuses. England's batsmen could barely put a bat to him in the Headingley Test of 1909, when, never short of a provocative aside, he took 7 for 58 and 4 for 27.

'Charlie Mac', though, was no real successor to Victoria's Jack Saunders, who, although described by his Test captain Joe Darling as 'the dirtiest chucker Australia ever had', took 79 wickets at moderate cost in 14 Tests between 1902 and 1908. He took five wickets in an innings in each of the last three Tests against England in 1907-08, and there is record of his field-setting in that series, when he bowled to F. L. Fane, as being eight men on the leg side. Against South Africa in 1902, he relished the matting surface at Johannesburg, taking 7 for 34. He approached from mid-on, with a 'corkscrew' run, sometimes brushing his ear with his bowling arm and sometimes bowling nearer roundarm. In common with many of the species, he pushed the ball through, especially when the pitch helped him, and was often then classified — like many another with the advantage of being left-handed — as 'unplayable'. Before he died on the operating table in 1927, he helped bestow another great gift upon Australian cricket: as one who had watched a young leg-spinner, Clarrie Grimmett, in New Zealand club matches, he wrote glowingly of him to Melbourne, where Grimmett was later to be received accordingly with more interest than was shown in Sydney when he began his quest for advancement.

Another Australian left-hander who rose to the very top — without playing Test cricket — was Frank Tarrant, a Victorian who made his reputation in England with Middlesex. Unquestionably close to being the finest cricketer never to have won Test honours, Tarrant batted and bowled his way into high places in the record book, and between 1907 and 1914 there was no better all-rounder to be seen. Even at 44, he came close to winning a belated Test cap against Gilligan's England side, having done almost enough to play for Australia 17 years previously, during a trip home in 1907-08. Between the world wars he compiled considerable wealth as a dealer in racehorses in India and Australia. It was said of him that he was about the only Australian seen in England who had no sort of throwing arm. But who needed a bazooka throw when he could score nearly 18,000 runs, including a highest of 250 not out, right-handed, and spin out nearly 1500 batsmen left-handed? In his eagerness, he often tried to spin the ball too much — the mark of the joyous amateur as opposed to the scheming pro; there was no legitimate arguing with the sort of talent that could make 182 not out and take 10 for 90, as Tarrant did for the Maharajah of Cooch Behar's XI at Poona. Only V. E. Walker and W. G. Grace rub shoulders with Frank Tarrant in having scored a century and taken all ten in a match.

A lesser-known Australian doing his bit in county cricket was Jack Cuffe, a Queenslander who played for Worcestershire, taking over 700 wickets in the dozen seasons before the Great War. He was little below Tarrant in ability. Handsome and wide-eared, he bowled his slows to such effect that in 1910 he hit the stumps eight times in taking 9 for 5 against Glamorgan, who were all out for 36. In that season he did the hat-trick against Hampshire, and in the next season he did the double. But against the toughest opposition in the land, Yorkshire, he had his field day: 9 for 38 at Bradford in 1907. He was another who might have been useful to his country if he had stayed at home. Instead, he enjoyed county cricket, league cricket, first-class umpiring, and finally, coaching at Repton School, near which establishment Cuffe drowned in 1931.

Of all the slow left-arm bowlers, however, the two who dominated the newspaper reports season after season throughout the 'golden' period 1900 to 1914 were Wilfred Rhodes and Colin Blythe, who were of similar classification, though different in temperament.

Rhodes was solid, calculating, Yorkshire through and through. Blythe, a Deptford-born cockney, was fragile of nerve, sensitive as a violinist, which indeed he was. Comparisons from their time are indeterminate. As one pundit might give Blythe best for bringing the ball in menacingly 'with the arm' (and Rhodes himself felt Blythe was better than he on a biting pitch), so another would place Rhodes ahead for his relentless, brainy pursuit of his victims whatever the conditions. For Rhodes, his all-time record of 4187 wickets could prove conclusive, even if his career stretched well beyond the war which was to cost Blythe his life. And, of course, Rhodes could bat. He worked his way from No. 11 in the England order to No. 2 with Hobbs, and shared in first- and tenth-wicket record stands against Australia.

For sheer destructive power, though, especially against soft opposition, Blythe left behind him almost an unrivalled picture. Five times he took 15 or more wickets in a match, once in a Test, against South Africa. Rhodes did it twice, once in the supreme setting of a Test match against Australia when he had the batsmen at his mercy on a damp pitch at Melbourne in 1903-04.

It was a sublime experience to talk with Wilfred Rhodes at length when he was 92, and long since deprived of his sight. In compensation, his memory was crystal clear, and from a lengthy, action-packed career — which had finished 40 years earlier — came a distillation of what mattered, the principal incidents garnished with fascinating trivia. After playing in Scotland as a professional, he had a trial with Warwickshire, who, in one of the most profoundly short-sighted decisions of all time, rejected him. When Yorkshire came to choose between Rhodes and a bowler named Albert Cordingley, Wilfred won — apparently on the toss of a coin by F. S. Jackson. Within five seasons Rhodes had banked 1000 wickets.

The old man remembered with astonishing clarity his earliest matches played before the 19th Century had elapsed. He remembered too, more understandably, his first Test match, when he opened the bowling with seamers. He could picture still in his mind's eye the ball which took Darling's off stump.

'I wanted to get at Victor Trumper,' came, in a rasping whisper, one of the most extraordinary statements ever to pass the lips of a bowler. 'Because he was a right-hander,' was the logical motive. In his turn, in a later confrontation, on a beautiful batting surface, Trumper, between overs, murmured: 'Please, Wilfred, give me some peace!'

As ever, C. B. Fry may be relied upon to describe with precision and some vividness what it was like to be out in the middle in particular circumstances. Rhodes he recalled thus: 'A few quick steps, easy steps and lovely swing of the left arm and the ball is doing odd things at the other end it is pitched where you do not like it; you have played forward when you do not want to; the ball has whipped away from you so quickly; it has come straight when you expected break; there is discomfort.'

Discomfort. There is the key word. All who have shuddered in the sinister vice-grip of classical slow bowling will understand. It is as unlike the mental anguish of facing truly fast bowling as the water torture is to the cat o'nine-tails.

Rhodes used to spin off the pad of his first finger; by showing the palm of the hand to the batsman, he could vary the pace cryptically. He never favoured a silly mid-off, since that deterred a man from hitting out at his bowling. He liked them to play forward — stretching further and further and further. This called for perfect control of flight and length. He had it. He had confidence too, based on common sense: after untold hours of practice in a shed in winter and later in the nets — often marking the ball with chalk to gauge the spin — he knew he should be able to bowl with that acquired accuracy in a game, shutting out all else.

Sometimes he was bound to lose, but this was all part of the philosophy. Jessop: 'We said if he gets a hundred today, he'll have to fetch 'em — and the wider we bowled the harder he hit 'em. I was hit for seven sixes in the match, six by Jessop and one by Champain...and I finished up with 14 wickets.' It would have been a fair bet that he knew the direction of each of those sixes, even 70 or so years afterwards. On another occasion, at Harrogate, South Africa's mighty striker, Sinclair, knocked a cabdriver off his cab with the force of a six-hit. Once in Ceylon, he missed out on a stumping victim when the umpire announced that the batsman had got back to safety before the appeal was made!

His modest recollection of Australia's dismissal for 36 at Edgbaston in 1902, when he took 7 for 17, was that the tourists 'made it look difficult, and worried themselves out'. On the 1903-04 tour, when Rhodes learned to put the ball through a little faster after batsmen started to get at him, he demolished Victoria (all out 15, Jack Saunders absent from the ground, caught napping) with 5 for 6, and seemed still, all those years later, to find it hard to forgive Bosanquet for spilling a catch from Harry Trott which would have given him a hat-trick. Another remembered let-down was Bob Wyatt's at Scarborough in 1930, when Bradman lifted old Wilfred's first ball to mid-off. At least it was something to have bowled competitively to both Grace and Bradman.

Rhodes made just on 40,000 runs as well, with a highest score of 267 not out, and like a good Yorkshireman, he recalled certain agonised pleasures. He was once out for 199 shortly after his partner had run one short for him. But though he was justifiably proud of his batting in a defensive sort of way, he is a slow bowler in most eyes — and perhaps the finest of all those who utilised their left arms. He captained Yorkshire — completely unofficially, of course — for many seasons. It would have been idiotic of any of the amateur skippers to have neglected to consult him on any matter of moment. But as a coach he was less than successful. After the extension of his playing career (he worked in a munitions factory in the First War, and there were those — not only in Yorkshire — who said he was finished in 1921), he went to Harrow School as coach. 'I was the first Yorkshire professional to retire,' he pointed out. 'The rest were chopped off.' At Harrow, he must have known much frustration. 'It wasn't a bit my style at all. They used to play forward every ball.' Sometimes he would hold onto the ball in mid-delivery and stare reprovingly at the boy already into the stereotyped forward defensive.

He himself used to enjoy hitting the ball to leg. Among the bowlers he admired was Gerry Hazlitt, the doomed young Australian off-spinner, who had a fast action but a slow delivery. 'He was a good one to cart to square leg!' And at Taunton, when he was 90 not out overnight, Rhodes once fetched three balls from Cranfield in the first over from way outside off stump to the boundary between square leg and mid-on. 'Why do you keep hitting them on that side?' the bowler called out laconically. 'There's no fielders there!'

Perhaps it is good therapy for all bowlers to belt a few runs from time to time.

He needed 41 Tests to harvest his 109 Australian wickets between 1899 and 1926, but for years he was more batsman than bowler. He finished his Ashes combat as a bowler — a somewhat reluctant hero — justifying a recall such as for which the England selectors have become renowned, by taking 2 for 35 and 4 for 44 at The Oval, and helping his side regain the Ashes. Every one of those wickets was a Test centurymaker.

Rhodes stands supreme with 16 seasonal doubles and 23 seasons with 100 or more wickets (three over 200). These figures will not prove him a better cricketer than Grace or Woolley or Sobers or Botham, but they do offer a weighty arguing point.

Ever the hardened pro, Wilfred Rhodes looked back near the end of his 95 years and saw how things might have been better. The wicket, he observed, was now an inch higher and an inch wider; and on top of that, the scope for lbw was greater: 'We had to pitch in line.'

Comparisons; comparisons. Leonard Crawley, the phenomenal hitter for Worcestershire and Essex during the 1920s and 1930s, moustache bristling, cravat proclaiming a military — almost piratical — mien, once sought in a letter to show how much better was one legendary bowler than another: Rhodes, he wrote, was 'far and away the best left-hand bowler I ever played. Compared to Verity his bowling was like a glass of fizz with a cup of cat's piss'. That would have set the 1934 Australians a'wondering.

A serious and more valid comparison is between Rhodes and his predecessor in the Yorkshire ranks, Bobby Peel, and the evidence suggests only that one — Peel — scored over the other in style. Rhodes spun more, but Peel had an easier and more rhythmic swing. So what? Rhodes might have retorted. Peel finished for himself at 40. At that age, Wilfred was little over halfway. He was still playing Test cricket in West Indies at 52.

For style, Kent's Colin Blythe stood almost alone. By bringing his left hand so far behind him prior to delivery that it almost entered his right hip-pocket, he initiated an arm swing which became a full, free, sweeping loop. Cardus loved many cricketers; his affection for 'Charlie' Blythe was beyond disguise. He saw him as 'the prettiest slow left-handed bowler of his, or surely any other, period'. Against the 'old soldier' guile of Rhodes, Blythe was 'all nervous sensibility'. The little chasse preceding delivery was 'almost timid', though his length 'forced the batsman to play just when the break was taking effect like a knife, and coming up from the earth at an angle which turned scientific strokeplay into vanity'.

Cardus, typically, had attributed all kinds of blue-blooded characteristics to Blythe. . . until the day he heard him speak to a team-mate: 'I'll 'it yer on top o' the nose in a minute!' he playfully called out. There was another tall and slender young man strolling the Kentish confines in those days: Frank Woolley, who bowled with a similar action, took a wonderfully large store of wickets (over 2000: Blythe took over 2500), including 5 for 29 and 5 for 20 against Australia at The Oval in 1912, and went on batting, for a quarter of a century, with a left-handed grace and command that enslaved grown men to a state of helpless schoolboy adulation for the rest of their lives.

Blythe was no star with the bat; but how he could bowl. Wandering over to the nets at Blackheath during a county match in 1898, he sent a few down, was spotted by Kent's coach, and was taken on straightaway. His first ball bowled Yorkshire's Frank Mitchell at Tonbridge in 1899, and another 'holy terror' was launched into the game, word spreading with customary speed through the county grapevine. With the avid slips field shortly to be joined by Woolley (who idolised and copied Blythe), and with wicketkeeper Fred Huish letting out deafening shrieks as he shared in the executions, Blythe — and Kent — sailed to glory. Statistically his best performance was 17 for 48 in a day at Northampton in 1907, when he seemed to be headed for the first all-20 in first-class cricket. Having taken 10 for 30 in the first innings, he had taken all seven in the follow-on when he put down a 'sitter' from Vials. That would have given him 18, with two to go, but the miss so upset him that, probably also by now fighting off exhaustion, he lost his touch and had no further success. Serious fatigue overtook him on other occasions, notably after he had defeated 15 South African batsmen for 99 in the Headingley Test of 1907, and 11 Australians for 112 at Edgbaston in 1909, an effort that left him at a numb standstill. Aligning this physical/mental fragility with Blythe's gift for probing a batsman with fearless full-length bowling even when under fierce attack is a wondrous exercise for the imagination. The secret must have been in Blythe's outlook, which was that of the true-born artist. When Lancashire's Reggie Spooner stroked him three times in succession through the covers, Blythe breathed a heartfelt 'Oh, Mr Spooner, I'd give all my bowling to be able to bat like that.'

Any batsman playing against Kent in those summers needed to be able to handle slow left-arm bowling. Blythe and his near-facsimile Woolley were backed, when necessary, by 'Punter' Humphreys, who was good enough to have taken on a major role with any other county. Warwickshire's batsmen must have yearned for the sight of a right-arm bowler after their visit to Tonbridge in 1913: Blythe and Woolley each 5 for 8. Though the pitch was awkward, Woolley went in and hit 76 not out to ensure a Kent victory.

Blythe was rather disappointing on his tours of Australia, where his health suffered, and South Africa, where he was less at ease on matting wickets. Only two items among a page and a half of small-type entries of his remarkable performances in *Wisden* refer to matches not on English fields. The obituary was published years before his friends would have wished. Among the first to enlist in the First World War, somehow having worked his way through the medical, Sgt Colin Blythe of the Kent Fortress Engineers, attached to the King's Own Yorkshire Light Infantry, was killed at Ypres on November 8, 1917. He was 38. His shrapnel-torn wallet was retrieved, and now resides in the pavilion at Canterbury, at the entrance to which ground is a large monument in his name. Blythe's body lies in a war cemetery at Ypres. Images of his dancing approach, fine-precision bowling, and ready smile beneath a high and wide forehead remained in the minds of all who had watched him.

10. Club to Test Cricket

Alonzo Drake — D.W. Carr — Warwick Armstrong —
Matthews' double hat-trick — Gerry Hazlitt

Rhodes, Blythe, Dennett, Cox, Hirst, Woolley, Dean, Llewellyn, Tarrant
. . . it was a left-armer's world in the decade leading up to the bloody, gassy,
crippling carnival of death known as the First World War. Fast, medium or
slow, all of these took 150 wickets in a season at least once; as did another,
Alonzo Drake, who twice in one week in 1914 bowled throughout both
innings of a match for Yorkshire unchanged with Major Booth (who was to
become a war casualty). Drake himself, a droll, even pessimistic, character,
laboured under a heart condition which was to cut him down at 34 in the
season following the war. All this tragedy lay mercifully and invisibly ahead
as the players went about their fun and games. 'Lonza' Drake took all ten
against Somerset on a newly-laid pitch at Weston in one of the matches
when none of the other nine Yorkshiremen got a bowl. He took them in
only 42 balls, for 35 runs, 11 of which came off one of his 8.5 overs. He
made most runs, 63, in the match too. A month earlier he had taken four
wickets in as many balls at Chesterfield, and it was clear that he, like
Dennett and one or two others, would have won England caps but for the
presence of Rhodes and Blythe — and the onset of the war.

One of the strangest tales concerned a club cricketer who rose to Test
honours with the rapidity of a character in a boy's comic-book. Douglas
Ward Carr, an ordinary cricketer at Oxford, seemed to have been lost to
the game when he injured his knee at football. In his thirties he jogged
along as a medium-pacer and batsman in Kentish club cricket — until his
imagination was captured by the South African googly brigade. Soon he
was bowling the 'deceiver' well enough to attract the county club's
attention. At the age of 37, in 1909, he played his first match for Kent,
taking 7 for 95 against his old university, was then left out but chosen
instead for the Gentlemen at The Oval and Lord's, and was invited to Old
Trafford for the Test match against Australia. He was omitted because the
ground was soft, and it seemed the real-life 'Spedegue' was to miss the top
rung of the fairy-tale ladder. But at The Oval, after three further successes
for Kent, he took the field for England, and, true to the script, spun
Gregory, Noble and Armstrong out in no time, having opened the bowling.
Here, though, MacLaren got things wrong. 'Daddy' Carr was kept on for

an hour and a half, lost his effectiveness, and finished with 5 for 146 off 34 overs. In the second innings he took 2 for 136 (Armstrong and Trumper) off 35 overs, and never played for his country again. Neither did poor MacLaren.

Carr, a schoolmaster, continued to play for Kent during the holidays — and even managed to lose a little weight. His pushed-through, low-arm, accurate, bouncing leg-breaks and googlies went on confusing the best of batsmen — until a fateful day in 1914, when Hobbs and Hayward hit him around at Blackheath. The county called upon his services no more; but he was 42 by now, and had at least enjoyed a late and remarkable career which, having yielded 334 wickets at 16.84, could serve as an inspiration to club spinners everywhere — in such time as current safety-first attitudes might properly be shelved.

Of the other spinners circulating in the period, left-hand all-rounder J. H. King of Leicestershire warrants mention, his puzzling flight bringing him 1100 wickets for a county which needed them desperately. Primarily a batsman, with a string of fine performances, he had his best bowling day at Aylestone Road against Yorkshire in 1911, when his 8 for 17 included a spell of seven wickets without a run off him in 20 balls. Cradling the ball in his right hand, then switching it, he bowled wide of the crease — around the wicket, as was common practice — and had nothing of a followthrough. Had he been with a more fashionable county, he might have played more than once for England.

One of the great days for spin came at the climax of a famous Eton v Harrow game at Lord's. In 1910, R. St L. Fowler gave his name to the match by taking 8 for 23 with off-breaks on a soft pitch to bring Eton victory by nine runs after Harrow had started out in need of only 55. The Army later claimed Fowler, who played little first-class cricket.

In these years Australia, with stocks so high that a good leg-spinner like Les Pye never aspired to a Test cap, were relying for orthodox slow bowling upon Bert Hopkins, whose pace was fairly brisk, the ball swerving and cutting from off. A genuine all-rounder, his most thrilling hour came at Lord's in 1902, when he had Fry and Ranji both for ducks. Turning the ball the other way — but not much — was Warwick Armstrong, whose Test career stretched from 1902 to 1921, during which time his weight crept up to more than 20st. In 50 Tests, 'using his bat like a teaspoon, and the bowling like weak tea', as Edmund Blunden put it, he scored 2863 runs, and bowling steadily at the leg stump, he lured 87 batsmen to destruction — much of it self-induced. Surviving film shows the 1905 Armstrong as quite athletic, with a smooth and steady approach, and a high delivery, his whole structure braced in a manner promising accuracy. His negative line brought many a protest, from crowds and from batsmen, MacLaren and Hayward on one notorious occasion, at Trent Bridge in 1905, kicking many of his deliveries away in contempt. He was unruffled. His 52 overs cost 67 runs. He was, after all, a master of the protest himself, once wandering off into the outfield during the Oval Test of 1921, leaving his bowlers to manage by themselves, and answering a spectator's enquiry as to the reason for his rudeness in reading a stray newspaper by saying that he was trying to find from the sports column who his opponents were. He wrote a book, *The Art of Cricket*, aimed principally at the young, which displayed his keen eye for detail, even down to advising bowlers not to lift heavy objects such as a cricket bag 'since such treatment interferes with the repose of the nerves and tends to stiffen the shoulders'. 'The Big Ship' stiffened many an Englishman's neck with his boorish behaviour on the field. When he died in 1947, he left an estate which in modern terms would have put him in the millionaire bracket. Whisky, which had helped him to a century at Melbourne when malaria was shaking his body, also made him his fortune. He became the Australian agent for Buchanan's.

Armstrong, fortunately, was almost alone in his enjoyment in constipating a cricket match with leg theory. What the crowds loved then, as ever, was an attacking leg-spinner, such as Arthur Mailey, whom Armstrong sometimes seemed to regard as merely a joke to change the flavour of things after Gregory and McDonald had knocked over the early batsmen. Less adventurous than Mailey in a handful of pre-1914 Tests was Jimmy Matthews from Victoria. Mention of his name invariably conjures recall of one amazing feat: his two hat-tricks not only in one Test match, but on the same day. The setting was Old Trafford, May 28, 1912, the opening game in the Triangular Tournament, and the real oddity was that Australia were playing *South Africa*. The Springboks were 265 for 7 in reply to Australia's 448 when Matthews, who specialised in the 'straight-break', bowled Beaumont; Sid Pegler was the unlucky second victim, lbw to a ball which may well have touched the bat first; and Tom Ward, the wicket-keeper, was also lbw. A small but privileged crowd was in attendance as South Africa followed on, and a couple of hours later Matthews did it again — this time a hat-trick of higher quality: Herby Taylor bowled; Schwarz caught-and-bowled; and Ward, again, also caught by the bowler, a good catch which he was unlikely to have missed in the circumstances. These six wickets were the only ones he took in the Test match. He may well have dedicated them, in the privacy of his mind, to the small son who had died earlier that year. When he himself died in 1943, aged 59, three of his sons were away on active service.

'Little Jimmy', long-faced and suntanned, took 85 wickets on the 1912 tour, a sound effort in a wet summer, though his only other Test return of note was 4 for 29 against South Africa at Lord's. Two Australians took over 100 wickets that season: Whitty, fast left-arm, and Gervys Hazlitt, earlier referred to, whose bowling action was suspect. Sydney-born, he played most of his cricket for Victoria, starting at the tender age of 17. At 19 he gained his first Test cap, and saw Australia home with 34 not out in an unbroken ninth-wicket stand of 56 with Cotter; but he did himself little good on his second appearance, for he hurled the ball wide from short cover when the last pair of Englishmen dashed for the single which brought a one-wicket victory at Melbourne. A straight throw would have given Test cricket its first tie over half a century before the actual event. Ah, what finishes they had in those days!

Hazlitt, a pleasant man, was on the outside looking in for some while after that, but in the last of his nine Tests, at The Oval in 1912, he went out in a flash of glory by taking 7 for 25 with brisk off-spinners on a drying wicket, his last five victims costing one run. If anything, the poor chap had bowled too well, for the pitch was still spiteful after the roller's effect had worn off, and Australia, batting again so soon, were skittled for 65, losing by a wide margin. England's victory at least assuaged any discomfort felt over Hazlitt's action. It was remarked that he threw many of his deliveries, and that he made a noticeable effort to bowl with a straighter arm later in the tour. The controversy was solved by his health. He played hardly any more cricket, and, being weak in the heart, like Yorkshire's Drake, died in 1915, aged only 27.

The war interrupted countless careers, and just as Jack Hobbs felt he never batted as well after 1918 as before 1914, so a number of leading bowlers lost their peak years. For others the pinnacle was merely postponed. Australia's Arthur Mailey was possibly a better bowler in 1915, when he was 29, than during the 1920s, when he bamboozled 99 batsmen in 21 Tests. For England, 'Tich' Freeman, J. W. Hearne, Parker, Astill, Fender, Jack Newman, Kilner, Jack White, 'Tich' Richmond, and the bowler of all sorts, Cecil Parkin, had all played county cricket before the fearful hiatus. Then the sun shone again, the deckchairs were dusted and brought outside, and cricket tripped its light fantastic for another 21 seasons.

11. Cartoons and Googlies

Arthur Mailey — 10 for 66 — 'individuals, not civil servants' — the dinner-jacketed bowler

Arthur Mailey played cricket as it was intended to be played and lived life as it was meant to be lived: never petty, always ready for a laugh, philosophical in both despair and ecstasy. Like Lindsay Hassett, he has most often been described as 'puckish'; like Puck, neither took life too seriously.

Such a whimsical nature would have been stretched severely by Mailey's world-famous and much-mocked figures of 4 for 362 off 64 overs for New South Wales against Victoria, who made 1107 at Melbourne in 1926-27. 'Just finding my length,' he murmured as the innings closed. 'My figures would have been a lot better if a cove in a tweed coat had held a couple of catches in the shilling enclosure.'

Mailey, known as 'George' to his team-mates, sustained the googly as a major agent of destruction. Had he not started a conversation with someone midway through his idle practice against the lavatory wall in Sydney's Domain, he might have gone on bowling leg-breaks and off-breaks, and contentedly seen out his playing days in the lower grades. As it was, his beginnings could hardly have been more humble. Born in a South Sydney slum and growing up in a two-roomed 'dwelling' on a sandhill, with a drunken father and tough, loving mother, Mailey soon found a hero: Victor Trumper. His photo hung on the hessian wall, and when the wind blew, he seemed to go through his whole repertoire of strokes. Came the day young Mailey was to bowl against his hero in a Redfern v Paddington grade match, and the theme for one of cricket literature's most touching and entertaining passages was shaped; for in his autobiography, written when he was 70, Mailey describes the frenzy of anticipation before the encounter — and the bi-emotional thrill of first being stroked to the boundary by the god-like Trumper and then deceiving him with a googly. 'I felt like a boy who had killed a dove,' he concluded. Lillee never said that of Boycott.

For Arthur Mailey, cricket and art were inextricably entwined. He had little formal schooling before working as a presser of seams into trousers, labourer, paperseller, bottle-collector, and well-paid glass-blower, an occupation that not only strengthened his fingers as he spun the 4ft pipe but also developed his stamina and his lung-power (though his appealing was described as a 'somewhat apologetic whimper'). At The Oval in 1926, according to umpire Frank Chester, he did not appeal *at all* when he could have had Hobbs lbw for nought. England's master went on to make 100.

As a youth, he practised the googly at home with an orange, once in a while smashing what little crockery there was, before graduating to an old cricket ball, which he carried everywhere — from the bottleworks to evening art class. 'I could so easily have thrown in the towel and drifted on to the scrapheap of human endeavour,' he wrote. He did give up cricket for a year, going fishing with his mother and crippled brother instead. But progress came in grade cricket, and in 1913 he was invited to tour the USA and Canada with a strong team which included several Test players, and then, with Trumper and others, to New Zealand. His Test debut must have been only months away when war broke out.

The war cost him two brothers; but now, approaching his 35th birthday, he was called at last to Test cricket. He made up for lost time. In four Tests of the 1920-21 series (Armstrong didn't use him in the second, at Melbourne) he took 36 wickets at an average cost of 26.28. The glass-blower's fingers spun the ball in all directions and to a crazy length, and in six of the eight innings he conceded over 100 runs; in the other two he went for 95 and 89. Truly the halcyon days of profligate spin — with telling results. Surely the only man ever to have learned of his Test selection while cleaning a water-meter in the shade of a coolibar tree, Arthur Mailey, as the diminutive, Buster Keaton-like follow-up to the fiery pace attack, made a deep impression as Australia steamrollered their way to five successive victories. He also made 25 per Test match, equal to eight weeks' wages.

This was the life, and when, within weeks, he reached England with Armstrong's side, he acquired a Fleet Street contract as a cartoonist for a princely 20 a week. Before the war he had tried in vain to draw professionally, even writing a somewhat pathetic letter to Clem Hill asking about opportunities in Adelaide. He was then drawing — under the pen-name of 'Bosey' — for the *Sportsman* and the *Referee*. Now, as a member of the Australian touring team and a popular artist of simple and ticklesome touch, he was much sought-after at the dinner-tables of the rich and famous. His writings, too, were to be of value — after a most unpromising start when his first assignment in Sydney, a local funeral, had him even getting the name of the corpse wrong. As R. S. Whitington wrote of him, 'Arthur, as a man and a bowler, was rarely strictly accurate'.

He played in only three of the 1921 Tests, but his dozen wickets were nearly all top batsmen. He ran through several county sides, and at Cheltenham in August he gleefully took all ten Gloucestershire wickets for 66 after Armstrong, having been knocked around a bit, tossed him the ball and sarcastically suggested Mailey should have a go at the good batsmen this time, while he would come on later to mop up the tailenders. Cornered many years later by a young clerk in the bank where he had his account, Mailey disappointed by dismissing the 10 for 66 as 'pure luck'. He also shrugged off his 9 for 121 against England at Melbourne, recalling that a few days after he had been presented with the ball, mounted in a silver ring, he looked out of the bedroom window to see his son bowling it against a brick wall.

Mailey's view of spin bowling was creed-like in essence. 'The mentality of the medium-pace bowler as a general rule,' he wrote, 'does not rate up to that of the more subtle type of bowler. With very few exceptions the great spin bowlers of cricket were personalities and men of character — not always pleasant but invariably interesting. They may have lacked the charm and friendliness of most of their faster confederates; they may have been more temperamental and less self-disciplined; but there seemed to be an absence of orthodoxy about them and they were able to meander through life as individuals, not as civil servants.'

One was even clever enough to return the catchy analysis of 10 for 66, and to name his book accordingly.

He was not beyond a spot of diabolical scheming. He used resin on his fingers — and warded off Johnny Douglas's challenge on the subject by pointing to the fast bowler's worn thumbnail, caused by raising the seam on the ball — and he was often seen shaking hands with his wicketkeeper, Bert Oldfield, who, in keeping with common practice, rubbed bird-lime on the palms for better grip. And, of course, Mailey studied opposing batsmen. He quickly espied that Hobbs could not with certainty pick his googly. He was playing leg-side balls as leg-breaks and off-side balls as wrong'uns. So Mailey flipped down a leggie outside off stump and had him caught at slip.

Once, a prearranged plan went wrong when a certain delivery was to be the googly, with Jack Gregory darting across from slip to take the catch down the leg side. Mailey forgot, found the outside edge, and Gregory nearly ruptured himself reversing to take the catch. 'I heard a devil of a scramble going on behind the stumps,' Hobbs said later.

In time, Hobbs began to read him better. Then, Mailey relied on flight variation based on degree of spin. He once bowled Hobbs with a full toss first thing in the morning, when England resumed at 283 for none. . .and did so again at The Oval in '26. Even the full toss was a difficult ball when committed to the stratosphere by the little Sydney gremlin.

Sometimes even Mailey, who learned more from Hugh Trumble than any other mentor, felt it prudent to retreat to more defensive bowling, especially when someone like Woolley — or Macartney in a grade match — was on the rampage. Then, he confessed, he felt a coward. Frank Woolley's straight-driving during the opening Test of 1924-25, at Sydney, was so fierce that Mailey reckoned he was letting the ball go then hopping behind the umpire for refuge.

Openly grateful to the splendid army of catchers supporting him — Oldfield behind the stumps, Gregory at slip, Macartney and Andrews in the covers, and Pellew and Taylor in the outfield — Mailey knew his secret lay in the top-spin accompanying the leg-break and wrong'un. Armstrong

— and Grimmett, who eventually took his place — bowled side-spinning leg-breaks, which did less in the air. He knew, too, that captaincy was a crucial factor. So few skippers knew then — and seem to know to this day — how to handle a spinner. Woodfull and Hassett were just two whom he felt lacked the necessary knowledge of the finer points of slow bowling. Vic Richardson, on the other hand, although certainly no spinner himself, seemed to be able to see the game through the eyes of a slow bowler. This was borne out on Australia's 1935-36 tour of South Africa, when Grimmett and O'Reilly took 71 wickets in the Tests, and almost 100 apiece on the tour.

Mailey himself made a good captain in grade cricket. He also proved a warm benefactor in the underprivileged neighbourhood of Balmain, seeing to it that the budding genius of Archie Jackson was allowed full scope, even to having his club subscription paid for him. Later he had the pleasure of informing the young man of his selection in the Australian XI. And while many bowlers are jealous of their skills, Mailey went so far as to give Ian Peebles an advisory net during the Manchester Test of 1930, responding to the Australian manager's rebuke by saying that 'slow bowling is an art, and art is international'.

The Oval Test of 1926, when Australia at last relinquished the Ashes, was Mailey's last. He arrived on the morning of the match still dressed in a dinner jacket: his car had broken down on the way back from a dinner engagement at East Grinstead the night before. At the end of a tiring day he put all he had into a faster leg-break and bowled Herbert Sutcliffe for 161. It was 30 years later that the imperturbable Yorkshireman got around to asking him: 'Oh, by the way, you old scoundrel, what was that ball you skittled me with at The Oval?'

It was not the only time he was seen in a dinner jacket. Once, in the early hours, with a bemused policeman his only spectator, he beat Neville Cardus (a like spirit) with a googly just to prove a point. The 'pitch' was the pavement in Piccadilly. The orange he spun would have brought back memories of the shack in Waterloo where it all began.

He didn't sleep much, either, on the eve of the pulsating last day at Adelaide in 1925, when he played gramophone records and had supper near dawn with Herby Collins and Johnny Taylor, Collins earlier having got rid of a bookmaker who offered 100 for Australia to throw the match. They won by 11 runs, Mailey taking the last wicket.

Eventually, the NSWCA, having ended Mailey's career when he was forced to choose between playing and writing, got around to giving him a testimonial. As a ceremonial, he bowled a ball to Taylor — and knocked his hob over. 'I should have bowled with my coat on more often!' he growled.

He ended his days in Cronulla, south of Sydney, bobbing about in his boat, and painting. His butcher's shop had a characteristic trade claim scrawled on the window: 'I used to bowl tripe; then I wrote it; now I sell it'. So beloved was he that Prime Minister Robert Menzies, who thought of him as 'a slow bowler of ingenious prodigality', made a long journey to see him on his deathbed. Mailey had not only the wry sense of timing to bow out of Test cricket with 99 wickets, but to abandon his worldly cares on New Year's Eve. How much more might he have achieved if batsmen were not allowed to pad his googly away with small fear of being lbw; or if the modern larger wicket and smaller ball had been at his disposal? He bowled Trumper out at the start of his playing days and Bradman at the end. And, keeping with the faith, he firmly believed that a fresh crop of spin bowlers would rise, bringing back a vital dimension to the game. The prayer goes on, perhaps to be answered only when no more than one ball is available per innings. The ghost with the 'puckish' face may then grin broadly, while the man in the tweed coat can rub his hands in anticipation of a catch, and the wicketkeeper can go back up to the stumps, where he belongs.

12. 'Tich' and Contemporaries

A.P. Freeman — 'Father' Marriott — Roy Kilner —
the 'chinaman' — Dick Tyldesley — Cecil Parkin —
Percy Fender — Charlie Parker — 'Farmer' White —
'Young Jack' Hearne — Ironmonger and Blackie

England's 'king of wrist-spin' in the 1920s was Alfred Percy Freeman, known far and wide (if that term may be permitted) as 'Tich'. Like Rhodes, he left an entry in the record books which is likely to remain into the 21st Century and beyond, for in the 1928 season he took 304 wickets, many of them completed by wicketkeeper Les Ames, who took 69 catches and made 52 stumpings. It began a phenomenal run by Freeman in which he took 2089 wickets in eight consecutive English seasons. In 1929 his Kentish gloveman, Ames, set a new record of 127 dismissals, 48 of them stumpings; and in 1932 Ames established a new high-mark with 64 stumpings in his 100 victims. Batsmen afraid of leaving the crease in the face of such an horrific statistical threat found Freeman even more difficult to counter. The tiny, long-nosed bowler with the shiny bald pate applied just enough spin to the ball and powered it into a teasing loop; and, like Old Clarke, he could take punishment knowing it was unlikely to last. The 19th-Century pioneer once said: 'At times it's enough to make you bite your thumbs to see your best balls pulled and sky-rocketed about — all luck — but you must console yourself with "Ah, that won't last long".' So it was with Freeman.

He had a hard time in Australia, taking only eight wickets at 57 in his two Tests there in 1924-25; but this was largely because no Australian regarded him with awe, since State cricket was bristling with bowlers of similar type. Nor did he have much success in South Africa, leaving the pundits to puzzle over why the bounce of harder pitches abroad was of no great use to him.

At home, though, until he was approaching 50, and then in the Birmingham League, he picked up wickets in spectacular profusion. Three times he took 10 wickets in an innings — a world record; five times he took nine, including 9 for 11 at Hove in 1922. Nine times he took between 15 and 17 wickets in a match, and spectators at Canterbury, Folkestone, Gravesend, Tonbridge, Maidstone and Tunbridge Wells all had something special to cluck about as the little wizard wove his spell. Of the 12 instances of over 250 wickets by a bowler in one season, six were achieved by 'Tich'

Freeman. Everything about him was small — apart from his annual wicket tallies — and with his dwarflike digits, the index finger came in for more work than is customary.

Starting in 1914 — when, aged 26, he succeeded D.W. Carr — Freeman, in only 19 seasons and five tours, gathered 3776 wickets (still second only to Rhodes) with flight that was often parabolic and an inch or two of turn this way — or that — or by sliding the top-spinner straight through. His precious aide, Ames, took time to work him out in the early days, but Frank Woolley, who could pick the well-hidden googly, was most helpful to the young keeper. The combination soon became one of those which cause batsmen restless nights before the encounter. A further menace was the big and fearless Percy Chapman, who intercepted sometimes even the hardest hits from his position a dozen yards away, sometimes making the catch, other times hurling the ball back for a run-out before the bat had completed its followthrough.

The contradiction of 'Tich' Freeman's long career was that against his mountain of first-class wickets, his performances for England are a molehill. He never played against Australia at home, and while he had a successful run in South Africa in 1927-28 (20 wickets in five Tests — and he briefly kept wicket when Stanyforth was injured), against West Indies in 1928 (five wickets in each innings of the Old Trafford Test), and in 1929 against South Africa (7 for 115 and 3 for 92 at Headingley and 7 for 71 and 5 for 100 at Old Trafford), his next — and final — Test, at The Oval, left him with figures of none for 169 after 49 overs of toil. Thereafter the selectors lost interest, preferring Dick Tyldesley, Robins, Peebles, Tommy Mitchell and young Freddie Brown for right-arm wrist-spin...and on one extraordinary occasion, C. S. Marriott, a Kent colleague of Freeman's, an amateur, who took 5 for 37 and 6 for 59 against West Indies at The Oval in 1933 in his one and only Test match.

'Father' Marriott, when he enrolled at Cambridge after a childhood in Ireland and Army service in the Great War, decided to bowl fastish leg-breaks on the perfect pitches of Fenner's. After three seasons with Lancashire, he took a job at Dulwich College, and thereafter played for Kent during the summer holidays, forming a penetrative partnership of contrasts with Freeman. Marriott, bringing his arm from behind his back, used the googly only once or twice at the start of a bowling spell ('to please Tich Freeman' — who liked to serve one up immediately to a new batsman), figuring that a big leg-break and a whisper of the propinquity of the wrong 'un were sufficient to disconcert. He was filled with admiration for his tiny bowling partner, from the way his sinewy arm delivered the googly with hardly a perceptible drop of the wrist to the manner in which Freeman took his sweater after being hit around: 'with a philosophic shrug, and a glint in his eye which said more plainly than words, "All right, enjoy yourselves — but I shall be back".'

Marriott unluckily never returned to Test cricket after that sensational debut in 1933. Knees trembling and mouth dry with excitement, he spun his first ball to George Headley, and achieved an encouraging maiden. His 11 for 96 remains among the best debut performances of all time...just as his book, *The Complete Leg-Break Bowler*, published shortly after his death in 1966, embodies perfectly the idiomatic enthusiasm of the leg-spinner: not that all the technical passages stand all tests, for Marriott insisted that one should *never* spin across the seam (wouldn't a briskly-spun leg-break which travels straight on after pitching on smooth leather be an additional problem for the batsman?) and he claimed that a ball which spun *up the slope* at Lord's (from the Nursery end) to bowl Hendren was a top-spinner *and not a googly.*

Marriott went back to his schoolmastering, Freeman to his home in Bearsted, aptly named 'Dunbowlin'. Others from the 1920s carried on their craft from the decade of Lindbergh, Lawrence and Lloyd George to the years of Huxley, Hitler and Jean Harlow. J. W. Hearne, Percy Fender, Charlie Parker, J. C. White and Vallance Jupp all spun a span across those years. Other mainline spinners, such as G. T. S. Stevens of Middlesex, T. L. Richmond of Notts, Dick Tyldesley of Lancashire, and Roy Kilner of Yorkshire bowled little, if at all, in the 'thirties.

Kilner's was a sad tale. Having established himself as a batsman before the First World War, he survived war wounds — one of them fortunately to his *right* wrist — and, encouraged by Wilfred Rhodes, soon became a key all-rounder for the county, batting and bowling left-handed. England used him nine times, with varying success, though he and Woolley, carrying a depleted attack, eventually brought about an Australian collapse at Adelaide in 1925. Four times he did the season's double, and when conditions were favourable he could be lethal, with accuracy and cunning variation. Comfortably-built and of no more than average height, Roy Kilner was a man of immense charm and popularity, and when he died in 1928, aged only 37, after contracting enteric fever while coaching in India, over 100,000 people lined the streets of Wombwell. The degree of hero-worship could be measured by the vast number of local lads of that era who were christened Roy.

There is a claim on Kilner's behalf that he was the first to bowl the 'chinaman' ball, though later Maurice Leyland, who was more than a doughty left-hand batsman for Yorkshire and England, began to spin from the side of the hand in the mid-1930s, and Ellis Achong, the West Indian of Chinese descent, is the most likely to have given his name to the delivery, even if he was not the first to bowl it.

The 'chinaman', in any case, needs explaining, since it means one thing in England and another in Australia. It is generally held in Australia that the 'chinaman' is the left-arm bowler's googly, which spins towards slip to the right-hand batsman. Englishmen seem to have accepted it as the ordinary left-armer's ball which spins in from the off. The former classification makes more sense, since the googly and the Chinese are both identified, to European eyes, with mystery.

Greville Stevens, 'Tich' Richmond and Dick Tyldesley were all successful right-arm bowlers equipped with the googly. Stevens, who attracted attention at 18 when he scored 466 not out in a school match in 1919, and played for the Gentlemen against the Players that summer, helped Oxford to honours and Middlesex to the County Championship next season, and by 1926, already a truly top-flight all-rounder, he was part of England's Ashes-winning combination, bowling Macartney in the Oval decider. Tall and filmstar handsome, Stevens, who bowled with tremendous life and spin, was endowed with the cheeriness vital to a slow bowler, and had one good set of figures for England — 5 for 105 and 5 for 90 in the Barbados Test of 1930 — before his business as a stockbroker claimed him completely.

Professionals, by contrast, went on and on. Called 'Tich' for the same reason as Freeman, Richmond was almost, but not quite, as good; and he would have gone on bowling for Notts appreciably longer had not he put on a disastrous amount of weight. From 1920 to 1926 he took over 100 wickets a season for the county, but when his powers waned in direct proportion to his waistline, he was sacked, taking up a new position as spin-bowler-in-chief for Sir Julien Cahn and his roving private team. Richmond played once for England, in 1921, and for Notts he took nine wickets in an innings twice, and eight on five occasions.

Tyldesley was another whose shape was related to the cricket ball he spun so cleverly. He turned it relatively little, but took many a wicket with the top-spinner, which, when sent down in profusion, so often bends a batsman's mind: the ball *must* spin from leg sooner or later, *surely*? Having already played against South Africa, he earned a place on the 1924-25 Australian tour by taking 6 for 18 for Lancashire against Yorkshire, and turning in some other promising performances at the psychological time. But he did nothing Down Under, and was to play the last of his seven Tests in 1930 at Headingley, when Don Bradman found him to be child's play. Cardus, who loved writing about Dick Tyldesley, could never forget the merry Lancastrian's lumbering, pitiful trot after the ball as it was hit past him time and again. Nevertheless, his figures for his county were formidable, and the committee must have thought long and hard before deciding not to meet his financial demands in 1931.

Tyldesley's hunting partner was very often Cecil Parkin, an outrageous character, a clown, a rebel, some thought a genius. In strict terms he does not belong in a book about slow bowlers — or fast — or medium. He was everything, and therefore less marginal than some slow to medium bowlers who belong in this story. Durham-born, tall and slim, he had a face like a North country comedian, and acted like one. He could bowl fast, swerve, spin either way in orthodox manner, and bowl the googly. He had a specialty, an unpleasant ball which climbed slowly to a great height and descended, full-toss, towards the bails. All this had the effect of speeding up the game. He either ran through sides, or the batsmen fed off him richly. It was mostly the former in 1923, when he took 209 wickets, and in 1924, when he did even better, his 200 wickets costing only 13.67 each. In 1920 his 9 for 85 for the Players against the Gentlemen at The Oval came from his full range of assortments; he was one of the easiest bowlers against whom to get flustered.

Ten times the England selectors trusted Parkin, and he returned five wickets twice against Australia, at Adelaide and Old Trafford; but England lost seven and drew two of the nine Tests he played in against Australia, and in his final appearance, against South Africa at Edgbaston in 1924, some uncomplimentary remarks about his captain, Arthur Gilligan, were published under his name and he was disciplined. A couple of years later he talked himself out of a job with Lancashire, so altogether this startling cricket jester and entertainer, by over-exuberance, cut short his own act.

First schooled by C. L. Townsend in the North-East, then influenced by S. F. Barnes, Parkin even went so far as to try out new deliveries on his long-suffering wife, who often had blackened fingernails — and once a black eye — to show for her loyalty. He wrote three spirited books, and it was one of his newspaper articles, urging that a professional should lead England if there was no amateur of sufficient quality, which prompted Lord Hawke's historic remark: 'Pray God no professional will ever captain England'.

Parkin's ashes were scattered in 1943 over the Old Trafford turf he so loved. He had not the good fortune to live to the ripe old age enjoyed by a cricketer very dissimilar in personality and background but alike in method: P. G. H. Fender. Though not quite the innovator and improviser that Parkin was, Percy Fender was a man of striking individuality. Surrey captain throughout the 1920s, scorer of the fastest-ever century, Test player surprisingly only 13 times, he dispensed a mixture of leg- and off-breaks, googlies (seldom used in 'good company', according to Mailey), faster yorkers, and even lobs, which were trundled down at Bournemouth in 1931 in protest at Hampshire's non-declaration. With a right- and left-hand batsman together, Fender sent his fielders from one side of the ground to the other after each single that day, and one over took 12 minutes.

He gave up fast-medium bowling as a young man when he saw the gross leg-spin put on by Joe Vine at the nets. Fender was entranced, and thenceforth devoted his considerable intellect to a kind of bowling demanding more than a strong shoulder. He switched from Sussex to Surrey before the First War, and, an elongated Charlie Chaplin figure, with curly, black hair, controlled moustache, spectacles and absurdly long sweater, he became a true Oval favourite — even though his uncompromising character and bent for outspokenness hardly endeared him to authority.

On the way to Australia in 1920, Fender was told by his skipper, J. W. H. T. Douglas, that his batting and bowling impressed him little. He thus had to wait until the third Test for his debut. But at Melbourne and Sydney he took five wickets in an innings. The remainder of his spasmodic Test career was a disappointment for one so original; yet in English domestic cricket he remained a great and successful entertainer with bat, ball and in the field. Suffice to recall his most astonishing achievement: against

Middlesex at Lord's, in 1927, either side of the lunch interval, Fender took 7 for 4 in 19 balls, six bowled, one lbw, with a mix of googlies and swerving cutters. Such is the potential of an inventive spinner when 'running hot' and backed by a favourable horoscope.

There seemed to be more bowlers in earlier days who based their method on wide variation, never simply prepared to lay back and wait for a batsman to make a mistake. There has always been more pleasure in fooling and surprising a batsman — preferably sending him back to the pavilion, though even that conclusion was not always essential to the satisfaction of the true Corinthians. Jack O'Connor, the Essex batsman, was willing to risk loss of accuracy by mixing off-breaks and leg-breaks; slow and simple-looking they may have been, but he fished in over 500 wickets. V. W. C. Jupp of Sussex and Northants, one of the most prolific and colourful all-rounders between the wars, could adapt to conditions with either nippy off-cutters or slow off-spin, intimidating the umpire with beetle-brows beneath his baldness, his dynamic little chunk of a body swivelling round in fierce appeal. Only Rhodes and Hirst bettered Jupp's 10 season doubles, and only three players have taken more than his five hat-tricks. (It might prompt some reflective thought to know that only one of the seven bowlers to take five or more hat-tricks could be considered on the faster side of medium pace: Schofield Haigh.)

Vallance Jupp also took all 10 in an innings — against Kent at Tunbridge Wells, when his side still lost by an innings, little Freeman taking eight wickets in each Northants innings — all of this upstaged a week later when Verity took 10 for 10 for Yorkshire against Notts at Headingley.

Yorkshire's George Macaulay was another adventurous bowler, often switching to off-spin around the wicket after a spell with the new ball. A rapacious cricketer, hungry for wickets, inconsolable when rain or bad light prevented him from getting out there to attack with vast off-spinners. Similar to Parkin in outlook — always ready for a joke, and using his mouth as much as his spinning fingers — Macaulay *versus* Macartney, the super-confident, aggressive little Australian batting maestro, was a contest to satisfy the gods of war, and when the 'Governor-General' swept to his century before lunch in the 1926 Headingley Test, the verbal exchanges between the two should have been recorded.

Jack Newman of Hampshire was also prepared to bowl all day, turning to off-spin after using the new ball with the equally trusty Alec Kennedy. Much-admired for his cricket and his character, Newman fell from grace just once, in 1922, when he did something which has become fashionable in modern times: kicked the stumps down. The Trent Bridge crowd were up to their familiar goading chants, and the bowler could not refrain from showing his contempt. His captain, the Hon. Lionel Tennyson, sent him from the field, made him apologise, told him not to do such a thing again, and gave him a fiver, knowing what a fundamentally good chap he was. Newman, a lifelong bachelor, lost a lot of lbw decisions through his habit of blocking the umpire's view in his followthrough.

Most counties had stock slow left-arm bowlers, and Hampshire's was Stuart Boyes, who was tall and graceful, and took over 1400 wickets for the county as well as almost 500 catches at short leg. The competition for a Test place was too severe to allow Boyes a cap; but Lancashire's Jack Iddon played five times for England in the 1930s, even if he was crowded out as a bowler. His slow left-arm work brought him over 500 wickets, including the distinction of 9 for 47 in a Roses match. He died in a car crash in 1946.

Two left-arm bowlers stood out in the 1920s, and the oddity was that Charlie Parker, who was considered by many of his opponents to be the finest slow left-arm bowler in the world, played only once for England. It was said that he once grabbed a selector by the lapels and asked for an explanation — which would hardly have helped his cause. Yet truly he earned, time and again, that too-easily-coined attribution: unplayable. He was recommended to Gloucestershire as early as 1903 by no less a judge than W. G. Grace, but it was years before he was able to fill Dennett's place. After the First War he dropped into the habit of taking over 100 — five times 200 — wickets in a summer. Only Rhodes and Freeman took more than his lifetime aggregate of 3278.

Six times he did the hat-trick (three in 1924, when he performed it twice in the Middlesex match at Bristol), and only Goddard and Verity stand alongside him in the list of those who have taken nine or more wickets in an innings on a staggering *nine* occasions. He followed his 9 for 44 (the other batsman was run out) against Essex at Gloucester in 1925 with 8 for 12 in the second innings, and holds a record even Freeman could not better: 26 wickets in three consecutive innings. One of numerous professional cricketers to cut a year or two off his age, he was born in 1882, and was thus 52 in his last season. Thirteen years earlier he had been awarded a benefit, which he commemorated with figures of 9 for 36 against Yorkshire, hitting the stumps with five successive balls, the second of which was a no-ball.

Weather-beaten of countenance, cap at a careless angle, Charlie Parker was a slow-bowling artist who approached his job with the overt aggression of a fast bowler. He was not insensitive. He could talk music and politics, and became a respected coach at Cranleigh. But no batsman ever felt completely at ease when facing him, especially with Wally Hammond at slip to hold everything edged into that area of 60 degrees. When Hammond held his world record 10 catches in the match against Surrey at Cheltenham in 1928, eight of them came off Parker. When his county tied against the 1930 Australians, it was Parker's 7 for 54 which swung the game, and he got Bradman in both innings. If there was a worn spot on a length, Parker could find it unerringly; and he was just fast enough, as Rhodes recalled, that 'you couldn't get at him'.

He retired just as the new lbw law came in in 1935, and must have rued painfully the fact that many more wickets would have come his way if he could have recaptured his youth, for now the 'arm ball' coming in to strike the pad could produce a wicket.

'Old Clarke', the one-eyed Nottingham ex-bricklayer: soda-water and a cigar for lunch.

David Frith

Bobby Peel, Yorkshire's brilliant but boozy left-arm spinner of the 1890s.

Right, Johnny Briggs, Lancashire's pride: 'the sun seemed always shining when Johnny was with us'.

Lower right, Off-spinner Hugh Trumble, whose Australia-England record of 141 Test wickets lasted 77 years, until Dennis Lillee broke it.

Below, 'Charlie' Blythe, the delicate Kentish cockney, who was killed in the First World War.

David F

David Frith

David F

Top performer of all — Wilfred Rhodes, whose tally of 4187 first-class wickets
is unmatched.

Which one was it? B.J.T. Bosanquet, father of the googly, asks the question

Above, the South African team which played against England in all five Tests of 1905-06. The googly quartet of Vogler (standing, second from right), Schwarz (seated, second from left), White (front, centre) and Faulkner (front, right), took 43 wickets in this series, 40 in the three Tests of 1907, and Vogler and Faulkner took 65 in the 1909-10 series.

Left, Charlie Parker: mysteriously only one Test cap.

Right, A.P. 'Tich' Freeman: 304 wickets in a season in days when cricket was a rich entertainment. *Below,* one of the author's all-time favourite pictures: Sutcliffe caught at slip by Gregory off the irrepressible little teaser Arthur Mailey, Melbourne Test, January 1925.

Left, lantern-jaw, hands like plates, raucous roar of appeal: that was Tom Goddard. *Below,* 'Grum' strikes: Hammond beaten and stumped by Oldfield off the persistent wizardry of Clarrie Grimmett, Trent Bridge 1934.

'Tiger' in full flight: the aggression of Bill O'Reilly suggests a fast bowler
though his standard pace was below (if only just) medium.

Left, 'Chuck' Fleetwood-Smith, to whose bowling there was no logical answer when his length and direction were on song. *Below,* the grip that produced the most startling of all analyses: 10 for 10. Hedley Verity, the calm Yorkshireman — killed in the Second World War.

Left, Doug Wright: batsmen smacked away his long-hops and full-tosses with mixed feelings, for the next ball could be unplayable. *Lower left,* there had never been anything like it: Jack Iverson's middle-finger grip and apparent each-way turn gave English batsmen nightmares. *Below,* South Africa's champion off-spinner Athol Rowan: 9 for 19 for Transvaal against the Australians.

eorge Tribe, rejected by Australia, reaped a rich harvest for Northants. So
lpless were the opposition at times that he tended to lose interest.

Above, sleeves down, cap firmly on, Sonny Ramadhin, the tiny Trinidadian dispatches another mystery ball. *Below,* Alf Valentine, from Jamaica, who took seven wickets in West Indies' first Test victory in England. His 'little pal', Ramadhin, took 11.

HIS WAS AUSTRALIA AS JIM LAKER SPUN ENGLAND

VICTORY AND THE ASHES

IR DONALD BRADMAN sees history made, says ...

GREATEST TEST MATCH BOWLING OF ALL TIME

bove, Jim Laker (left) and Tony Lock, Surrey and England's lethal spin pair rough the 1950s. *Below,* ten little Australians, all in a row: Laker's anchester massacre, 1956 — 9 for 37 and 10 for 53.

Above, the balletic step of Johnny Wardle: good when orthodox and alm⚫
magic when he bowled from the back of the hand — though Yorkshire did⚫
like it. *Below,* the ritual kiss of luck: another over by Hugh Tayfield, Sou⚫
Africa's top Test wicket-taker with 170.

The brilliant South Australian, Bruce Dooland, who spun out 770 batsmen in only five seasons of county cricket with Notts.

Subhash Gupte, the confident little Indian. For Garry Sobers, he was simply the best spinner he faced.

ove, in the path of Iverson — though never quite as lethal — came Johnny
leeson. Below, a celebrated triumph: Richie Benaud, bowling round the
cket, gets through to Peter May's stumps and sends Australia headlong
wards Ashes victory, Old Trafford 1961.

Central

Above, a terror on damp pitches, Derek Underwood (7 for 50) edges England closer to a sensational victory at The Oval in 1968, having Graham McKenzie caught inches from the bat. *Right,* Robin Hobbs, the last of English leg-spinners of the modern age, deceives Pakistan's Burki.

Patrick Eagar

The guile of Lance Gibbs. The spindly West Indian off-spinner held the world Test record with 309 wickets until Lillee passed him. Gibbs, though, stood supreme with his workload of 27115 balls.

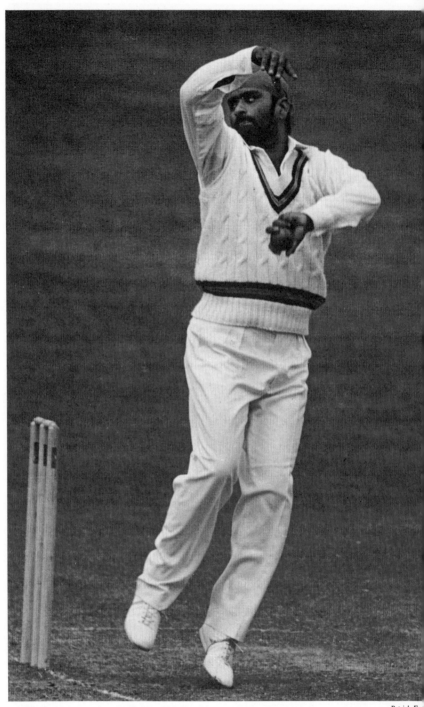

Patrick Ea...

The popular Bishan Bedi, with his comfortable, bobbing action and patkas of many colours, spun his way to an Indian record of 266 Test wickets.

Above, the genius with the withered arm: Chandrasekhar, who spun like a top, but at such a brisk pace that batsmen could often only play him with a prayer. *Below,* off-spin in five decades: Fred Titmus of Middlesex and England began his career in 1949 and was still fooling batsmen out in the 1980s.

Patrick Eagar

Built like a fast bowler, with steely wrists, Intikhab Alam was the first Pakistani to take 1000 first-class wickets.

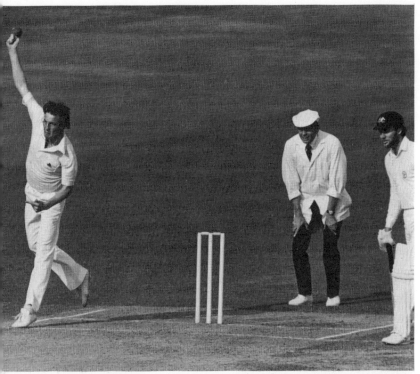

bove, languid, classical motion: John Emburey, England's best off-spinner,
as banned because of his participation in a forbidden tour of South Africa.
elow, Abdul Qadir, who mesmerised England in 1982 with leg-spin variations,
d Iqbal Qasim, the left-armer, who quietly moved to 100 Test wickets. This
air kept spin to the fore for Pakistan.

'Roo' Yardley, lean as a kangaroo dog. In an era of pace bowling, he won
cherished accolade for spin by winning the International Cricketer of the Ye
Award in 1982.

The other leading slow left-armer was J. C. White of Somerset, who played only a few games after 1935. His fruitful career stretched from 1909, and brought him over 2300 modestly-priced wickets. He was not a vicious spinner of the ball in the Parker mould. First spotted by Tyler, he preferred from the start to do his work in the air, and his gift for controlling the flight of the ball was uncanny. All through a hot afternoon 'Farmer' White would roll down over after over, the seeming innocence of his bowling causing distant spectators to wonder why the batsmen did not pick him off at will. But any who had been out in the middle realised that to attack was a very risky exercise against the 'hung' ball, the testing curve, and the pinpoint accuracy linked to a covering off-side field.

He came from the village of Stogumber, a quiet man, rosy-cheeked, with fair hair which was to turn to silver-grey. He was blooded by Somerset as a teenager, and in 1914, at 23, just before the world stopped on its axis for four years, he took 83 cheap Championship wickets and topped the county's bowling. Upon resumption in 1919, he dropped immediately into the groove, and took 100 or more wickets that season and in the 13 that followed, compelling even the Hobbses and the Hammonds to watch him closely even on hard, fast pitches. In that first post-war season he took 16 wickets in a day against Worcestershire at Bath, and tortured that same county two years later with 10 for 76 in the first innings at Worcester. In 1923 he took his only hat-trick; it was at Lord's, and it converted a likely Middlesex victory into a draw.

Jack White captained the county and became one of the very few spin bowlers to lead England. Taciturn in his modesty, he knew a quiet and deep pleasure in his achievements on the 1928-29 tour of Australia. M. A. Noble rated his contribution as at least as important to England's cause as Hammond's 905 Test runs, and there have been very few demonstrations of sustained skill and stamina to equal White's in the third Test, at Melbourne, and the next, a month later, at Adelaide. In those four innings he wheeled down 57, 56.5, 60 and 64.5 six-ball overs for a total of 87 maidens and 19 wickets (13 at Adelaide) for 427 runs. His cost per over was 1.79 runs; his cost per wicket 22.47. Like Rhodes before him, he had defied popular opinion that an English slow left-arm bowler would be murdered on hard Australian tracks. The pitch at Brisbane in the opening match became a sticky horror, and White took 4 for 7 to finish Australia off for 66, and defeat by a savage 675 runs. In the eight-day fifth Test, when he took over the captaincy from a below-par Chapman, he bowled another 75.3 overs in the first innings, taking 2 for 136. It was Mailey-like industry, but without the lavish cost.

'The Farmer's' stout effort was directed at such heavy scorers as Bradman, Woodfull, Kippax, Ryder, Hendry and the brilliant youngster Jackson, with tempting gaps left in the leg-side field by way of traps, and a fortified cover field positioned like a dyke, Hobbs, 46 but still a good field, leading the patrol. How many times White must have murmured 'Well fielded, cock' to his colleagues, especially Percy Chapman, his skipper, who cut off everything within yards at short mid-off, aggravating the Australians' frustration.

Whether he was taking punishment — which he occasionally did, of course, in such a lengthy career — or bowling Gloucestershire out for 22 (as he did in 1920, taking 7 for 10, although Somerset eventually lost) he was calm and unemotional — an irritating adversary. In summary, he was as Noble wrote, 'able to call the tune and compel the batsmen to dance to it'.

Of the right-arm spinners to be seen either side of the Great War, J. W. Hearne was perhaps endowed with most genius. Indeed, but for persistent frail health, he might have placed his name on the highest pedestal of all-rounders. As it was, his long career, 1909 to 1936, produced figures matched by very few: 37,252 runs, average 40.98, 96 centuries, and 1839 wickets with leg-breaks and googlies at 24.44. 'Young Jack' played for England 24 times, and made a century against Australia at Melbourne in 1911-12 when still a few weeks short of his 21st birthday. A couple of years later he took 5 for 49 against South Africa at Johannesburg, but thereafter his rich promise was unfulfilled at Test level.

Immaculately straight-batted and stylish, he played some memorably long and attractive innings, usually in company with Patsy Hendren or Frank Tarrant, with both of whom he had stands in excess of 300. As a bowler, Hearne began a remarkable line of Middlesex leg-spinners between the wars. A small, light man, with a nice sense of humour, he was dapper and neat in all he did. His approach to the crease was one of the briefest ever seen, and though he fell short of bowling greatness, he possessed two of the requisite qualities: the ability to turn the ball just enough and on a fine length, and the nature to take punishment without panicking. Illness, injury, and fatigue curtailed his performances, notably early in the 1920-21 series, when his talents were direly needed against Australia, but he achieved the double five times, and though he did less bowling as the 1920s drew to a close, he reserved his best statistical performance for 1933, when he shook Derbyshire with 9 for 61 at Chesterfield in a match that proved a leg-spinners' delight: Sims took 8 for 47 in the first innings, and Tommy Mitchell bagged 7 for 86 for the home side. Twenty-six out of 32 wickets in the match fell to the wrist merchants.

Hearne, in his years of fading elegance, had so much remembered success to warm him, going back a quarter of a century to the afternoon at Lord's when he had a spell of 7 for 2 against Essex. Health was the gift he lacked in its full bounty, though he was to live till 1965, his 75th year.

Australia were less lucky in that a player of equal faculty showed his worth in the early 1920s in his homeland and in Lancashire league cricket, only to die at 27 of peritonitis. Frank O'Keeffe, strongly-built and determined, moved from NSW to Victoria in 1921 in quest of greater opportunity. There was much competition, but he showed his worth against Armstrong's touring team upon their return with innings of 177 and 144 at Sydney, and then made a further big century and took wickets with leg-spin in two State matches. Remembering Trott, Tarrant and others, he decided to make a name for himself in county cricket, and began with a league contract with Church. The climate, however, did not agree with even such a robust constitution, and only a few months before he qualified to play for Lancashire, he was dead, much mourned by the friends he had made. Into his short life he had crammed a lot of experience, even playing cricket in France while shellfire burst nearby. Legend has it at the Carlton club, Melbourne that O'Keeffe was the first captain to have his fielders walking in briskly as he ran in to bowl. His premature loss left many a lovely spinner unbowled and boundary unhit.

A further tale of opportunity lost, if only passingly, concerned Sam Staples of Notts. Basically an off-spinner of slow-medium pace, his big chance came after four successful seasons when he was chosen to go to Australia in 1928. He was kitted out, took his place in the team photo, and sailed on the *Moldavia*, only to be stricken with back muscle trouble and confined to bed. Within the month he was shipping back to England at his own request. His bowling would have been invaluable at least in the later stages of the gruelling tour. He played a few years more, the last Notts slow bowler to open the attack, and finished with over 1300 wickets.

One of the most colourful players in the 1920s was the tall, erect Frank Ryan, born in New Jersey, USA, in 1888, and educated at Bedford Grammar School. Briefly with Hampshire, he went, penniless, to Glamorgan and took over 900 wickets for the Welsh county, spinning the ball vast distances with the fingers of his left hand. An erratic genius who could 'bowl like a drain', he took 37 wickets in three matches in 1925. One morning he was discovered asleep under the pitch-covers! When he left Basingstoke he owed John Arlott's father £1 — a debt for which that great commentator's parent never forgave him. Ryan, who had a keen eye for women, fell prey to drugs, but survived to become an inspector for the War Graves Commission after the Second World War.

Of the stalwarts who served their counties for almost a lifetime, Ewart Astill of Leicestershire has an exalted place. Bowling mainly off-breaks with a high action, he played for the county for a third of a century, beginning in 1906, when he was 18 and had attracted notice for his cricket with a Sunday school team. Fine-featured and athletic, Astill came so near to carving out for himself an illustrious Test career, winning all kinds of accolades and representative honours. At the end of it all, he had 2431 wickets, but only 25 in nine Tests in South Africa and West Indies. He was, then, essentially a county cricketer, who thrived on work, and with George Geary he carried Leicestershire through many a match in the 1920s and 1930s, twice bowling unchanged right through a match with him, and five times taking a dozen or more wickets. His nine doubles place him fourth below Rhodes, Hirst and Jupp, and, above and beyond his impressive figures, as a team-mate and opponent he was a joy to know. A superb billiards-player, he also sang well and played the piano. Small wonder he became a popular and successful coach for his old county and then at Tonbridge School.

Long before Astill's career ended, there was concern that spin bowling was going into decline. In his book *The Quest for Bowlers*, published in 1926, C. T. B. Turner, the master bowler from Australia (who could hardly be classified as a slow bowler, though his speed, 55 m.p.h., measured at Woolwich Arsenal in 1888, would seem to compare with Bedi's), expressed alarm at the preoccupation in the mid-1920s with 'swerve' bowling now that pitches seemed less to favour spin. Turner himself had spun from the off at a brisk pace, and formed a lethal partnership with Jack Ferris, left-arm medium to slow-medium. Between them they had taken 482 first-class wickets on the 1888 tour, and 365 in 1890. 'Terror' Turner raced to 101 wickets in only 17 Tests, with the low average of 16.53, a fitting reward for one who used to rise at 4.30 a.m., prepare the Cobb & Co. mail-coaches, then make his way to the cricket ground — while still the majority of the population of Bathurst had yet to stir — and practise bowling until he could bowl a designed length and spin anything from one inch to twelve at a solitary stump.

Turner's small (and now rare) book may have been prompted by the desire — at 64, and married to his third wife, who survived him — to make a few shillings (he left 202 in 1944), for the alleged dearth of spinners in Australia, as in England, is not substantiated by the list of bowlers concerned. What may have perturbed Turner was that many of them were getting on in years. Yet they, more than fast bowlers, fielders and batsmen, could view their weight in years as an advertisement for their experience, their greater wisdom. The return of Rhodes for the Oval Test of '26 said it all.

Grimmett, even older than he confessed at the time, eventually displaced Mailey in the Australian XI, and proved to be a major figure for ten years. His story follows at length. Of the others in Australia, Ironmonger and Blackie, because of their age, are now regarded as figures of fun. Bert Ironmonger, born in Queensland, was in his 47th year when called up from the Victorian ranks to play his first Test match. He had lost the forefinger of his left hand, and fired the ball out from the stub rather as one would release a marble. It undoubtedly accounted for a unique nip to the delivery, and caused some to wonder if his action was legal, though he was never called for throwing. A modest, reliable man, Ironmonger, a labourer by trade, must have been surprised to find himself in national colours at Brisbane in 1928 at such an advanced age, and after toiling through almost 100 overs in that Test and 68 at Sydney, taking six wickets for 306 runs, he would have thought his international days were done. Yet he was a killer on a rain-affected wicket, like Underwood, whose pace is similar, though Ironmonger had a higher action and got more bounce. Called up again two years later, he took 11 for 79 against West Indies at Melbourne, 9 for 66 in the match against South Africa a year later at Brisbane, seven wickets in the Melbourne Test, and, when they returned to that ground for the final Test, he bettered all his and most others' figures with 5 for 6 and 6 for 18, giving everyone another excuse to drag out that moot adjective 'unplayable'. The Springboks were upturned for 36 and 45, and the match aggregate of 234 is the lowest in a completed Test match. To Ironmonger was attributed the story about a clueless batsman being wanted on the phone as he went out to bat, the caller being asked to hang on since it wouldn't be for long. At Melbourne in 1932 it was the wretched South Africans who would not have kept a caller waiting.

'Dainty' Ironmonger (he was apt to be clumsy, and had trouble with his old legs) was useful to Australia in the Bodyline series, by which time, as we now know from the recent rediscovery of his birth certificate, he was 50 years of age. With a bushman's lumbering gait and leathery countenance, Bert Ironmonger took 74 wickets at only 17.97 in only 14 Tests, all played at an age when the average cricketer has settled for a comfortable seat, a mug of beer, and a range of disparaging spectator remarks.

Don Blackie was even older, if by only two days, having been born on April 5, 1882, at Bendigo. He could little have guessed, when he joined Melbourne's Prahran club in 1906 at the age of 24, that he would one day play for Australia, and that that one day was 22 years away. His off-breaks spun with clever swerve from a great height (he was a wiry, bow-legged 6ft 3ins), brought him a record of 798 wickets in VCA club cricket, but just as he had to wait a long time for State honours (in 1924-25, when he was 42, and had already retired for a while), so he had to age a bit more before the Test selectors decided he was their man. Then, against the 1928-29 England XI, after the breakdown of Gregory and illness of Kelleway, 'Rock' Blackie took 4 for 148 at Sydney in his first Test, and 6 for 94 at Melbourne in the next. His career finished with the Adelaide Test, but his 14 wickets at 31.71 placed him second only to Tim Wall in the averages, and he was free to go back, pride enhanced, to spinning them out for his club (now St Kilda) until his fifties, starting his run out near mid-off with whom he would exchange a chuckling remark, wrapping his long fingers around the ball and coming in to bowl at about Ian Johnson's pace, with a wide swing of the arm which extracted maximum curve, especially into a breeze.

Like Blackie, Ron Oxenham, who toiled for Queensland at slow-medium, was given only part of one Ashes Test series (also the '28-29 games), and four later Tests, but with only moderate success. His best ball was one which floated in. It got him many an lbw, although only two Ceylon batsmen fell this way when Oxenham, then 44, started the 1935-36 Tarrant/Ryder tour of the sub-continent by taking 9 for 18 against All-Ceylon, the other seven batsmen being bowled.

The most-capped Australian off-spinner of the 1920s was Arthur Richardson, another who was no sprightly youth, and whose solid runmaking capacity gave him the edge over the Blackies and Ironmongers. And yet he never took more than two wickets in a Test innings. When England — in the immortal outlines of Hobbs and Sutcliffe — fought through a period of sticky-wicket hazards at The Oval in 1926, to set up a splendid and patriotically-rousing victory, it was thought by the more keen-eyed judges that Richardson, bowling off-breaks around the wicket with a leg trap, was made to look more difficult than he was by the artful England pair, who were content for Collins to keep him on. Ray McNamee of NSW might have been a contender, had he more batting ability. During his three seasons at the top, he took 72 wickets at 30, and knew the uniquely contrasting experience of bowling at Victoria in Melbourne while they piled up 1107 (McNamee 0 for 124) and at the same opposition at home in Sydney a month later (though they now lacked Woodfull, Ponsford and Ryder), when the 'Vics' crashed for 35 (McNamee 7 for 21). Australia's 1926-27 season was one of the queerest.

As always, there were batsmen around who bowled spin well but not so often. Herbie Collins was a left-arm spinner of real class before it fell to him to concentrate on his batting, which got Australia out of several tight spots. Austin Punch, a consistent NSW batsman, was a fine leg-spinner who had few opportunities. Bert Hartkopf, on the other hand, was a genuine all-rounder whose leg-spin won him a Test cap in 1924-25. He scored 80, but Hobbs and Sutcliffe had an opening stand of 283, and when England had done, Hartkopf, of German ancestry, had one wicket (last man Strudwick) for 120.

Elsewhere around the world, spin prospered in the hands and fingers of bowlers whose names meant little internationally, since their countries, India, New Zealand, and West Indies, were just starting out as Test-playing forces — and then without the blare of publicity known to modern cricket, whether it be for a new nation such as Sri Lanka or the more 'box-office' Test series. The ageless C. K. Nayudu, fearless batsman, was also a skilful slow-medium bowler with mystical changes of pace. New Zealand had a fine all-rounder in Durham-born Roger Blunt, who bowled leg-spin and took 3 for 17 and 2 for 17 in the Kiwis' first-ever Test, against England at Christchurch in 1930. A specialist leg-spin/googly bowler of the highest class and same vintage was Billy Merritt, who had a remarkable tour of England in 1927 when 18 years of age and with only four first-class matches behind him. He took 169 wickets in all matches at under 20 apiece; but in his six subsequent Test appearances things went wrong for him. He left a good impression at Lord's, however, on the 1931 tour, when he took 7 for 28 against a strong MCC side, Blunt taking 3 for 13. It was remarked that neither bowled a loose ball, a fair achievement in 91 deliveries. Bowling a bad slow ball is easier than falling off a chair.

Merritt, who moved into league cricket and then on to Northamptonshire, for whom he played either side of the war, is remembered as probably the best yet of New Zealand's googly bowlers — always excluding Clarrie Grimmett, if his birthplace is not to be over-looked.

West Indies had some interesting spinners, C. R. 'Snuffy' Browne dispensing fastish leg-breaks at times so persuasively that batsmen were near-helpless, as at Derby in 1928, when he took 8 for 81, and against Barbados ten years later, when he finished with 7 for 13. A magistrate, he became the first black West Indian to be made an honorary life member of

MCC. George Gladstone, a Jamaican of mysterious origins, was a man of stamina. His slow left-arm bowling tended to seal up one end all afternoon, and against the 1929-30 MCC team he bowled 75 overs, taking 9 for 252 in the match. This won him a Test cap, and while England piled up 849 (Sandham 325), he toiled through 42 overs to take 1 for 139, with 0 for 50 in the second innings. He may have played in only one Test match, but it lasted fully nine days. Apart from Joe Small (slow-medium off-breaks), there was not much other Caribbean spin to be seen in high places.

South Africa, in contrast, abounded in top-class slow bowlers in that decade. Jimmy Blanckenberg, who already had a reputation before the Great War, was considered by Australian captain Herbie Collins to have been the best slow bowler he ever faced. Tireless, he could bowl long spells to a perfect length, spinning and swinging both ways, and he was a constant menace to England in the 1922-23 series, when he took 25 wickets. Born in 1893, Blanckenberg has been listed for years as 'presumed dead', in a statement which failed to sting him into reappearance, if such were possible.

At the turn of the century George Rowe had been the principal slow left-arm bowler among Springboks — just before the googly army took up arms. He took over 100 wickets on both the 1894 and 1901 tours of England. Next in the line was Claude Carter, a Natalian who played for Cornwall. He picked up 28 wickets in his 10 Tests, and toured England in 1912 and 1924. Later came Cyril Vincent, whose cricket was restricted by business responsibilities. Still, he played in 25 Tests, excelling at Leeds in 1935, when he took eight top England wickets with immaculate flighted left-arm spin.

Henry Promnitz, of the intense gaze and triangular face, was a top-spin-googly 'mystery' bowler from Border, and in the first of his two Tests, at Johannesburg in 1927, he got enough work off the mat to take five good English wickets for 58 in 37 overs. But his Test career was not to blossom, even though in 1935-36 Stan McCabe couldn't tell which way he was spinning. In 1983, when he died, Promnitz had been South Africa's oldest surviving Test player at 79. There were two other classy leg-spinners coming up: 'Tuppy' Owen-Smith, who made a great impression at 20 in his only series, against England in 1929, and the bright-eyed Quentin McMillan, from Transvaal, whose wiles earned 36 wickets in 13 Tests. He also had a field day against South Australia on the '31-32 tour, taking 9 for 53, only to retire in favour of a business career at the end of the tour.

Owen-Smith had a mere five first-class games behind him when he toured England with the 1929 Springboks, and his genius as an all-round cricketer was soon apparent, even if he bowled little in these his only five Tests. A century at Headingley, when he added a record 103 for the tenth wicket in only 63 minutes with 'Sandy' Bell, almost saved the match for South Africa. Owen-Smith's 100 runs before lunch included a straight six off 'Tich' Freeman and a pulled six off Jack White, and in those far-off sporting days it was natural that the crowd booed Duckworth when he shouted for a stumping against the youngster when he was 99. Owen-Smith returned as a Rhodes scholar, won Blues at Oxford for cricket, boxing and rugby, and captained England at the latter sport. He continued his cricket with Middlesex, who were crowded out with leg-spinners. Still, he took the ball often enough to claim 100 wickets in three seasons at moderate cost.

Denis Tomlinson, though capped only once, was a leg-break bowler of great importance to Rhodesia, and there were numerous others, in all countries, who practised the art in cricket's slow-bowling heyday, when almost every team had one if not two 'leggers' and the game moved faster — one way or the other. The greatest pair, though, lived in sunny Australia.

13. Aussie Demons — and Verity

Clarrie Grimmett — Bill O'Reilly — Fleetwood-Smith —
Hedley Verity — Walter Robins — Ian Peebles —
Jim Sims — Tommy Mitchell — John Clay —
Tom Goddard

Grimmett and O'Reilly! Even the Hammonds, Sutcliffes and Nourses lost a little sleep before or even after facing Australia's lethal combination of the 1930s. What a contrast the two presented: Grimmett, small and stooped, always in a cap, crinkled face not given to much expression, and a gentle, bobbing action culminating in a roundarm delivery, the wrist and fingers the crackling power-point of operation; O'Reilly, tall as a eucalypt, bald head defiant to the sun, face screwed up in an agony of belligerence, the ungainly, bounding approach climaxing in a windmill whirl of arms — all this supported by a verbal aggression now seen as ancestral to the latterday oaths, so much sharper, of the Lillees and Sarfrazes.

Clarrie Grimmett was born near Dunedin, New Zealand, on Christmas Day, 1891, and, after some Plunket Shield cricket, ventured to Australia. In Sydney he played only grade cricket, earning a rebuke from M. A. Noble for slipping through his overs too fast (1½ minutes). Moving on to Melbourne, where the old left-armer Jack Saunders helped him, he had a few Shield matches for Victoria; but he had to go further, to Adelaide, before his talents were truly appreciated. Earning a living as a signwriter, Grimmett eventually was called up by Australia at the age of 33, and took 5 for 45 and 6 for 37 on debut at Sydney, bowling Woolley with a wrong'un to record the first of 216 Test wickets in 37 Tests. The first man to take 200 Test wickets, Grimmett actually took 13 in his last Test, at Durban in 1935-36, a series in which he captured a record 44 wickets, with O'Reilly bagging 27. Jack Fingleton and Bill Brown crouched courageously in the leg-trap for both bowlers throughout that hot summer tour.

They called Grimmett 'Grum' or 'The Fox' or 'Scarlet' or 'The Gnome', nicknames all rubbed with affection as well as respect. He preferred to practise alone. He was jealous of his secret methods, and was going to give nothing away to prospective opposing batsmen in the nets. In the early days he trained his fox terrier to fetch the ball — the dog apparently could count up to six, and retrieved only at the end of an 'over' — while he never ceased to search for new variations. He spent years perfecting the 'flipper', a ball which quite unexpectedly skidded through, bringing numerous lbws. Benaud, Pepper and Dooland all inherited it. And even after the Test selectors had abandoned him, he worked on new kinds of delivery, some of which captured top wickets even when he was in his late forties. In season 1939-40 he showed what he was still worth by taking a record 73 first-class wickets. He never got over his omission from the 1938 tour of England, which would have been his fourth.

When Mailey ceased to play for Australia, Grimmett took over the into-the-wind end. He spun less than his predecessor, and concentrated on pinpoint accuracy: the 'miser' compared to the 'millionaire'. In perfect batting conditions he would peg away at the leg stump, enjoying long spells in which he planned a batsman's downfall perhaps over a 10-over period or longer. Relentless. Unflappable. Though Bert Oldfield completed many a dismissal for him, Grimmett had less than complete faith in the smooth and clever wicketkeeper, an attitude some way justified by surviving film which shows a leg-stump googly beating the gloves and a top-spinner buzzing between the Prince of Keeper's pads. Indeed, many of Grimmett's wickets were lbw and caught-and-bowled.

During the 1930 tour of England he met Bosanquet, who asked 'Am I responsible for you?' Not surprisingly, the spin brethren talked for hours, their scientific discussion at the end of the pier at Hove ending at two in the morning. Grimmett took 29 Test wickets on that tour, a return which, in truth, had as much to do with Australia's success as Bradman's 974 runs. His 10 for 37 against Yorkshire did nothing to lessen the opinion that the Northerners can't handle leg-spin; yet 134 other wickets came his way that summer, average 16.85.

In each of the next two home series, against West Indies and South Africa, he gathered 33 wickets, and back in England he took 25 more (O'Reilly 28). It seems highly unlikely that England would have amassed such scores as 658 for 8 and 903 for 7 if little old Grimmett had been around during the 1938 series.

Naturally he was hit from time to time. Hammond overcame the leg-stump attack by stepping away and belting him through the covers. For a time, batsmen knew the flipper was coming by the sound of the snapping fingers...until Grimmett countered by clicking the fingers of his left hand as he sent down a standard leg-break. Deception was his business, and cool was his nature. Hempelman, the schoolmaster who instructed boy Grimmett to forsake fast bowling (he soon afterwards spun out 14 batsmen for six runs in a match for Wellington Schools), deserves a grateful thought.

So too does Reg Bettington, a highly-talented all-round sportsman and leg-spin/googly bowler from Sydney, who captained NSW after a string of successes for Oxford and Middlesex. Bill O'Reilly, having been dropped for the next Shield match after failing to impress, took 5 for 22 against Victoria. Bettington, his skipper, promptly declared himself unavailable for the next match, against Queensland, and O'Reilly was reprieved. Within the month he was playing for Australia, and on the way to achievements seldom matched in the history of the game.

His hostility, beamed from a considerable height, his awkward bounce, fizzing googly, and sharp leg-spin brought him 102 wickets in only 19 Tests against England in four series, and his record in grade cricket in Sydney rivals that in league cricket of S. F. Barnes, who also had the skill and reputation to sweep away lesser opposition at will. For St George, 'Tiger' O'Reilly took 766 wickets at 8.7 apiece, 1943-44 being his best season, when he took an astounding 147 at 8.2. Five times he performed the hat-trick — something that eluded him in first-class cricket.

Bluff and kindly off the field, as becomes a schoolmaster, O'Reilly was born on December 20, 1905, at White Cliffs, in opal country in western NSW. His grandfather came from Ulster, and was a policeman in the time and vicinity of the Ned Kelly gang. Young Bill was a talented tennis-player and athlete, but his bowling was soon noticed, with its virile spin, the fast yorker, and the accompanying hollered appeal. His brother, Jack, having seen Mailey bowling in Sydney, passed on details of the wrong'un, a ball of which 'Tiger' quickly became master. He learned early what it was like to bowl to a champion. At Bowral, playing for Wingello, O'Reilly toiled while 17-year-old Don Bradman hit 234 not out. When the match resumed the following week, O'Reilly spun a leg-break round young Bradman's legs first ball and sent stumps everywhere. The admiration between these two champions of Australian cricket was to last a lifetime. Together they were to win numerous matches for St George, NSW and their country.

O'Reilly taught himself to bowl with a gnarled banksia root for a ball. The gruelling heat and irritating dust inescapable in bush cricket sorts out the weaklings. The Tiger must have thought back to his tough beginnings as he laboured through 85 overs at The Oval in his last Test against England, taking 3 for 178 while Hutton made 364 and his special enemy, the left-handed Leyland, scored 187. O'Reilly was once asked his views on bowlers who ran out non-striking batsmen who backed up too early. He replied that in his time no batsman was that eager to get down the other end to face his bowling. Even at The Oval in 1938, this was so.

He did get to within a whisker of taking a Test hat-trick. In 1934, at Old Trafford, soon after his request for a change of ball had been met, he had Cyril Walters caught, bowled Wyatt next ball, and conceded four to a thin inside edge by a bewildered Hammond before bowling him all over the place with the fourth ball. Hendren and the persistent Leyland saved England that time with a massive stand. Oddly, the batsman who handled the O'Reilly blitzkriegs best of all was the tiny Lindsay Hassett, whose dominance spawned some hilarious repartee between the two.

William Joseph O'Reilly, like Frank Allan before him, was 'a bowler of a century', only he, unlike the earlier man, proved it almost every time he took the ball in his huge hand, in three countries — plus New Zealand, whom he crushed with 5 for 14 and 3 for 19 in his sole post-war Test appearance, when he was 40. For years afterwards he wrote trenchantly on the game, never missing a chance to carry the cause of an apparently dying art. Of all the budding spinners in recent years, Kerry O'Keeffe, who began with the same club, St George, most felt the pressure of the old champion's belief in him. Indeed, there were those who thought that the Tiger saw in the young top-spinner a vision of himself. There can never be another O'Reilly.

Nor — though we have seen Sincock and Hourn — can there be a likeness to O'Reilly's contemporary, Leslie Fleetwood-Smith, who was the founder of prodigious left-arm googly bowling in Australia. Born in 1910, he made his debut for Victoria when only 21, and might have progressed further during the Bodyline tour of 1932-33 had not Hammond murdered him in the early State game. As it was, he caught the selectors' attention with an analysis of 9 for 36 against Tasmania. Like all of his species, when he was on the spot he toyed with batsmen's minds and bats.

'Chuck' Fleetwood-Smith, with his shiny black hair parted near the middle, toothbrush moustache, and disregard for authority (he went gliding one Sunday in England, flouting a clause in his tour contract), was the most devastating spinner O'Reilly ever saw. His ability to send the ball into super-fast rotation was practically peerless. Given the ability to land it always on a length, he would have been the greatest bowler who ever lived. Instead, he looked to be so only once in a while. He took 106 wickets on the 1934 tour of England, but played in no Tests, Grimmett and O'Reilly, with support from another leg-spinner, Chipperfield, doing everything that was necessary. But after three Tests in South Africa, Fleetwood-Smith helped turn the tide against England in that extraordinary 1936-37 Test series, when, two-down, Australia won the next three to take the rubber. Fleetwood-Smith took 19 wickets in those three Tests, ten of them at Adelaide — where the series was levelled — including the vital wicket of Hammond. It would never have happened but for a broken right arm as a schoolboy, which compelled him to start again with his unaccustomed arm.

In all first-class cricket he took 597 wickets at only 22.64 apiece, a record which might surprise those who associate him with looseness. Mailey, equally famed for his lavish spin and for sometimes tossing them all over the place, took 779 wickets at 24.10. O'Reilly, to seal any argument, took 774 at 16.60.

Like O'Reilly, Fleetwood-Smith had a hard time at The Oval in 1938, taking just Hammond's wicket for 298 runs off 87 overs, having had Hutton missed off a possible stumping by Ben Barnett when 40. This was probably the signal for 'Chuck' to start mimicking bird-calls, something he did to relieve tension. In later years the lack of control in his bowling transferred to his way of life. A pub traveller for a time, he partook too heartily of the merchandise, and soon after his second marriage broke up he contracted a ghastly combination of chest ailments which would have finished off someone less gritty. Then came arrest for vagrancy, a good-behaviour bond, and partial recovery. But bronchitis finished him soon afterwards at the age of 60. The similarity of life's pattern to that of Percy Chapman, England captain of just such a debonair nature, was horribly real.

Spin, then, carried Australia to many a triumph in the 1930s, when Bradman, McCabe, Ponsford, Woodfull, Brown and Fingleton put runs on the board in lavish quantities. Besides the big three — O'Reilly, Grimmett and Fleetwood-Smith — there was Frank Ward, who, hardly adequately, took Grimmett's place as a leg-spinner, and was another to meet a sad end, living in isolation with only a dog as a companion; and the penetrative, talkative, left-arm bowler Bill Hunt, who was given only one Test; leg-spin/googly man Hugh Chivers, English-born, who took 151 wickets for NSW; 'Perker' Lee, an off-spinner who won two Test caps; Fred Mair, who bowled medium-pace and then leg-breaks and googlies, and was highly-regarded, even if his only representative cricket was in India for Tarrant's side; Alec Hurwood, slow-medium off-spinner, who took 11 wickets against West Indies in his only two Tests; and Percy Hornibrook, the Queensland left-arm orthodox spinner, who had to wait some time for Test recognition, and wrote his name on one match, at The Oval in 1930, when his 7 for 92 polished off England by an innings. Woodfull was glad of Hornibrook's ability to get Duleepsinhji out, an ability which Grimmett lacked: the Queenslander dismissed the Indian four times in the Tests and eight times in all during the tour. Hornibrook, a dentist, also had a habit of extracting Macartney in matches at home. Yet he was inconsistent, and, to his credit, his own harshest critic.

Elsewhere around the world, leg-spin held its own, West Indians C. B. 'Bertie' Clarke, of the teasing loop and spitting googly, doing well on the 1939 tour of England and returning to bowl successfully in county cricket after the war (batsmen could take no liberties at The Oval in 1982 when, at 64, and recently a father, he played in a Test veterans' game); and John Cameron seeing through a curious career which began with prodigious googly bowling at Taunton School, all ten in an innings at Lord's in 1932 for The Rest v Lord's Schools, more batting than bowling success for Cambridge and Somerset, and eventually two Tests for West Indies in 1939, when he was vice-captain. By then the googly had gone. It is a temperamental bird. Sometimes it dominates and sometimes, disliked by the contorted shoulder muscles, it emigrates, often forever.

O. C. 'Tommy' Scott was a leg-spinner from Jamaica, and in the Kingston Test of 1930, when Sandham scored 325 and England 849, his home crowd watched him toil through 80.2 overs to take 5 for 266, still the most runs conceded by a West Indies bowler. In the second innings he dropped back into the groove for a further 25 overs, taking 4 for 108 this time. Nine wickets for 374 under a Jamaican sun: a recipe for sleepless nights or perhaps eternal sleep. Less than a fortnight earlier, Scott had bowled 75 overs in the island game against MCC: a 36-year-old full of heart.

One of the most dramatic performances of the 1930s in Test cricket came from a South African, the cocky little Xenophon Balaskas, whose 'leggers' and 'googles' spun his country to their first-ever victory on English soil, at Lord's in 1935. Fascinated by spin from the age of seven, he was also a fine bat who later made a century against New Zealand. His bowling, though, delivered at a brisk pace, usually at leg stump, brought him the greatest fame. Almost half a century later he could recall clearly how each of his English victims fell — Wyatt to a top-spinner, and Leyland; Ames bowled before he could lift his bat, Errol Holmes caught at short leg off the googly...Balaskas, named 'the black Greek' by sour Yorkshire batsmen after he had skittled them at Bramall Lane just before the Lord's Test, took almost 150 wickets in all cricket just before the 1947 Springbok team for England was chosen; but he was omitted. One of the selectors knew about the bad knee he had hoped to keep secret. At 70 he was still enthusiastically coaching schoolboys in Johannesburg, hoping to 'produce a Fleetwood-Smith'.

New Zealand, the kicking boy of Test cricket for years to come, entrusted their slow bowling quota to such as Cyril Allcott, a left-handed all-rounder whose six Test wickets cost 90 each, and 'Giff' Vivian, also left-handed, who picked up the wickets of Sutcliffe and Ames on his Test debut, at The Oval, when he was still not yet 19. The tall Norm Gallichan was another Kiwi left-arm bowler who at least claimed Hammond's wicket in his only Test, at Old Trafford in 1937. Most interesting was Sydney-born Doug Freeman, a schoolboy of 18½, 6ft 3ins tall, gangling, long-fingered, like C. L. Townsend. Freeman played in two Tests against England in 1933, at Christchurch and Auckland, Hammond scoring 227 and 336 not out; Freeman 0 for 78 and 1 for 91. He enjoyed the experience. After all, these two games represented 40 per cent of his total first-class cricket. The wicket he did obtain, Sutcliffe, came from a long-hop.

As for India, her great days still some decades away, the brave and noble C. K. Nayudu, referred to previously, who captained his country in 1932 in its first Test, was a prolific batsman who also bowled slow-medium with steadiness, enough movement to worry, and a lovely pace-change — altogether a living case of Oriental intrigue. He was fit enough, too, to play a final first-class match at the age of 69. His brother, C. S. Nayudu, was a talented leg-spinner, not elegant but troublesome, though his 11 Tests produced only two horribly expensive wickets. Mushtaq Ali, who made a great name for himself as a batsman in an era of high scoring, was initially a slow left-arm bowler. Lala Amarnath, whose Test career stretched almost 20 years, was also no mean bowler, though his brief run-up led to inswingers and occasional leg-cutters, with little use of the wrist. R. J. Jamshedji, slow left-arm, played once for India in 1933-34, at the age of 41. India's early bowling strength lay in pace, with Nissar and Amar Singh the chief protagonists. The inspiration of spin bowling came with the 1933-34 MCC tour, when, as the world reeled from the Bodyline series of a year before, Verity, James Langridge and C. S. Marriott, with Les Townsend of Derbyshire bowling medium-pace off-spin, displayed the art of slow bowling in several guises.

Langridge, brother of high-scoring John, also of Sussex, had tuberculosis as a boy, but recovered to become a trusty county left-hand all-rounder who won eight Test caps. It would have been more but for Verity. 'Jas' Langridge was hardly an attractive batsman, but he made lots of runs. Nor was he a model of fluency as a bowler, having built a sort of curtsy into his short approach. But he claimed over 1500 wickets, and did the double four times. Once, at Bramall Lane, his left arm scythed down nine Yorkshiremen in an innings for 34, and at Cheltenham he once took seven wickets for eight runs. He played a record number of matches (622) for Sussex, and found the edge of the bat so often that the scorebook entry c Langridge (John) b Langridge (Jas) became almost as commonplace in the newspapers as the weather forecast. He took 7 for 56 against West Indies at Old Trafford in 1933, a gratifying enough experience, but he was denied a cap against Australia. Taken there in 1946 at the age of 40, he was chosen for the third Test but had to stand down with a groin injury. His career ended sadly, though. Jim Langridge, then 45, was knocked senseless and twitching by a bouncer from the Cambridge Springbok Cuan McCarthy in 1952.

In all truth, Langridge would probably not have made his Australian tour if Hedley Verity had still been alive. Verity was *the* left-arm slow bowler of the 1930s. In his final county match, at Hove in 1939, when war was blotting out the sun, he took 7 for 9 (including Jim Langridge), raising his tally of first-class wickets to 1956, all taken within the decade. He would doubtless join the elite who had taken 2000 wickets when cricket was resumed next summer or the summer following? He was still only 34.

No. The Yorkshireman had bowled his last competitive ball. A captain in the Green Howards, he was leading his men through a cornfield in Sicily, under severe fire, when he was hit in the chest, captured, and died in a prisoner-of-war hospital. He was 38, and mourned not only as a courageous soldier but as a gentleman and a superior cricketer. No-one this century who has taken over 1500 wickets can match his average of only 14.90, and no-one in the history of the game can match his innings figures of 10 for 10 against Notts at Headingley in 1932 (which surpassed his 10 for 36 on the same ground a year earlier against Warwickshire). With a hat-trick and two further two-wickets-in-two-balls, he took 7 for 3 with his last 16 deliveries to finish with 19.4-16-10-10 on a 'congenial' if not 'sticky' pitch, a ludicrous set of figures.

Verity was tall, religious and reserved. He played league cricket while awaiting the call of his county, which came in 1930, when he was 25 and his legendary predecessor, Rhodes, 52. Rhodes and Emmott Robinson were of the calculating school that would instil into a youngster like Hedley Verity that the afternoon's return of 7 for 26 was all well and good, but it could have been 7 for 22 had there not been a short ball which was cut to the boundary. He took a longish run to the crease, and bowled, usually, faster than Rhodes — at a pace comparable to Underwood's. He had a lethal specialty in the fast yorker, which usually dipped in, and tossed the ball higher on damp or crumbling pitches. He looked mechanical, but behind every ball was scheming, highly intelligent thought. And he believed in length as a faithful Muslim believes in the koran.

Yorkshire took the County Championship seven times during Verity's ten seasons, summers that saw him seven times take nine wickets in an innings, in addition to the pair of all-tens. No kissing and hugging. Just an unerringly accurate series of balls posing, in the main, unanswerable questions, and a steady trek back to the pavilion by too timid or too blindly aggressive batsmen. With the hostility of his friend Bill Bowes at the other end, many an amateur batsman, having skipped the Notts match so as to preserve himself from Larwood and Voce, thought long and hard about availability for the Yorkshire match.

The occasions when Verity was punished stood out more sharply against his overall reputation, none more famously than when South Africa's 'Jock' Cameron smashed him for 30 runs, six boundaries, in an over at Sheffield in 1935. Wicketkeeper Arthur Wood cheered the bowler up by saying, 'You've got him in two minds, Hedley. He doesn't know whether to hit you for four or six!' A beautiful one-liner echoed thousands of times since at all levels.

Verity took 144 wickets for England in 40 Tests, 59 of them against Australia, at 28.06. His first big strike was at Madras in '33-34 (7 for 49 and 4 for 104), but four months later, at Lord's, came his most memorable performance. On a pitch affected by rain, but not, as England keeper Les Ames asserted, by any means unplayable, Verity plundered 7 for 61 and 8 for 43 to give England a rare innings victory over Australia. Ponsford wasn't playing, but Bradman was, and on the final day Verity took 14 wickets for 80 runs. Howard Marshall, the BBC commentator, could scarcely keep up with events, an embarrassment which led to the installation of a resident scorer in the broadcasting box. The follow-on was the key to it all, and Verity saw to it that Australia fell seven short of avoiding it. Woodfull surprisingly ordered only the medium roller, and the pitch later became quite spiteful, especially for a side which had known only hard wickets during the tour. Bowling round the wicket, Verity by his very accuracy wore a patch for himself on a difficult length. In the second innings he picked up six wickets in the last hour of the match. 'Verity's match'. To very few falls the honour of having a Test named after them.

Verity missed the gruelling 1934-35 tour of West Indies, where he would have been hard-worked as well as useful. Warwickshire's George Paine got his chance, and took 17 wickets at reasonable cost in the four Tests. But he was no Verity, even if he had topped the national averages for the previous summer. His county team-mate Eric Hollies rolled his leg-breaks to the top of the bowling averages (10 wickets at 21.70) against West Indies, having barely recovered from deplorable seasickness — with cabin-mate Paine — on the banana-boat as it chugged across the Atlantic.

Hollies took 7 for 50 in the Georgetown Test, figures he was never to approach in the remainder of his intermittent Test career, which extended to 1950.

During the 1930s, when the prolific 'Tich' Freeman might have expected to have been a fixture in the England XI, the selectors, obviously lacking in faith in the Kentish midget (was he, like Fender, overlooked because he either was, or was supposed to be, Jewish?), preferred amateur players such as Robins, Peebles, Stevens (in the 1920s) and Freddie Brown. Tommy Mitchell, the bespectacled Derbyshire leg-spinner, a product of colliery cricket, won five Test caps, and Jim Sims of Middlesex four. But the effervescent R. W. V. Robins played in 19 Tests, taking 64 wickets at 27.46 besides making runs, including a century against South Africa; and Ian Peebles played in 13 Tests before shoulder injury robbed him of his sting.

Walter (never Wally) Robins was an attractive cricketer. Fair-haired and small of build, he advanced down the pitch as a batsman in the George Gunn mould — without quite the same results — and bowled leg-breaks and hard-to-read googlies in lively fashion. A vital wrong'un bowled Bradman for 131 at Trent Bridge in 1930 in his first English Test and led to England's sole victory that season. Although sometimes erratic, Robins bowled at such a brisk pace in his earlier days that batsmen tensed in opposition. Before long, however, he was persuaded to slow down and toss the ball more into the air. He may never have been as effective a force again. His best Test figures were 6 for 32 against West Indies at Lord's in 1933; and after a long career he finished with almost a thousand wickets in addition to nearly 14,000 runs. He captained Middlesex both sides of the war and served as Test selector and tour manager. No-one, including the umpire who was told to 'stick' his sweater, 'seaxes and all', was ever in any doubt as to Robins's mood. He may even have put a name to the left-arm bowler's mystery ball, for when stumped off West Indian Ellis Achong, he turned to Learie Constantine and thundered, 'Fancy getting out to a bloody chinaman!' 'Do you mean the bowler or the ball?' replied Constantine.

'Robbie' was ever interested in the history and technicalities of the game, a quality which aided him as a captain. Arthur Mailey considered he would have been the best of captains for any other slow bowler, and that he might have been more effective if he had been more interested in reaping a rich harvest of wickets than in the scientific side of bowling.

Cooler by far was his tall friend Ian Peebles, Scottish-born and a prodigy who played for England in South Africa in 1927-28, when barely 20, after having been spotted by Aubrey Faulkner, whose secretary he was, and 'Plum' Warner. He had already played for Gentlemen v Players, though not for any county. Joining Middlesex, he took 120 wickets in 1929, his easy approach, high action and beautiful blend of leg-spinners and googlies rendering him the talk not only of society but of cricket circles. Peebles was a man of charm, a product of his time. He went up to Oxford, and seemed a natural choice for England in 1930 when something — *anything* — had to be found to stop Bradman. With scores of 131 at Nottingham, 254 at Lord's, and 334 at Leeds, the mighty little Australian might set his sights on 400 at Manchester. Peebles didn't let him. Having shaken Woodfull with a bouncing googly, he deceived the Don and then had him dropped at slip by — of all fieldsmen — Hammond. It mattered little. Soon Peebles put a leg-break on the perfect grid reference, and Duleepsinhji pocketed the catch. Bradman was out for only 14.

Peebles finished the innings with 3 for 150 off 55 overs in an Australian innings of only 345, so it could hardly be said that his skipper, Chapman, had less than the utmost faith in him. But in his only other Australian Test, the one which followed, Peebles delivered 71 overs in an innings of 695 to take 6 for 204, three of them tailenders. After successes in South Africa that winter and at home against New Zealand in 1931 came disaster. His right shoulder was not functioning as it should, and the zip went from his bowling. Further county cricket and captaincy lay ahead, but his former powers were no more. It was 'an appalling shock'. He thought much about the game and wrote with much delight and insight, one of his more important offerings being a treatise on illegal bowling actions, with a suggested definition and remedy. He put his name to 923 first-class wickets — and to one of the odder scorebook entries during a South African tour: 'absent — bathing'.

Seen beside the elegant Peebles, Jim Sims looked somewhat lugubrious, though behind the heavy eyebrows and simian features lurked a wit. In a long career he took over 1500 wickets, including all ten for 90 for East v West at Kingston-upon-Thames in 1948. His googly was one of the best in the business, but he made no impact in Australia on the 1936-37 tour. He had started his career as a batsman, but his years at the crease are chiefly remembered for his classic remark before facing Larwood: he said he was not exactly nervous, but a 'trifle apprehensive'.

Someone even more in the comic vein, judged on appearance, was small, bespectacled Tommy Mitchell of Derbyshire, who, with sleeves buttoned at the wrist, looked less like a professional cricketer than a junior bank clerk out for a bit of teasing fun. In fact, his spinning prowess lifted him out of the dark confines of a coalmine. Mitchell liked to mix standard off-breaks in with his leg-spinners and googlies, but his limitations at Test level were revealed in more ways than one. An unduly long spell against Australia owed much to his captain's policy of 'giving him a bowl since he was a chosen member of the team'. When, a year later, that skipper, Walters, had been succeeded by Bob Wyatt, Mitchell found the new captain instructing and coaching him from mid-on between each delivery. The baggy-trousered little man from Derbyshire soon tired of this, and told his leader in vivid language to bowl himself. Mitchell's 1483 wickets cost only 20 each, and from 1929 to 1938 he never failed to take 100 in a season. In 1935 he took 10 for 64 at Leicester. Small wonder he resented being told how to bowl in the Test match a fortnight later.

Slow bowling held its head high in the 1930s. Glamorgan had master off-spinner John Clay, a cultured man who began as a fast-medium bowler. He took almost 1300 wickets for the Welsh county at just under 20 in a career stretching from 1921 to 1949, and yet played only once for England.

An important founder member of Glamorgan in first-class cricket, Clay, at the age of 50, had the pleasure of taking the wicket which gave his county their first Championship title, his final appeal being greeted by a cry from umpire and fellow-Welshman Dai Davies: 'He's out, and we've won!' In the previous match Clay took 5 for 15 to help demolish Surrey for 50 — a total equal to his age. It all helped pay off the years of unavailing effort for Glamorgan.

J. C. Clay's halcyon years were before the war, and a taste of his control comes in the details of 11 consecutive maiden overs against Somerset and 10 against Northamptonshire, the feat of a bowler who commands not only complete skill but also rigid concentration. His colleague Emrys Davies had plenty of the latter quality. A left-handed all-rounder, he was the first to do the season's double for Glamorgan (1935), and in 1937, after making 274 with Dyson for the first wicket, he did the hat-trick against hapless Leicestershire. His flighted bowling brought him 903 wickets, though he never attempted to put much spin on the ball.

Across the Bristol Channel there towered a lantern-jawed man who could, in contrast, seemingly rasp a sliver of leather off the ball, so vicious was the spin-power applied by his huge fingers. Tom Goddard was yet another to start out as a fast bowler. He was built for it. But a stint at Lord's saw him converted, and immediately that brisk delivery, giving rise to sharp spin (sometimes unaccountably from leg) and awkward bounce, was winning dramatic success, much of it at the end of a raucous, deep-throated roar of appeal. Gloucestershire, with their responsive pitches, knew they had a treasure. By his retirement in 1952, when he was past 50, he ranked fifth in the world with 2979 wickets at just under 20 apiece. His eight Test caps add further mystery when it is considered that three (Freeman, Parker and Goddard) of those top five bowlers in the game's history earned no more than 21 caps between them.

Twice Goddard made the best of an England cap. At Manchester in 1937 (the year he took all ten against Worcestershire) he took 6 for 29 against New Zealand, and just over a year later he took a hat-trick against South Africa at Johannesburg. In the following English summer he took 17 wickets in a day — helped by a cross-wind — against Kent at Bristol. Only Blythe and Verity share that distinction. Neither would have shouted so loudly and often for lbws and catches. Goddard bowled the ball which clinched Gloucestershire a tie against the 1930 Australians. Hammond described the cry as 'How wuz her, then?' Her wuz out. Eighteen years later Goddard took 0 for 186 against the Australians, for whom Morris, told to hit the veteran hard, scored 290. And Bradman, concise of memory, had suggested to his own off-spinner, Ian Johnson, that he might study the Gloucestershire man! Goddard's front foot turned in at the point of delivery, bringing his left shoulder round, his left side upright and stiff, preventing a falling-away. A fearsome proposition.

In the substantial shadows of Goddard and Charlie Parker stole the kindly and gentle Reg Sinfield, an all-rounder who served Gloucestershire well for 15 years up to the war, managing only one Test match, in 1938, after narrowly missing selection for the previous tour of Australia. 'They'd have won the Ashes if they'd had me!' he cheerfully told *Wisden Cricket Monthly* in 1982, looking back from his 81 years. A teenage sailor in the Great War, Sinfield remained the jolly Jack Tar. Spotting a ladybird on his shirt, he interpreted it as a sign of luck and promptly persuaded his captain to put him on to bowl. His floating spinners ran through the 1935 South Africans. His sole Test appearance brought him Bradman's wicket, which was something, and his happy toils for Gloucestershire brought him more than 1100 wickets. Lucky were the thousands of boys who later received the benefit of his fatherly coaching.

Sinfield was himself fortunate in that he planned to retire after the 1939 season. For some, there were still many peak years left when Hitler's war put an end to leg-breaks and off-breaks on England's green fields. Many a ball was spun in service camps in desert and jungle, even in prisoner-of-war compound; but political and military history was now slicing a deep division across cricket history. To cast around the counties is to net a shoal of spinners who might have spun merrily on from 1939 to 1945. Some resumed after the war, since extra weight and age and loss of practice were less serious handicaps than with pace bowlers. And after the immediate post-war 'happy glow', so much of the old gaiety drained from the game. The inswingers and off-spinners came into their own as the revised lbw law began to bite. Leg-spin's days were not exactly numbered, but they were shrinking, rather like the ball itself in vision as it disappeared out into the road, dispatched by a Wellard or a Miller.

Among those who lost precious years to the Second World War were Worcestershire's Peter Jackson, fair-haired, modest, with huge hands, a purveyor of medium-pace and brisk off-spin, and Frank Smailes of Yorkshire, another with the two strings to his bow, who took all ten against Derbyshire a few months before he donned khaki, and who had to wait until 1946, when he was past his best, before he won an England cap. He it was who found Hedley Verity's grave in Italy and arranged for a headstone to be erected. Verity was never truly replaced in the Yorkshire side, although his substitute when away on England duty was often Horace Fisher, who not only made Yorkshire history by demanding — and getting — his county cap for providing such a service, but wrote the oddity of a hat-trick of lbws into the book. An off-spinner to write his name into the records of spectacular deeds — with one ball if not three — was Jack Davies, who, as a Cambridge undergraduate, flighted an off-spinner to bring about Bradman's downfall for a duck in 1934. With the solemn face of an Alastair Sim, Davies played as an amateur for Kent until the early 1950s, having served as a colonel and senior psychologist during the war — a compelling coupling of rank for any slow bowler. Also with Kent, though serving in later years as scorer, not, like Davies, with the Bank of England, was Claude Lewis, a slow left-armer not in the same class as Blythe or Woolley, but claimant to a barely-noticed hat-trick either side of a lunch interval at Trent Bridge in 1939.

Len Wilkinson was a hopeful, fair-haired, young leg-spin/googly bowler from Lancashire who topped MCC's bowling on the tour of South Africa in 1938-39; but he was not very effective in the high-scoring Tests on the pluperfect pitches, and his efforts left him somewhat exhausted for the final English season before the war. Lancashire had been unlucky to lose the services of Frank Sibbles after an elbow injury in 1937, when he might still have had some seasons left. Crinkly-haired and mild of manner — Cardus said he never appealed, only asked a question — Sibbles took over 900 wickets with off-spin, with best figures of 8 for 24 at Weston.

Another who might have continued but for the hostilities was J.H. Parks, father of Jim junior, of Sussex. He was predominantly a batsman, but his slow to medium inswingers and off-cutters took him to a unique double in 1937 when he passed the 3000 runs and 100 wickets marks. His son, like many a wicketkeeper, could bowl a sharply-spun leg-break or googly given the chance. Hampshire, meanwhile, had two quality off-spinners in their ranks as the 1930s drew tensely to a close. Gerry Hill, after sometimes using the new ball, would apply his fighting skills to long, worrying, probing spells, while Charlie Knott, a slight figure, developed after the war into the finest amateur bowler Hampshire had ever produced. He never quite made it into the England team, but his loose, side-on action brought him over 600 wickets at fair cost, with a hat-trick at Lord's for Gentlemen v Players in 1950. A player whom Hampshire messed about was Jim Bailey, an all-rounder who bowled slow left-arm. He was recruited in 1927 when 19, yet it was 21 years before he surprised everyone by taking 109 Championship wickets — and topping Hampshire's batting too — having been released for many years in which he served on the Lord's ground staff and in the Lancashire League. During his great season, when he was 40, he had the pleasure of hearing himself described as perhaps the finest slow left-arm bowler in England.

But if one figure might exemplify the determination of the pre-war school, but with its willing spirit, to resume cricket combat after the war, it might be Freddie Brown, the huge, rosy-cheeked 'schoolboy' who went as a now-forgotten member of the 1932-33 'Bodyline' team to Australia, only to return 18 years later, at the age of 40, as England's captain, to win his country's emotional first post-war victory, still twisting down his bounding leg-spinners between bouts of medium-pace, white neckerchief round his hot, red neck. Keeping his thumb off the ball, Brown would impart almost audible spin, mixing in a good googly. Not renowned for accuracy, still he could bowl the occasional ball to which there seemed no answer. Being the only Peruvian-born Test cricketer was his novelty. Being captured at Tobruk and interned was his misfortune. Reviving Northants cricket after the war with his special brand of bluff, no-nonsense leadership was his first pride. Winning Australian hearts — and a Test match at Melbourne — was the next. This mighty hitter and spin bowler became president of MCC, chairman of the NCA, and a CBE. Truly the performance of a John Bull who had the heart to bowl leg-spin even when under fire.

14. The Unplayable

Doug Wright — Eric Hollies — Roly Jenkins —
Peter Smith — George Tribe — Jack Walsh —
Colin McCool — Bruce Dooland — Ian Johnson —
Athol Rowan — 'Tufty' Mann

'I owe Aubrey Faulkner everything,' Doug Wright once said, with
characteristic modesty. It is possible that of all the bowlers in the game's
history, Douglas Vivian Parson Wright of Kent and England could bowl
the most lethal ball. Numerous master batsmen — and confused wicketkeepers — acknowledged that *on his day* he could be — here's that word
again — unplayable. With his technique, running in from over 15 yards,
hopping and skipping as he went, and whipping over a wristy and finger-
spun ball that would dip, bounce and deviate crazily off the pitch, to expect
long-term accuracy was to display a dismal ignorance of physics. Many a
batsman fed greedily on Wright's long-hops and full tosses; many profited
from screaming edges; and many trudged back to the pavilion knowing
they could not have saved themselves even if given good warning. There
was a 'touch of the south wind hostility about him,' thought Mailey. 'The
more he was attacked the harder he blew, the longer and faster he ran.' He
blew hard enough in taking seven hat-tricks in first-class cricket — a world
record. So swift was his quicker ball that Godfrey Evans needed to signal to
the slips to go deeper — a flapping backwards of his gloves down beside his
knees — to obviate the risk of any of them sustaining a broken nose or wrist
should the ball be edged.

Wright first played for Kent in 1932, and by his retirement 25 years later
he had taken 2056 wickets at 23.98. Significantly, his 108 Test wickets cost
63 per cent more. He took 7 for 105 against Australia at Sydney in 1946-47
— a match England might have won if Edrich had not missed Bradman off
Wright in the second innings — having taken 5 for 167 at Brisbane in the
opening Test. In all six completed Australian innings he conceded well over
100 runs. He took five in each innings against South Africa at Lord's in
1947, and 5 for 48 against New Zealand at Wellington. But, the occasional
'dream ball' notwithstanding, he was known as an unlucky bowler, a tag
not unconnected with his technique. He thought his best bowling
performance was at Sydney in 1946, when he took 1 for 169! He might
have prospered to a greater degree in Test cricket of another age, for his
captains were continually tempted to bowl him for long spells. As a shock
bowler in, say, Brearley's team of the late 1970s Wright could have been a
consistent worldbeater. If only more captains and coaches could absorb the

fact that Wright, while most expensive of modern spinners, also had the best striking rate. The game never moved faster in terms of runs *and* wickets than when this man was in action. But by the 1980s leg-spin had become a dirty word.

There was nothing dirty about it after Hitler's war. It was bowled with abandon in county and Test cricket, in all nations. Warwickshire's retiring little Eric Hollies, another with pre-war Test experience (how he hated that boat journey to and from West Indies), trundled away, seldom spinning even as much as Grimmett but commanding the same lethal accuracy.

Utterly unjustly, Hollies made his indelible mark with just one famous ball. Don Bradman, making his farewell appearance in Tests, was bowled second ball for a duck by Hollies' googly at The Oval in 1948. Four runs would have given batting's greatest practitioner a lifetime Test average of 100. Fair-haired Hollies did not play in a Test on the 1950-51 Australian tour, but he had fun at the Australians' expense in two matches for Warwickshire, taking 8 for 107 (Brown and Morris both out hit-wicket!) in 1948, and 7 for 59 five years later. The 1948 performance, during which he felt he had the beating of Bradman with the googly — but withheld it for the time being — was conceivably his best-ever feat, though statistically his 10 for 49 against Notts at Edgbaston in 1946 was top. It was no ordinary all-ten either, for he needed no assistance, bowling seven and having the other three lbw. A product of the Black Country, Hollies took 2323 first-class wickets, which outnumbered the runs that this quiet, wry, artful character nudged. He led Warwickshire in his final season, 1957, and bowled 78 balls against Leicestershire without conceding a run. Flight and relentless accuracy were his strengths, and while Mailey bracketed him with Tommy Mitchell as 'lacking tenacious stubbornness', the one having a nervousness, the other too prone to clowning — making them 'liabilities in the hurlyburly of Test cricket' — to remember Eric Hollies only for *that* ball at The Oval in 1948 is like remembering Chaplin as no more than a tramp who once made a dramatic meal of a boot.

Roly Jenkins of Worcestershire was a more outgoing personality. Born in 1918, on November 24 (cricket's most distinguished birthday? — Sutcliffe, Barrington, Titmus and Botham), Jenkins made his county debut, on £2 a week, in 1938. He went on to play nine times for England, beginning in South Africa in 1948-49 (taking a wicket with his third ball), when he was a late substitute for Hollies, though the Warwickshire man was preferred next summer, even though Jenkins took 189 wickets (only a dozen of them with the googly) and performed the double. The neglect may have had something to do with frivolous remarks uttered during the match against MCC.

He believed in tossing the ball up: 'putting it above the batsman's eyes'. Absence of footwork against him usually proved doom-laden. He played every match as if it were a Test match, and therefore his internationals took no extra out of him. He did claim, however, that it takes quite as much physical effort to bowl slow as fast. It would with a bowler of his style. He had a seven-pace, rolling, crabwise approach to the crease, usually still wearing his cap, and dispatched the ball after a flurry of arms, hips and shoulders as his whole body went into the delivery. A swift dart to the off side after followthrough made him a wonderful fielder to his own bowling. He told Peter Barnsley in an interview that 'when I was batting, the ball looked like a Mills bomb, but when I was bowling it seemed like a football'. He once belted 47 in a quarter of an hour as Worcestershire made 131 in under 40 minutes to beat Notts. His three hat-tricks were all against Surrey, with two in one match (1949), and even if his efforts proved tiring, he was still teasing them out in the Birmingham League at the age of 55. He left an oft-quoted line in the annals when, upon being told that the batsman he had just abused for playing and missing was a reverend gentleman, he addressed him thus: 'Well, with your bloody luck you're bound to finish up as Archbishop of Canterbury!'

T.P.B. Smith, the Essex leg-spin/googly bowler, in contrast to Jenkins, took little out of himself in the run-up — for it was a 'walk-up'. His right leg kicked round karate-style, in R.W.V. Robins fashion, and he imparted a brisk spin that brought about the downfall of 1610 opponents, a record for Essex. With his neat Ronald Colman moustache and slicked hair, he served the county from 1929 to 1951, achieving the double in 1947, when he scored 163 against Derbyshire at Chesterfield while batting No.11, the highest ever by a last man, his stand with Frank Vigar (another very useful Essex leg-spinner) realising 218. Peter Smith was the victim of a cruel hoax in 1933, when he responded to a false telegram calling him to The Oval to play for England against West Indies. It was 13 years before he was to win his Test cap, though his four appearances for England were unsuccessful. He toiled while Bradman and Barnes put on 405 at Sydney in 1946. Yet two months later, on the same ground, he spun his way to a glorious 9 for 121 in NSW's first innings, a record for a touring Englishman in Australia. He took nine in an innings three more times in county matches during the succeeding 18 months. Smith could hold his length when under fire, as when Hugh Bartlett savaged him for 28 runs off an over: he never wavered. Perhaps experience builds confidence, but the fatalistic attitude is essential as epitomised by Arthur Mailey.

Thus, it is unusual for a teenager to bowl a steady length against mature attacking batsmen. Such a youngster was Ian Bedford, whom Walter Hammond considered the only newcomer after the war to show 'the fire of genius'. In 1947, while still at school, Bedford took 25 cheap wickets for champions Middlesex, and was marked down as one for the future. But his form fell away, and though he was called back to captain the county in 1961, he made modest use of himself, and was destined to dominate club cricket in the confines of north London, collapsing and dying while playing at Buckhurst Hill when only 36.

The post-war years were happy years for spin. So much of it was to be seen on the county circuit. Bert 'Dusty' Rhodes of Derbyshire turned the ball either way, taking over 600 wickets in a long and faithful career which included four hat-tricks. Lancashire left-hand batsman Jack Ikin was a handy leg-spin/googly man whose use was restricted. Ellis Robinson's off-spin was delivered closer to medium-pace, with a wide turn that brought him 129 low-cost wickets in Championship matches for Yorkshire in the formative summer of 1946, reminding spectators of the effectiveness of the combination of Verity, Bowes and Robinson in the last pre-war season. Robinson was also a brilliant close fieldsman, but his confidence was apt to waver, and he sought fresh fields with a move to Somerset, whom he continued to serve for the first three seasons of the 1950s. Ted James began a successful career as a slow-medium off-spinner for Sussex in 1948, and Stan Trick (was there ever a better name for a slow bowler?) began promisingly for Glamorgan in 1948, his slow left-arm spin, coming from a great height, convincing Fred Root that here was an England bowler in the making. Len Muncer, after years as a prisoner of the Japanese, turned from leg-spin to off-spin — and from Middlesex to Glamorgan — to help the Welsh county to their first Championship in 1948. When Muncer took 9 for 62 against Essex, he had the dubious pleasure of catching the tenth batsman. His calculated spin was too much for Sussex (15 for 201) and Notts (11 for 82) that summer.

It was a halcyon period, too, for the slow left-armers. For one extraordinary summer — 1946 — Arthur Booth emerged from league cricket in Yorkshire to take 111 wickets at only 11 apiece to top the national averages. Then he submerged himself again in club cricket and coaching. Tubby, popular Horace Hazell diddled out almost 1000 batsmen for Somerset, smiling all the way, never quite in the class of Jack White, but capable of commanding respect from even the most rumbustious hitter. In 1949, at Taunton, he sent down 105 consecutive deliveries from which no run was taken by Gloucestershire (chiefly Tom Graveney), a world record until Nadkarni beat it.

Bill Roberts, who died of cancer in 1951 aged only 36, was seen at one stage as the successor to Hedley Verity, having done well against touring teams for Lancashire and in the 1945 'Victory Tests'. Another Lancastrian, Vince Broderick, played with much success for Northants, and won a place in two Test trials before passing his peak. There were the occasionals like Denis Compton, whose left-arm mixture — often forgotten in the glow of his supreme batsmanship — brought him over 600 wickets, and Donald Carr, whose unorthodox and often erratic variety won him 328. John McMahon, who never returned to Australia after the war, was a force for Surrey until Tony Lock's rivalry persuaded him to move on to Somerset. Tall, laconic McMahon gave the ball a buzz and had a well-concealed googly that even the most eminent often missed.

But the English left-arm spinners who stood out were Jack Young, Dick Howorth and Cecil 'Sam' Cook. Young's cool and erudite bowling helped Middlesex to many a triumph, and served England on eight occasions, one of them at Trent Bridge in 1948, when he locked Bradman and Hassett in a vice for 11 successive maiden overs. Two years later he exceeded even this with 13 in a row against Glamorgan. Short, squarely-built and genial, the philosophical Young displayed slow left-arm bowling as a gentle, scheming pastime, far removed from the crashing blitz of the pace men. Howorth, one of the few to bag a wicket with his first ball in Test cricket, took over 1300 first-class wickets, like Young, though never more than seven in an innings. In 1947 he made over 1500 runs and took over 150 wickets, the product of an extremely thoughtful approach. He never sought lavish turn but concentrated on flight variations and that old indispensable, accuracy Cook, capped in his first season, 1946, in which he took over 100 wickets one with his first ball, took over 1700 wickets, many of them on the responsive West Country wickets. A plumber, he flushed out numerous opponents with the gentlest flick of his finger, on one occasion dispatching nine angry Yorkshiremen for 42 on the sandy Bristol pitch. His one Test appearance, in 1947, was a disaster. The South Africans took 127 runs of his 30 overs, and made him long for his wrenches and ball-cocks. Impatient at the lack of spin in the Trent Bridge wicket, he wheeled down an inswinger which Alan Melville swept for six. Slight, bronzed and round-faced, Cook moved easily into umpiring after he had floated down his final delivery not so much in anger as humble service, having maintained a long splendid and honourable line of 'Glo'shire' spinners.

All the Test countries apart from West Indies were ripe with spin bowlers in the post-war seasons, none more so than Australia. Curiously, many of them emigrated to England, where, it was said, the easy pickings in county cricket softened them and made them lesser bowlers. None was cleverer than George Tribe, whose orthodox left-arm spin was converted to wrist spin in order to exploit the law permitting lbws from outside off stump. Missing selection in Bradman's 1948 team, little Tribe sought success in England and spun his way from the leagues into the Northamptonshire side, where he prospered to the tune of seven seasonal doubles, only one fewer than the great Tarrant, and making a nonsense of his poor figures in his three 1946-47 Tests against England. A haul of 99 wickets with a Commonwealth team in India, the land of spin, enhanced his reputation as probably the finest left-arm spin bowler in the world, perplexing the best of them with balls spun from the side, over the top, and through the back of his hand. That hand came in useful in another way, according to Jim Laker. When Tribe's appeals for lbw against a maharajah were continually turned down, he lifted the umpire — who was even smaller than himself — and shouted, 'Don't be such a bloody fool! Have another look!' The umpire, upon further consideration, gave the illustrious batsman out Inevitably Tribe was branded 'unlucky', so often beating bat, stumps and keeper. If, when Len Hutton — and wicketkeeper Don Tallon — had misread him so frequently at Sydney, the ball had gone to hand, his figures might have prompted Australia's selectors to retain faith in him. It was Northants' good fortune. Their nimble, fair-headed Victorian import went on to claim a county record of 175 wickets in 1955, when 15 of them came in a match against the hapless Yorkshiremen. Even that seemed expensive when, three seasons later, he routed them with 15 for 31 at Northampton, taking 8 for 4 with his last 24 balls in the second innings. As always, his wicketkeeper, Keith Andrew, handled him with poetic composure. Tribe, as Australian team-mate Jock Livingston recalled, would bowl over the wicket, then around, searching for the rough into which he would pitch the ball. With a busy season to endure, he would never spin the flesh off his fingers on unyielding batting pitches.

Jack Walsh was another Australian to move into country cricket with terrifying effect. Sydney-born, he joined Sir Julien Cahn's band of professionals before the war, having modelled himself on Fleetwood-Smith. Walsh spun the ball just about as widely as any bowler in history, and used this lavish turn to mesmerise newcomers. Then came the prodigious variety, enough to have a batsman praying for the restoration of the fast bowlers. He served Leicestershire for a dozen post-war seasons, reaping over 1100 wickets and also made a few runs, without ever taking that side of the game too seriously. It was always a privilege to him that he played cricket for a living, and he adorned the game with a chuckling attitude that would have been a lesson to many who came later.

Colin McCool, another from NSW, won 14 Test caps before deciding his future lay in England. During the 1948 tour of England he was relegated to the self-styled 'ground staff', unable to get into the Test side in a summer when the ridiculous 55-overs new-ball rule made it a game for pace bowlers. Tossing the ball high from a roundarm action, McCool worked his spell by flight, followed by appreciable spin. Yet his Test century at Melbourne (he had made 95 in his Ashes debut) was a portent, for his batting brought him quite as much success as his bowling in the years ahead, when the seam began to tear painfully into his soft spinning finger. When cricketers think about the next segment of their lives as their 40th birthday dawns, McCool set about carving out five years of continuously fine performances for Somerset, for whom he made a dozen centuries, took some brilliant catches, and lured over 200 batsmen to destruction, eight of them for 74 at Nottingham. The lad who went to Victor Trumper's old school and practised in the narrow streets of Paddington, Sydney, knew he was up against it when, already an 'old man', he entered county cricket; but by the time he left it he was greatly admired and respected. His son, Russel, was born in Taunton, and had ambitions to follow in his father's footsteps in the early 1980s — by which time Colin McCool was virtually a recluse, farming north of Sydney.

There are those who will claim that there has never been a better leg-spinner than Bruce Dooland from Adelaide. After war service in the Pacific islands with a commando unit, he represented his State (taking a hat-trick against Victoria) and his country. But his success in three Tests was not spectacular enough to hold him there, so he trod the increasingly well-worn path to England, playing firstly for a handsome fee in league cricket, and then for Nottinghamshire. County cricket became the perfect platform for him. From 1953 to 1957, five seasons, he took 770 wickets at 18.86, fooling five or more batsmen in an innings on as many as 76 occasions. It was as if Tich Freeman was back. Not that Dooland, tall and graceful, had much in common with the little Kent man apart from the prolific haul of wickets. The Australian, who spun hard through each and every day, relied mostly on the leg-break, with top-spinners and, to a lesser extent, wrong'uns. Having learnt the 'flipper' from Clarrie Grimmett, Dooland in time passed on to Richie Benaud the secrets of the back-spun, skidding ball which foxed so many batsmen as they aimed pull-strokes well above the line, to be adjudged lbw. Dooland, mindful of its difficulty, called it the 'post-graduate delivery'.

A top baseballer too in his younger days, Dooland was chosen twice for the Players against the Gentlemen, and had a very successful tour of India with a Commonwealth side. Twice he did the double, and seldom indeed could any county have had such good value from an overseas signing. There was much sadness around the Trent when Dooland returned to Australia.

Other Australians ventured to England and made impressions. Cec Pepper, a mountainous NSW country-born player who once smashed a 23-minute century in a Services match in England, was a stalwart of the Australian Services XI. Never one to think twice before making comment, Pepper made himself unpopular with batsman and umpire when appeals against Bradman were refused. The same thing happened during a Commonwealth tour of India which he abandoned in disgust before the scheduled end. Meanwhile he was carving a name for himself as an entertainer and drawcard for various northern league clubs, belting fast fifties and hundreds for fat cash collections and zipping through his googlies and flippers to the mortification of inept batsmen who tried to play him off the pitch. Later he became an umpire, sharing matches occasionally with the equally talkative Bill Alley. Pepper was nothing if not aptly named.

Vic Jackson, like Jack Walsh, played for Cahn's XI in the 1930s and joined Leicestershire after the war. They were flat-mates and were capped by the county on the same day. But they were very different in method: Walsh, the left-arm mystery man, Jackson, the steady batsman and off-spinner, one of only three bowlers to have taken all ten wickets in a Sydney first-grade match. A model professional, he scored over 14,000 runs for Leicestershire (28.53) and took 930 wickets. He was only 48 when he died, victim of a level-crossing smash that also took the life of a nephew of Jack Fingleton.

Jack Manning, a curly-haired orthodox left-arm spinner from Adelaide, played most of his first-class cricket for Northants, and three times in the late 1950s he exceeded 100 wickets for the county, pushing the ball through at a pace which discouraged much forward footwork. He was rather unlucky to miss the 1953 Australian tour of England. Perhaps Doug Ring filled his spot. Ring, a large, hearty Victorian (Tasmanian-born), had toured with the all-conquering 1948 side without getting much opportunity. In 1953 he played in only one of the Tests, the Watson-Bailey epic at Lord's, when he eventually dismissed both batsmen. There was not a great deal of flight about his leg-spinners and googlies, but there was about his batting. He pulled ferociously and loved to send an on-drive sailing over the fence. Ironically, Ring is another bowler to be remembered chiefly for a batting exploit. In the 1951-52 series against West Indies, he and the lumbering Bill Johnston saw Australia home by one wicket at Melbourne after adding 38 while the opposition panicked.

The slow bowler in whom Australia had the greatest faith in the immediate post-war years was Ian Johnson, whose off-spinners were delivered with a bent arm (legacy of a boyhood accident) and a deliberate movement which troubled many purists. He was never called for throwing. He did, though, trouble England's master batsman Len Hutton, causing a cry to go up that the great Yorkshireman had a weakness against the off-break. Johnson just achieved the Test double of 1000 runs and 100 wickets in his 45 appearances, and following the retirement of Lindsay Hassett he was favoured above Miller and Morris for the Test captaincy, becoming one of the select few bowlers who have led Australia. A diplomatic man, he had flown Beaufighters during the war while the precious years of young manhood were whittled away for him — and countless others — while green fields lay idle. He was quickly into his stride when Test cricket resumed, and proved highly useful as middle-order batsman and slips field as well as spin bowler. At Sydney against England in 1946 he had 1 for 3 after flighting down 88 balls, finishing with 6 for 42. He toured England in 1948, but missed out in 1953. Three years later, however, he skippered his country, only to run into Laker, whom he tried in vain to emulate. This much may be said for him, though: he was more successful than Laker on Australian, South African and West Indian pitches. Crinkly-haired, high of forehead, Johnson did his work through the air, but disliked performing around the wicket, as did Lance Gibbs of a later generation. Johnson, a CBE, served as secretary of Melbourne Cricket Club for a quarter of a century.

Elsewhere, spin was in the hands and fingers of Indians Amir Elahi, a jolly man who had been inspired by C.S. Marriott, and who had shown his worth before the war with a googly used with discretion; Sarwate, a tall leg-spinner and later high-scoring batsman, best remembered for his tenth-wicket stand of 249 against Surrey with Banerjee in 1946; wavy-haired, Shinde, a skilful leg-spinner who survived spells of 75 and 85 overs in domestic cricket to take 6 for 91 against England at Delhi in 1951-52 and bowl Peter May neck and crop a few months later at Leeds, three years before his death from typhoid. To none of these fell the honour of bowling the ball which Bradman tucked away to reach his 100th century. Harising-hani Kischenchand, an occasional leg-spinner, carved his name into history thus one sunny afternoon in Sydney. In West Indies, ugly little Wilfred Ferguson, hardly taller than Tich Freeman, and bald and fat to go with it, was a key bowler for a time, taking 11 English wickets for 229 on his hometown mat at Port-of-Spain in a 1948 Test, exploiting the breeze like a wizard.

In New Zealand, Tom Burtt, a thick-set left-arm spinner from Canterbury, took a record 128 wickets on the 1949 English tour, tying down batsmen over after over with probing accuracy and toiling through 45 overs at Old Trafford for his best Test figures, 6 for 162. His 10 Tests brought him 33 rather costly wickets.

Apart from England and Australia, South Africa boasted the best array of slow bowlers. Athol Rowan, brother of batsman Eric, had some wonderful days, not least when he took 9 for 19 for Transvaal against the 1949-50 Australians (15 for 68 in the match). Only a smart response by Ian Johnson (6 for 22) enabled the tourists to sneak home by 15 runs when Transvaal needed only 69 to win. In such conditions, a run is truly a run. Rowan carried a war injury which compelled him sometimes to wear a leg-iron. After dragging himself to the crease, he released the ball off his index finger, seam upright, spinning, mainly from the off, after brisk work by the wrist. His 15 Tests returned him 54 wickets at 38.59. Martin Hanley of Western Province played for South Africa no more than once, which surprised the perceptive and much-travelled Tom Reddick, who first saw him playing for the Desert Air Force at Trent Bridge, when his floating, sharply-turning off-spin claimed seven eminent wickets. Tall and fair, Hanley suffered from finger tenderness; but Reddick rated him with J.C. Clay as the best he had seen on hard batsmen's pitches. (Goddard won the accolade on a helpful wicket.)

V.I. (Ian) Smith from Natal also had some great moments. On the 1947 tour of England he bowled 78.1 overs in the opening Test, at Trent Bridge, taking 7 for 189. Five weeks later, having been dropped from South Africa's Test team, his leg-breaks bamboozled Derbyshire to the extent that they were all out for 32, Smith 6 for 1 off 4.5 overs, finishing with the hat-trick. As he had taken 7 for 65 in the first innings, Derby was to remain one of his favourite spots on earth.

In Ian Smith's debut Test there also appeared for the first time a slight figure in glasses who introduced himself to cricket at the highest level by bowling eight consecutive maiden overs to those man-eaters Compton and Edrich. This was N.B.F. Mann, an escapee in Italy during the war, when he was hidden in a barn by peasants. He died in 1952, after operations for cancer, his 32nd birthday yet to come, and he was much mourned. If nothing else, 'Tufty' Mann, excruciatingly accurate left-arm slow bowler, had delicately marked for himself repeated glories, heading South Africa's bowling averages against England in the Test series of 1947, 1948-49 and 1951 and finishing second against the 1949-50 Australians, against whom he was less effective. Originally with Natal (he was amateur golf champion of the province at 16), he played for Eastern Province after the war, soon setting a then world record of 542 balls in an innings (v Transvaal at Johannesburg), from which only 69 runs were taken. His contemporaries at Cambridge in 1939 would have been surprised when he rose to become an automatic choice for South Africa for 19 consecutive Tests, during which he seven times bowled 50 overs or more in an innings — only once conceding 100 runs. The pain of his insidious illness finally forced him into hospital before the Oval Test of 1951, and his loss was one of those major tragedies which are heightened in effect when set against a sporting or artistic background.

One further peripatetic cricketer warrants mention: Syd Hird, a product of Balmain, Sydney, where he was a boyhood friend of Archie Jackson. Hird, a leg-spin/googly all-rounder, came only as close as 12th man to the Australian Test team — during the 1932-33 Bodyline series, after he had taken 6 for 135 for NSW against MCC. The oddity was that three of his wickets came with the help of substitutes, Pataudi and Brown being stumped by replacement wicketkeeper Hammy Love. Hird soon was off to England, an alternative to unemployment. There he turned to off-spin, which has always been considered more professional in the Old Country. He was tremendously successful for Ramsbottom in the Lancashire League, where he first gained a contract when Bradman declined; but after the war Hird settled in South Africa, where he made a century in his first major match and became captain of Eastern Province. A smart captain too. When Border needed only 42 in their second innings to win outright, Hird suggested that a new ball would be a waste, so they used the ball from the first innings. Getting a firm grip on it, Hird proceeded to spin out five batsmen for 16, slow left-armer Thwaits taking 4 for 13, and the match was won by seven runs, Border all out 34.

15. Perfect Pairings

Jim Laker — Tony Lock — Johnny Wardle —
Roy Tattersall — Bob Appleyard — Jack Iverson —
Richie Benaud — Lindsay Kline — Ramadhin and
Valentine — Hugh Tayfield — 'Fergie' Gupte —
'Vinoo' Mankad

The decade of the 'fifties began, in the context of slow bowling, with the romance of two unknown youngsters from the Caribbean who took England by surprise, and ended with another surprise: the sudden emergence of a long-promising Australian spinner as not only a match-winner but as a captain quite out of the ordinary. The West Indians were Ramadhin and Valentine, the Australian Benaud. And in between, there was much excitement to be had in the sphere of Test cricket, thanks to an Australian mystery man named Iverson and a cool operator from South Africa named Tayfield.

Yet the decade will be forever branded with the names of a pair of English spinners whose exploits, sometimes on nasty playing surfaces, struck terror into the hearts of opponents just as if they were about to face the fiercest of express bowlers.

Laker and Lock, the perfect pairing. Even their names joined to make a kind of music, the tone contingent upon whose side you were on. Jim Laker was born in Frizinghall, Yorkshire on February 9, 1922, and might have played for his native county but for the outbreak of war. When he came back, after service in the Middle East, where his off-spinners had been praised by T.P.B. Smith and the great South African batsman Dudley Nourse, Laker wondered if Yorkshire would be interested. But Ellis Robinson was installed seemingly for good, so Laker set about furthering his career in the bank. A trial for Essex was missed because of a raw spinning finger, but soon after taking all ten wickets in a club match — an achievement he was to make almost commonplace — the young man received his historic invitation to show his wares at The Oval. He and John McMahon came through the trial with flying colours, and little more than a year later Laker won his first Test cap, making his mark with 7 for 103 in West Indies' first innings at Bridgetown in January 1948. In the second, 'Foffie' Williams smacked him for 6, 6, 4, 4 as he raced to a half-hour fifty, so at international level Laker tasted at the very start the kind of extremes experienced by all bowlers who toss the ball up. Against the Australians a few months later he took some stick in the Tests, though at Lord's against Bradman — the only batsman for whom he ever felt any sense of awe — he beat the great man time and again in one memorable over from the Nursery ('wrong') end.

The first sensational performance of Laker's first-class career came in the Test trial at Bradford in 1950, when he took 8 for 2. An inexperienced reporter asked him if these were his best-ever figures. Despite taking 166 wickets at 15.32 that season Laker was not chosen for Australia that winter. Nor, having helped towards England's successful Ashes campaign in 1953, did he go to Australia in 1954. But in 1956 he did enough not only to guarantee himself a game as long as he could bring his arm over; he stepped up among the immortals with figures unmatched in the history of the first-class game.

The first blow against the bewildered Australians came in the shape of 10 for 88 in their first innings against Surrey. Laker got five of them with straight balls, and considered this a better performance, considering the soundness of the pitch, than his later feat at Manchester. He got the maximum narrowly, Miller having been dropped at extra cover off Lock when nine were down. Came the fourth Test, at Old Trafford, and after England had scored 459, the Surrey off-spinner trotted in, half-lope half-waltz, to take 9 for 37 off 16.4 overs, blowing Australia over for 84. Lock took the other wicket (Burke), having sent down 14 dangerous but otherwise unrewarded overs. Following on, the Australians soon found themselves facing the spin twins again, and from the Stretford end Laker began to weave his spell. He got Harvey and Mackay for a 'pair' apiece, and as the sun began to make things difficult on the uncovered and rain-dampened pitch, the Australians became utterly desperate. Colin McDonald and Ian Craig fought bravely and sensibly, but most of the others might have been blind for all their ability to resist. Benaud wasted much time whacking the pitch between deliveries and Ian Johnson tried one of the most outrageous bluffs by appealing to the umpires because sawdust was getting in his eyes. Laker's fingers, as he came up towards his 50th over, began to ache. Then Lindwall fell to a catch by Lock and became Laker's ninth wicket; and Maddocks, two overs later, was struck on the pads. Laker swung round, ankles crossed in familiar pose, and umpire Frank Lee flicked up his index finger. On July 31, 1956, Jim Laker, the tall, taciturn Surrey Yorkshire-man, completed match figures of 68-27-90-19. Technically the record of 19 in a match could be broken. No-one present that day believed it ever would. As for Laker, his quiet humour manifested itself in the next Test, at The Oval, when Tyson took the first Australian wicket. 'I've got nothing left to play for now,' Laker murmured to his nearest team-mate.

At Old Trafford, after rounds of interviews and handshakes and autograph-signings that cannot have done his giant spinning finger much good, Laker climbed into his car and headed back for London, where he was about to take 4 for 41 against ... the Australians. Somewhere along the way he stopped for a beer and a sandwich. And he sat unrecognised in the corner while all the customers buzzed excitedly among themselves about the Test match.

During the 1956 series against Australia, Laker took a record 46 wickets. During the season, in all matches he took 132 — and 63 of them were members of the wretched Australian touring team. The Old Trafford pitch came in for much criticism, naturally enough chiefly from Australians. Yet it is said that Don Bradman, now a journalist, thought at the start that it was a beauty, just what Ian Johnson's men had been waiting for. England seemed to prove him right with their big first innings, Richardson and Sheppard making centuries, Cowdrey 80. A quarter of a century later Australia's coach, Peter Philpott, stated that he had never seen such an atrocious pitch as that at Old Trafford at the start of the 1981 Test. He felt it would break up on the second day. But on Day 5 Australia, batting fourth, carried their total to an heroic 402. Philpott, a shrewd man, misread what is evidently a tricky pitch to decipher. Perhaps Bradman did so too in 1956: or was it a case of failing Australian nerve and batting technique?

Whatever his victims' thoughts on the subject, many of them made it quite clear that they would seek — and expect — revenge if Laker ever managed that tour of Australia. But when at last he made it, in 1958-59, although he failed to take 19 wickets in each of the Tests, he was so much the master bowler that his 15 Test wickets cost only 21 each, and he also finished top of the tour averages.

He retired after that, coming back briefly with Essex. His career tally was 1944 wickets at 18.41, 1395 of them for Surrey, whom he helped substantially towards their seven consecutive Championships in the 1950s. The Oval pitches came in for repeated and heavy criticism, helpful to bowlers as they were after Bert Lock's preparation, part of which involved the application of his secret-recipe 'treacle'. Surrey made their runs fast and set their mighty bowling attack loose in their quest for outright victory. At Stuart Surridge's disposal were Bedser, Loader, Laker and Lock, with an array of magnificent close catchers. Not that this attack was successful only at home. They were a menace anywhere, as Surrey's 121 victories in 196 Championship matches (1952-58) shows. Laker felt the wickets at Kennington were 'sporting but not dangerous'. A century against a full-strength Surrey, though, particularly at The Oval, was in those days to be warmly cherished.

Jim Laker, with his 193 Test wickets and glittering string of performances behind him, became a popular television commentator. In contrast, his 'spin twin', Tony Lock, took off to Australia, where, years later, he became naturalised. He was aggressive in speech and manner, casual in dress and attitude. When he first presented himself at The Oval he had a mop of red hair and was wirily-built. When he eventually retired as captain of Western Australia, to become a roving cricket coach in that vast State, he surprised friends in England by turning up at the 1980 Centenary Test celebrations with a girth that staggered and an accent that confused. The bald dome they had long recognised.

'Locky' was Surrey-born, and became as ferocious a spin bowler as the world has seen, Barnes and O'Reilly notwithstanding. In the winter of 1951-52, soon after getting his county cap, he practised at an indoor school in Croydon. The roof-beams were low, so he had to abandon trajectory. Then his speed increased, flight having been lost. The next summer brought him his first England cap, but his modified action brought him trouble: umpire Fred Price called him for throwing during Surrey's match against the Indians. He was stunned.

Not until he was touring West Indies with the 1953-54 MCC team did Lock fall foul of the umpires again, Perry Burke calling him in the opening Test in Jamaica and both umpires calling him in the Barbados match. He had recently made himself a national hero by taking 5 for 45 in the Oval Test when England beat Australia to regain the Ashes after 19 years, so the concern was deep, especially when stories began to circulate that Lock and Fred Trueman had been difficult to control during the Caribbean tour. Yet many county cricketers were not in the least surprised at the judgments against Lock. In a well-aired remark, Essex batsman Doug Insole spoke for more than a few others when he questioned whether Lock had just bowled him out or run him out. Indeed, Lock's faster ball, the 'thunderbolt', was so fast that, like Bill O'Reilly's 'Irish special', it might almost knock a wicketkeeper off his feet.

Tony Lock continued to produce the goods for Surrey as they charged to victory after victory; but the Test selectors were worried. The no-balling gave them reservations. Lock meanwhile had further problems. His spinning finger continually tore after heavy use, causing him to miss games. He missed the 1954-55 tour of Australia, like Laker and Trueman, such was England's bowling strength. That winter Lock worked on his action, and from then onwards it was only his occasional faster ball which offended. He was called in only one further match, at Cardiff in 1959.

By then he was an established cricketer of enormous value: a penetrative spinner, useful tailend hitter, fearless and brilliant backward short-leg fieldsman, and a player who breathed the fire of hostility into his team-mates. In 'Laker's year' he matched his pal by taking all ten Kent wickets at Blackheath, and in 1957 he took 11 for 48 against West Indies on his home track, The Oval. He simply slaughtered the New Zealanders who toured in the following summer: 9 for 29 in the Lord's Test, 11 for 65 in the next at Leeds, 7 for 35 in the second innings at Old Trafford. This time he had to be taken to Australia. And here is where the startling transformation had its first leg. On the 1958-59 MCC tour, Lock, bowling much too fast, and, by misguided orders, over instead of round the wicket, took five wickets in four Tests at 75 apiece. Four years later, overlooked for the 1962-63 tour, he accepted an offer to play for Western Australia and had the immediate satisfaction of being part of a State victory over Dexter's team. He came to terms with Australian conditions, became an artful, flighty spinner, bullying, inspiring leader, and elevated cricket in Australia's vastest State to a position of pride.

Not that England was finished with him. Leicestershire signed him up in

1965, and benefited from his skill and his enthusiasm. And the Test selectors chose him in 1963 against West Indies, his diving, one-handed catch to get rid of Sobers at Headingley being worthy of the Palladium. Yet again they called him up in an emergency in 1968, when, aged 38 and with a dreadful knee, he scored a valiant 89 at Georgetown. Truly a cricketer to have the last laugh. He finished with 174 wickets in 49 Tests, with no evenness whatsoever about his figures. He became a monarch in Perth cricket, just occasionally falling from grace, as when he was sent from the field in 1964-65 to wash the friars balsam from his spinning finger. He raised himself high in the lists with 2844 first-class wickets at 19.24, and had the courage and tenacity to remodel his style after the umpires had condemned him. There never has been a more aggressive spin bowler.

His arch rival, Johnny Wardle of Yorkshire, was also highly noticeable on a cricket field. Deceptively, the clown who let the crowd think he had misfielded, when the ball was in his grasp all the time, was undemonstrative almost to the point of surliness off the field. Like Lock, his intermittent Test appearances left him puzzled — stung at times, when the question mark over his rival's bowling action was taken into account. Wardle's action was pure, traditional. The left hand swung up from behind the backside. Abroad, he sometimes bowled over-the-wrist stuff: with great success. He practised on deck while sailing to Australia in 1954, and rattled the Australians when given the chance at Sydney in the final Test. His whirlwind left-hand hitting low in the order did England some good as well. Jim Laker thought Wardle's unorthodox deliveries in South Africa two years later were the best bit of spin bowling he ever saw. His googly turned less sharply than those of Tribe and Walsh; but the wonder of it was that a Yorkshireman was bowling it at top level at all. 'It's surprising how you can get a good player out,' he once said, in his Les Dawson voice, 'by doing something you shouldn't be doing!' Despite his success with off-breaks and googlies, there were those who felt that his county forerunners, Rhodes and Verity, never used them, so why should he? One reason: results. He was a businesslike cricketer. There was nothing truly devil-may-care about Wardle.

Some ill-advised comments in a national newspaper concerning the Yorkshire captaincy late in 1958 caused his invitation to tour Australia to be withdrawn by MCC, and his first-class career finished there and then, with an impressive total of 1846 wickets at only 18.97 each. In his 28 Tests he took 102 wickets at hardly greater cost. Later he spun out many a Minor County player opposing Cambridgeshire, and irresistibly displayed that 'devil' in a Lord's Taverners match at Lord's by toying abominably with TV person David Frost — much to the delight of the crowd — before sending him back for a duck, something nobody is supposed to suffer in a charity match. A proud product of Ardley, near Barnsley, Johnny Wardle was the kind of artist and 'character' whose absence was so deeply lamented in the duller years ahead. His square shoulders, flaxen hair and graceful action were never to be forgotten by those who watched him.

The rivalry for the left-armer's position in the 1950s was between Lock and Wardle, but in 1948 it seemed another from that category was going to assist England for a long time to come. This was Malcolm Hilton, who, when a tender 19 years of age, dismissed Don Bradman twice in the Australians' match against Lancashire. The first time the batsman snicked a ball into his stumps; the second, Hilton beat him three times and then had him stumped. Small wonder the shy lad from Oldham was toasted at lunch and clapped heartily by club members. Not so long ago he had been developing his skill on a cinder pitch behind his home. The toothy Hilton played only four times for England, running into the mighty West Indians in 1950 and Eric Rowan in 1951, when he took 3 for 176 in a marathon spell at Leeds. That winter in India he had moments to remember when he took 4 for 32 and 5 for 61 on a turning pitch at Kanpur. Thereafter it was county cricket, his tally for Lancashire being a creditable 926 wickets at less than 19.

A contemporary of similar method was Bob Berry, who went from Lancashire to Worcestershire to Derbyshire, and picked up two Test caps against the 1950 West Indians. The first of them was wreathed in high promise, for he took 5 for 63 and 4 for 53 at Old Trafford in England's only victory of the series, flighting the ball bravely and using his brain quite as much as his bowling arm. But Weekes, Worrell, Walcott and Co. found him no trouble in the next Test, at Lord's. Although the ebullient little Berry toured Australia that winter, he was no threat. In 1953 he joined an elite by taking 10 for 102 in an innings against Worcestershire, his next county, at Blackpool, and when his wanderings were through, he rested with 703 wickets and became a publican.

Lancashire bristled with spin in this period. Ken Grieves, the Australian cricketer/footballer, was a valuable batsman and fieldsman who took over 200 wickets with leg-breaks and googlies. Then came Tommy Greenhough, who emerged to tempt the Test selectors late in the 1950s and had the pleasure of taking 5 for 35 at Lord's against the harassed Indians. He came close to a hat-trick then, and only a rare bad day by Godfrey Evans stopped him from improving even further on those figures. In the last Test, at The Oval, Greenhough bowled what John Arlott thought was the ball of the season — and that commentator was watching cricket almost every day of the summer. It pitched leg, fooled keeper Swetman too, and took Ghorpade's off stump. But the young leg-spinner had a problem. His copybook side-on action, with its high arm, sent him following through down the pitch, something which did not enamour him of the umpires. Erratic form as he tried to modify his technique, together with the brisk competition for places and persistent injury, relegated him to county ranks. He finished with a worthy 707 wickets for Lancashire at 21.98.

The greatest of that county's spinners in that era was Roy Tattersall, a modest, tall, thin, long-necked former medium-pacer from Bolton who captured headlines in 1950 by taking 193 dirt-cheap wickets. That winter he was flown as a reinforcement to Australia, where his ungainly left-handed batting — he managed 10 in a vital last-wicket stand of 74 with Reg Simpson — helped England to their first victory over Australia since the war. 'Tatt' did not spin a lot, though he did enough on a damp pitch to make batting a nightmare. His height made for distinct bounce, and had it not been for J.C. Laker, he would have played many more times for England. As it was, he won 16 caps and took 58 wickets for his country, the best of his three field days being a Saturday at Lord's in 1951 when he took nine South African wickets, including innings figures of 7 for 52. His best figures for Lancashire were 9 for 40 against Notts, including a hat-trick. That same year he upset himself almost as much as the beneficiary by taking 13 for 69 and ruining Somerset's Bertie Buse's benefit match at Bath, which was all over in a day.

Just as sensational as Tattersall's arrival upon the scene was that of Bob Appleyard, who made his debut for Yorkshire in 1950 and in the following season took 200 wickets. He was not exactly slow, for he cut the ball off the seam and employed a cunning pace change with a most awkward bounce following a flight which was hardly ever a straight line if viewed from above. Jumping just before delivery, he imparted a certain life to the ball, and his accuracy was killing. Tragically, so almost was the illness which assailed him soon after his glorious season. He fought off the tuberculosis, but some of his sting was lost forever. Still he played for England nine times between 1954 (the season of his return) and 1956, serving Hutton well as support for Tyson and Statham in Australia, bowling mainly at the leg stump, and having a major hand in destroying New Zealand at Auckland for the lowest of all Test scores: 26 all out, Appleyard 4 for 7. He was not re-engaged after the 1958 season, this doughty cricketer from whom sometimes captains had difficulty prising the ball if they wished to take him off. His 708 wickets at 15.48 pose the haunting question of how well he might have done if blessed with good health.

As for the leg-spinners of the time, Yorkshire had Eddie Leadbeater, who failed in his two Tests in India in 1951-52 and moved later to Warwickshire. He was still clever enough with his leg-break and top-spinner to top the Huddersfield League averages in 1979, when he was 52. Bill Greensmith of Essex took over 700 wickets for the county, though never 100 in a season. Yorkshire-born and blooded early, Greensmith had no hat-trick or all-ten to offset two entries in the record book that tend to drown the memory of his once-rich promise. In 1953 Jim de Courcy, batting for the Australians at Southend, smashed 28 runs off a Greensmith over, and eight years later, at Chelmsford, Denis Lindsay hit him for 30 (five successive sixes) in the match against the South African Fezelas. No use being a leg-spinner if you have a strong urge to drown yourself after an onslaught like that.

A skilled leg-spinner from Ceylon, Gamini Goonesena, practised his art for Notts and NSW, having shown his ability with the bat in making a double-century for Cambridge in the 1957 Varsity match. His 674 wickets, captured from a low arm action, cost only 24.38 apiece, and had his country, now Sri Lanka, then been a Test nation he might not only have been handed a lot of Test caps, but the captaincy as well, for so solid was his confidence that even under fire from the big guns he was unlikely to have wilted.

Supreme among off-spinners who did not gain Test honours was Don Shepherd of Glamorgan. Few of his 2174 county victims would not have been prepared to grant that he would not have disgraced his neighbouring country, England, in international cricket. Many must have been the occasions when his name crossed the lips of Test selectors. After a positive approach to the crease, he propped somewhat as his arms whirled, and the resultant delivery was usually a fierce off-cutter. His long career began in 1950, and he still had something left when, at 42, he contributed much towards Glamorgan's 1969 Championship success. He had begun as an out-and-out medium-pacer, but the wicked break from off at just below medium pace, with the cordon of short-leg catchers, headed by the brilliant Peter Walker, himself a talented spinner (left-arm), and Wilfred Wooller, ready to pocket anything airborne, took him to a total of wickets, 2218, such as no bowler has touched without also playing Test cricket. Someone had to claim this oddity. Shepherd must often have wondered why it had to be him, just as batsman Alan Jones did almost everything in the game except win an England Test cap.

A Glamorgan spinner of that time who did catch the Test selectors' eye was the tall off-spinner Jim McConnon, who was preferred to Laker for the 1954-55 Australian tour after representing twice against Pakistan in 1954. His figures for his county were good: 799 wickets at 19.59; but he lacked the extra edge to succeed at the highest level. He went off to league cricket halfway through the 1950s, but returned to bolster his county, by which time Laker had made the Test spot his own.

Off-spin was whipped down by Brian Close, whose extraordinary career began with a season's double for Yorkshire in 1949 and finished in the colours of Somerset 28 years later. With a low arm, heavy body action and tons of optimism, the bald and bold 'Closey' might not have been the epitome of subtlety, but he found ways and means of getting over 1100 batsmen out; and if his groans were anything to go by, he was dead unlucky not to have got 1100 more. Over in the West Country, 'Bomber' Wells, before trying his luck with Notts, picked up over 500 wickets during the 1950s without taking too much out of himself. Sometimes he shortened his two-pace 'run-up' to one pace; and sometimes, when the poor batsman was taken by surprise and pulled away from the stumps, Wells stopped his arm near its apogee, and continued on from the freeze position as soon as the batsman was settled. Like all the other off-spin merchants of the time, before the restriction on numbers of leg-side fieldsmen, he owed much to his close catchers. Tubby, bespectacled, and always full of zany conversation, this popular little black-haired printer later took himself off to Nottinghamshire, for whom he took over 400 further wickets during the first half of the 1960s. He was probably the worst runner between wickets that the game has known, seeming to take a macabre pleasure in his reputation. His off-spin bowling, though, was almost certainly under-rated (except by many who faced it) because of his constant jesting. Cricket becomes so much more worthwhile when a genuine clown is around. Sadly, they seem to be forbidden at Test level, except when Derek Randall slips in under the canvas.

There were other, genuine, serious off-spinners vying for higher honours. Martin Horton of Worcestershire, later New Zealand's national coach, was in the all-rounder class, and made it into the England side twice in 1959, though he did more with the bat than the ball. The extremely tall Alan Oakman, free-striking batsman, off-spinner and predatory short-leg fielder, was another to finish with 700-plus wickets — and two Test caps — though his England appearances saw him taking catches for Laker (seven of them) rather than bowling a stream of overs. Edwin Smith emerged from the coalmines of Derbyshire to serve his county throughout the 'fifties and 'sixties, buzzing off-spinners that shook his quiffs of black hair, though only once did he take 100 wickets in a season for the county: in 1955, when he recorded his best figures, 9 for 46 against Scotland in Edinburgh: another to enter Test selectors' conversation, though only when the principal off-spinners in the land were injured or out of form. A sad case was Basil Bridge, who showed much promise for Warwickshire, taking 123 first-class wickets in 1961, more than a few snapped up by M.J.K. Smith in the leg-trap. Soon, though, Bridge, having coached in South Africa during the winter, suddenly lost all control. His problem was compared with 'golfer's twitch' and no amount of counsel, hypnosis and psychiatry could pull him together. There have been similar examples among fast bowlers, each a reminder that bowling is not the straightforward pastime, unconnected with nerve-control, that some may suppose it to be.

One of the more interesting characters weaving a spell at that time was Robin Marlar, who went to Sussex via Harrow and Cambridge. In later life he turned to commentary of such fire-spraying nature that he might have passed for an ex-fast bowler. But Marlar was an artist of the off-spun ball, with a springy action and long, loose arm. He was an inventive, game skipper whose team, it was once said, followed him 'out of sheer curiosity'. He sometimes underbowled himself — the old problem of bowler-captains — though on one occasion he showed astonishing stamina by bowling for 5½ hours against Worcestershire, taking 6 for 111 off 58.5 overs. That same summer saw him demolish Lancashire with 6 for 73 and 9 for 46. Never renowned as a batsman, Marlar did thrash the 1956 Australians for a 33-minute half-century. His accuracy was nagging, and on a moist pitch he could turn the ball lethally. A stint as librarian to the Duke of Norfolk preceded a successful business career, from which Marlar could look back on a haul of 740 wickets for the county, none of which could have given him more pleasure than the seven he took for Gents v Players. And he did bowl Jack Robertson with the biggest off-break that gentle master had ever seen.

A final thought on English leg-spinners of the period. Many took a turn at the crease only once in a while, such as Colin Cowdrey, whose either-way turn had looked so promising at school, and who once gave enormous pleasure to the crowd at Sydney — when Alan Davidson hit him far away onto the top of the old Brewongle stand. But a bouncy little Yorkshireman who served English cricket twice over was Johnny Lawrence, who played all his county career for Somerset, taking almost 800 wickets and fielding marvellously at short leg. Then, when he opened a coaching school near Leeds, he became Geoff Boycott's personal 'technique doctor', helping the most dedicated of opening batsmen through mental and physical crises as they occurred. Who said spin bowlers were not to be trusted?

Australia discovered an amazing bowler at the start of the 1950s. Jack Iverson, a 'rum sort of character' according to McCool, was a big, ungainly chap who began playing around with a table-tennis ball while on active service in New Guinea. Holding a cricket ball between his thumb and a bent, long, strong middle finger, he could make it spin sharply from the off with an action that often seemed, to the batsman, to be imparting leg-spin. He flicked the ball as would a man disposing of a burnt-out cigarette. Lumbering in against the Englishmen in the 1950-51 series, Iverson mesmerised most of them, taking 18 wickets at 15.24, including 6 for 27 at Sydney to wrap up the third Test. Brown's men hardly used their feet, and paid the penalty. Turning occasionally from leg and with a curious googly sometimes tossed in, he deployed a silly mid-on and silly point, and let his sinister reputation as a genuine mystery bowler do the rest to the tormented Poms. As the series wore on he became less of a bogey as his opponents played him as an off-spinner, Hutton and Simpson in particular handling him with greater ease. Washbrook must have continued to lose many a night's sleep. Iverson was 35 when he humbled England.

'Big Jake', who had been a fast bowler at Geelong College, took 75 wickets in all matches at seven apiece on the 1949-50 tour of New Zealand. He had decided to play sub-district cricket in Melbourne after watching some blind cricketers at play. He told his wife of his admiration for their courage and that he was intent on proving that his bent-finger method could be successful. His English opponents were often made to look sightless too. However, in State matches he was less of a demon. Miller and Morris sorted him out, identifying the higher-tossed ball as the top-spinner, stepping to leg and hammering him hard — a ploy which quickly proved that Iverson could not absorb punishment. His Test career was limited to that series against England, though he did tour India with a Common-wealth team, revealing himself to a multi-national side as a companion of unparticular habits. Paul Gibb remembered his handshake as so strong that you wondered what had got hold of you'. He bowled an underarm ball on that tour — and took a wicket with it. Parked out on mid-on, he would never field a ball if he could kick it on to a team-mate; and with the bat (a dirty old chunk of wood held together by twine) he was as clueless as the most feeble of his adversaries when facing his own flicked deliveries.

Iverson, the phenomenon, withdrew from the game when he realised hi limitation as insurmountable, and resumed work in the family real estate business. He took his own life in 1973, when he was 58.

As Australia looked to the future, the leg-spin department was entrusted to a young trainee newspaperman from the Parramatta district, west o Sydney. His leg-spinning father had once taken all 20 wickets for 65 in a club match, though the son, Richie Benaud, had enough determination and built-in confidence never to need outside inspiration, even if a boyhood glimpse of Grimmett did him no harm. Constant practice and the long term faith of the selectors paid off in the end in the most dramatic fashion He came in off a bustling approach and twirled his wrist-spin through off a rubbery, flowing action, left shoulder well round, back foot square with the crease. His accuracy was riveting, his control of direction for leg-spinner top-spinner, wrong'un — and 'flipper' — awesome.

He came good in the fullest sense during the 1957-58 tour of South Africa, when he took 30 wickets and scored over 300 runs in the five Tests A year later, when Ian Craig faded through illness, Benaud was the surprise (to the outside world) choice as Australia's skipper. And a new age dawned. His demonstrative enthusiasm, his tactical control, his bowling which troubled Peter May and the lesser English batsmen, and his vigorou batting led Australia to an unexpected 4-0 victory, and two years later he in tandem with West Indies' captain Frank Worrell, injected such spirit into an ailing sport that the 1960-61 series went down as one of the half dozen most inspired and exciting of all time.

A few months later, Benaud, his powerful right shoulder at last giving in to wear and tear, steered his country to another Ashes success, the climax coming at Old Trafford when England were cruising to victory. In a measure of desperation, he bowled round the wicket, aiming at the rough o the footmarks — a ploy featuring in few coaching books — and brought off a spectacular victory by taking 6 for 70. In the next Ashes series, against Dexter's side in 1962-63, he kept his Test captaincy record intact with a 1-1 result, though his own powers were waning. The bursitis had virtually cost him his googly, though so canny was he that it took opponents a long time to find out. Benaud handed over the captaincy to Bob Simpson during the 1963-64 series against South Africa, his last, and rested with a then-unique double of over 2000 runs and 200 wickets in 63 Tests, his bowling reward of 248 at 27.03 standing as an Australian record until Lillee beat it. Among his batting exploits, a 78-minute Test century at Kingston, Jamaica in 195? will live on; so will his 11 sixes in an innings at Scarborough in 1953 — a tour he would otherwise rather forget — when Wardle and Tattersall were crucified. Of all his dazzling gully catches, the left-hander which ended Cowdrey's innings at Lord's in 1956 stands out; of all his testing spells none could have enraptured onlookers more than his 7 for 18 for NSW against the 1962-63 MCC team, when even Graveney, who usually played him fairly well, had no answer. Parfitt, the left-hander, played him dozens of times with his right pad that afternoon, drawing from an exasperated

Hillite the cry: 'Tie ya bat to ya pad, Parfitt! You'll make some runs that way!'

Benaud, like so many spinners over half a century, took benefit from Bill O'Reilly's counsel, and he in his turn has helped many a player with the right word. The mature face which looks out from the television screen in the 1980s was only just over 18 when it first contemplated an opposing batsman in a first-class match. Its owner, who once played the nerve game with Peter May to the extent of 24 consecutive googlies, allied a deep talent to no less than an average allocation of luck which included a chance meeting with a chemist in New Zealand in 1957 who was able to prescribe a calamine/boracic treatment for Benaud's red-raw spinning finger. His tally of 945 first-class wickets might not have accrued otherwise.

A team-mate of Benaud's on his first tour of England, in 1953, was Jack Hill, known to some as 'Larry' (Olivier) because of theatrical gestures when he beat a batsman. Hill bowled a top-spinner which hummed off the pitch almost, it seemed, at Tate's pace. Seldom was there movement either way, but the apparent acceleration after pitching caused batsmen headaches, and he was expected to be a success in England. But neither there nor in the West Indies did the Victorian prosper. Varicose veins did not help his cause.

Jack Wilson, the egg-shaped little left-arm spinner from South Australia, won a trip to England in 1956, finding his way into the Bombay Test on the way home after only one bright moment in the Old Country: he took 7 for 11 and 5 for 50 against Gloucestershire with his high-tossed googly mixture on a sandy Bristol track. It was a bizarre match. In the county's first innings of 44, Wilson took six wickets while not a run was taken off his bowling; and Australia's wicketkeepers, Langley and Maddocks, both took the new ball, such was the balance of the side. Wilson's feat would have had Bristol's spin demons down the decades smiling gleefully, and, if nothing else, gave the tour selectors some kind of justification when the final analyses were made.

Wilson got one Test cap. Some talented Australian contemporaries were less fortunate. Brian Flynn, a leg-spinner for Queensland, once took eight wickets in an innings of a Shield match, while NSW had Fred Johnston, a balding leg-spinner, and Bob Roxby, whose move to South Australia did not pay off. NSW were also well served for a couple of seasons by Jack Treanor, who came from Benaud's club, Cumberland. Wal Walmsley went from Sydney to Tasmania, Queensland, New Zealand and the Lancashire League, making runs and spinning successfully wherever he went. Test players Graeme Hole, of the Hollywood looks, and Jim Burke were often used by State and country, the former a conventional off-spinner whose three Test victims were Hutton, Christiani and Waite, and the latter a blatant 'pusher' who, surprisingly, was never called for throwing. A puckish and perhaps knowing grin spread over Burke's countenance when the matter was raised — and whenever this courageous and somewhat frail opening batsman took a first-class wicket. A 'dart-thrower' was the more common epithet used by opponents. This talented pianist and mimic, whose suicide in 1979 profoundly shocked all who knew him, put Peter May into his modest bag of Test wickets, and once took 4 for 37 in a Test at Calcutta, a feat which gave him quite as much satisfaction as his marathon innings of 161 in the previous Test, at Bombay. Keith Slater was another with a suspicious action during the late 1950s, when throwing and dragging, mainly among fast bowlers, was threatening the fibre of the game. Slater, from Western Australia, bowled both medium-pace and off-spin, and it was when he sent down his faster ball that umpires and players grew concerned. He was no-balled for chucking on two occasions seven years apart, having betweentimes attracted the attention of the Test selectors with a spell of 4 for 8 for his State against the 1958-59 MCC team.

Australia's best spin discovery of the late 'fifties was Lindsay Kline, a lightweight, blond Victorian who bowled left-arm wrist-spin, with the googly, from a run-up culminating in a kangaroo hop. He became the first Australian for 45 years to perform a Test hat-trick when he spun out three tailenders to complete an innings victory over South Africa at Cape Town in January 1958 — and yet is more often remembered for withstanding the full fury of the West Indies attack for almost two hours at Adelaide three years later to help force an unlikely draw in company with Ken Mackay: this after having got out more than a dozen times in the nets before making his way to the middle. Kline was properly positioned in the order at No.11, but after that valiant day at Adelaide he and Mackay became national heroes. Yet this turned out to be the last of Kline's 13 Tests. He picked up hepatitis in India, but toured England in 1961 and did well. But there was no room for him in the Test side. He finished with 34 Test wickets — including 7 for 75 in Australia's victory over Pakistan at Lahore — at an average of 22.82, five runs better than the cost for his 276 first-class wickets. Had contemporaries but realised it, Kline was one of a dying breed.

Before passing on from Australia, one further character warrants a mention. Bill Tallon, older brother of the great wicketkeeper, took a few expensive wickets for Queensland just before the war with leg-breaks and googlies. He stuttered and was not shy of inserting the odd swearword, with which knowledge the reader may taste some extra spice in a tale told by the late Bill concerning his treatment by big-hitting Cec Pepper. Tallon had taken a couple of early wickets. But then Pepper smashed him straight for six. The bowler watched open-mouthed as the ball sailed away, and became the 'only cricketer to get a s-s-s-s-sunburnt roof to his mouth'. The next ball allegedly went over square leg and out of the ground. When it came back from the schoolroom it had penetrated it had algebra sums written all over it. When the next ball was walloped out into Vulture Street, it came back plastered with tram-tickets. At last Tallon deceived Pepper, who sent the ball steepling almost out of sight. The unlucky fielder waited, did a two-step or two, and fluffed the catch. Full of apology, he heard Bill Tallon call out: 'Hard luck, s-s-s-son, but don't w-w-w-worry, anybody'd drop a ball covered in s-s-s-snow.' Tallon's other story, about getting one for none, two for none, then getting Bradman out: 'Beauty! Three for three-hundred-and-bloody-fifty!' packaged nicely the kind of breezy outlook advisable in all who aim to bowl slow. Tallon's family pride was restored in due course by the wonderful deeds behind and in front of the stumps by young brother Don.

Sonny Ramadhin and Alf Valentine had played two matches each when chosen to go to England in 1950 with the West Indies team captained by John Goddard. Ramadhin, 5ft 4ins and nine stone in weight, came from Esperance Village, Trinidad, and was only 20. He came in busily to the crease, sleeves buttoned at the wrist, cap usually firmly over his shining black hair, threw his left arm across his face, and twirled his right bowling arm windmill-style. With no obvious change of action he bowled leg-breaks, off-breaks and straight balls. He was baffling. England's batting cream was apt to turn sour that summer as Ramadhin spun out 26 batsmen in the four Tests and a record of 135 on the tour (at 14.88) while Valentine, born in Kingston, Jamaica in 1930, captured 33 Test wickets with his fizzing left-armers, and 123 on the tour. No-one else took more than six wickets for West Indies in the Test series, and Gomez, with 55, was third in the tour bowling aggregates. What contrast there is in 'Ram and Val's' figures against those of the 1980 West Indians, whose five fast bowlers took all 81 wickets in the five Tests.

Valentine was toothy, bespectacled (he got his first glasses on the National Health that summer), crinkly-haired, and kept his left index finger in order by constant applications of surgical spirit. Still it wore and sometimes bled, for he bowled almost 1200 overs on the tour, including 92 in England's second innings at Trent Bridge. There, Ramadhin also wheeled down 81, their combined haul amounting to 8 for 275. West Indies won that one, having won the previous Test, at Lord's, their exciting first-ever Test win on English soil. Ram and Val contributed 18 wickets for 279 runs in that historic encounter. Further successes in the Oval Test match, viewed alongside the power batting of Weekes, Worrell and Walcott and the firm opening partnership of Stollmeyer and Rae, elevated West Indies to world class. It was something of a surprise when Australia bounced them and outbatted them in the 'world championship' series of 1951-52.

Valentine put enormous spin on the ball, which naturally caused it to curve some distance. With his accuracy, he compelled batsmen to watch him closely and make at least four swift calculations. From the briefest of run-ups, the ball cradled in a curled wrist, he could afford an energetic full sweep of the arm — his knuckles almost brushed the pitch after letting the ball go — without becoming unduly tired. It was natural that there should soon be a calypso composed about this modest yet lethal pair.

Valentine's 92-overs record was soon beaten, by Ghulam Ahmed, the Indian off-spinner, who sent down 92.3 overs for Hyderabad against Holkar — just three balls more. In 1957, however, Ramadhin reclaimed this heroic mark for West Indies by bowling 98 overs (588 balls) in

England's second innings in the Edgbaston Test. But it marked the end of him as a matchwinner. Having taken 7 for 49 on the first day of the series — which performance caused Englishmen to sigh 'Here we go again' — Ramadhin was shut out by Colin Cowdrey's left pad in the second innings. If one innings did more than any other to have the lbw law widened in scope, it was this. Cowdrey made 154, Peter May finished 285 not out, and their stand was worth 411. Ramadhin, frustrated almost to tears by perhaps a hundred refused appeals, felt the spirit of the game had been transgressed. The batsmen, playing every ball as an off-break, had employed professionalism of a high order — even if both were amateurs.

There had been an earlier occasion when Ramadhin's temperament was put to the severest test. During the Melbourne Test of 1951-52, when Ring and Johnston conjured an unlikely 38 for the tenth wicket to steal victory, Ramadhin limped from the field, overcome by the pressure and the confusion of having half-a-dozen 'captains' barking orders.

He was so small and exercised such magical powers that one thought of him rather as a concert violinist than as a sporting combatant. Like Iverson, he was probably destined to last only a short time. And yet while he played in Test matches, Ramadhin made the game immensely more interesting. He finished with 158 wickets in 43 Tests, which was a West Indies record at the time. Having married an English girl and settled down to the life of a publican in Lancashire, he played for more local clubs than can comfortably be chronicled. In one match he even made 90, with Cec Pepper in the opposition. Sonny Ramadhin's batting average in Tests was 8.20.

Alf Valentine went off to the USA, leaving 139 wickets in the book from his 36 Tests. He never improved on the 8 for 104 with which he shocked England at Manchester in 1950, when he was not only stepping onto a Test field for the first time, but seeing Test cricket for the first time. Then, he was asking when So-and-so was due to come in, only to be told that he had just got him out.

Ramadhin and Valentine: the stuff of legends. Yet a generation later all the kids in the Caribbean — and who can blame them? — want to bat like Viv Richards or bowl at least as fast as Michael Holding.

In the 1950s spin was still seen as very much part of the West Indian game. Charran Singh from Trinidad played in two Tests against England in the 1959-60 series, picking up three distinguished wickets with the help of a clever slower ball; but this left-armer's place in history owes more to his innocent incitement of a riot at Queen's Park Oval, Port of Spain. A clear run-out, his dismissal was the signal for bottle-throwing and field invasions by spectators who simply could not stomach seeing their side in trouble.

A most promising cricketer tragically killed in a road accident in England in 1959 was 'Collie' Smith, a young, underprivileged Jamaican who scored a century against Australia in his maiden Test at the age of 21 and another two years later in his first Test against England. His bowling showed promise. Off-spin was not exactly recognised as a West Indian specialty.

But Smith had his special hero: Jim Laker, whom he had idolized since seeing him in Jamaica in 1948. Young Smith's off-breaks brought him 48 Test wickets before his life ended on that dreadful night in Staffordshire.

Also travelling in that car was Garry Sobers, then only 23. He became the greatest all-round cricketer the world had ever seen — except to those who clung loyally to WG's reputation, or had fond favourites for the title whom they would never jettison: Rhodes, Gregory, Miller, and later Botham. Sobers, later deservedly knighted, took over 1000 wickets, 235 of them in Test matches, and no-one will ever be able to separate those taken with fast, swing bowling from those resulting from spin. Even when he bowled spin, Sobers, depending upon mood, state of pitch and position of the match, might bowl conventional left-arm spin or he might toss down briskly-spun over-the-wrist balls. Had he been a duffer with the bat, he still might well have won dozens of caps as a bowler. He had that elusive facility — denied to other pace bowlers who tried, such as Alan Davidson and Bill Johnston — of bowling slow stuff quite as effectively as fast.

New Zealand's Geoff Rabone mixed it, though he would not wish to share the same paragraph as Sobers. And Alex Moir was a specialist leg-spin/googly bowler who shares the New Zealand record of 15 wickets in a match (v Central Districts, New Plymouth, 1953-54). A springy, stocky, genial man, Moir, with apparent connivance by his team-mates, bowled consecutive overs either side of tea in a Test match against England at Wellington in 1951, emulating the rudely defiant Armstrong. Moir paid heavily for his 28 Test wickets, but enhanced the game's standing when he refused to run out West Indian opener Allan Rae after he had slipped over, with no run at stake. Just the sort of thing Mailey would have done.

Moir's younger spin partner in the Otago side was Jack Alabaster, who was actually chosen to tour Pakistan and India in 1955-56 without having played in a first-class match. Slower than Moir, and as yet without his powerful turn, Alabaster struggled throughout. But, back home, he had a small hand in New Zealand's first-ever Test victory, having Weekes caught and bowling Binns as the West Indians crashed for 77 at Eden Park, Auckland. By the time Jack Alabaster, of the shambling run-up, had played the last of his 21 Tests he had taken 49 wickets, though never more than four in an innings.

In South African Test cricket the cause of spin had been upheld, not all that spectacularly, by the leg-spin of Percy Mansell and Clive van Ryneveld. Mansell was born in Shropshire and wore the kind of glasses that made him resemble a village librarian. Sometimes bothered by heart-strain, he was a steady bowler, useful batsman and neat and efficient slip fielder. van Ryneveld, whose admission as a barrister in 1952 caused him to miss the 1952-53 tour of Australia, when his presence could have improved the 2-2 result, had played for England at rugby and devastated Cambridge in the 1948 Varsity match at Lord's, when his leg-spin and virile googly accounted for seven wickets for 57. Tall and handsome, a Rhodes scholar like Owen-Smith, he became South Africa's captain against England and

Australia, though his performances with either bat or ball were not out of the ordinary. He was one of those 'leggers' who could be erratic almost beyond hope one day, and a world-beater the next.

Of course, all else was overshadowed in the 1950s by the cool, accurate and highly successful off-spin of Hugh Tayfield, the wide-shouldered Natalian who first rocked the cricket world by taking 7 for 23 on a sticky wicket in his third Test match, against the 1949-50 Australians, at Durban. In an amazing match, Australia, all out for a record low against the Springboks of 75, fought back by dismissing the home side for 99 in their second innings (Johnston and Johnson sharing nine wickets) and then scoring 336 to win by five wickets, thanks to Neil Harvey's magnificent unbeaten 151.

Tayfield, tall, with black hair and dark eyes, used to kiss his Springbok cap before handing it to the umpire, and his habit of stubbing his toecap into the ground before floating in to bowl gave him the nickname 'Toey'. He reverted to being Athol Rowan's understudy on the 1951 tour of England, but in Australia just over a year later he won lasting fame with 30 wickets in the five Tests, many of them the product of stupendous catching either among his bevy of fielders half a pitch-length forward of the bat or on the fence. Bowling the perfect length and maintaining an unflappable presence, Tayfield struck hardest at Melbourne in the second Test, when his 6 for 84 and 7 for 81 supported Endean's 162 not out and levelled the series. His triumphs were all recalled 30 years later when Tayfield was next seen at Australian grounds and was regarded, rightly or wrongly, as an agent for the SACU, who were hard on course to lure top cricketers to a South Africa which had been politically isolated in sport for 12 years.

Tayfield was that good that many considered Laker not necessarily to be his superior, particularly on hard wickets. The South African slew the New Zealanders at home and abroad, his 6 for 13 at Ellis Park, Johannesburg including a spell of 5 for 0 in 32 balls. In 1955, in England, he took 26 wickets in five Tests, nine at Leeds and eight at The Oval, where he had a spell of 52 overs in five hours' play, taking 4 for 54 in that time. It was computerised accuracy: a strangehold in which a carefully-placed field played a vital role too. A man of lesser mental strength would not have been equipped to bowl steadily on after 40 or so overs for a mere 1 for 70 and turn it into 6 for 115.

England in 1956-57 seized up against him as he conceded only 2.23 runs per eight-ball over (1.67 per six-ball over). Using the breeze at Durban, Tayfield broke the South African Test record with 8 for 69 and set a new first-class mark of 137 consecutive scoreless balls. At the Wanderers, Johannesburg, in the next Test, he improved it still further with 9 for 113, taking his side to a 17-run victory as last England batsman Loader was caught at long-on by a substitute who happened to be Tayfield's brother, Arthur. Hugh was chaired from the field, having weathered early punishment from Insole and Cowdrey to complete another killing spell of almost five hours. At Port Elizabeth, on a poor pitch which spawned frequent shooters, Tayfield did it again, manoeuvring his way to 6 for 78 on the fourth day to steal victory by 58 runs and square the series. It was not without a good deal of additional discomfort, for he was nursing a knee injury; but his bag for the series, 37 wickets, was a South African record, beating Vogler's 36 in 1909-10 also against England. Since Tayfield had also taken six wickets in each innings at Pretoria on an underprepared pitch at the start of the tour, May's batsmen were heartily sick of the sight of him come March. Cowdrey, for one, was glad to leave it all behind. He described Tayfield as being 'not a bowler who ever frightened you, but if you were going to score any runs at all off him, he had to be hammered'. This particular high-class batsman confessed he could never achieve this object with any sort of consistency. Springbok skipper Jackie McGlew has described how this courageous and indefatigable off-spinner was 'utterly convinced that no batsman could survive indefinitely while he was bowling'. Tayfield's lustful eagerness to join the action — and stay in it — matched Macartney's with the bat.

Against Australia in 1957-58 Tayfield was less effective, and in England in 1960, when he played the last of his 37 Tests, he failed to take a wicket in two of the five Tests, even though he took most wickets (123) on the tour. His final tally was 170, easily a record for South Africa in Test cricket as the curtains were drawn in 1970.

In Pakistan the 1950s saw the curtains just being opened, with the formative years giving way to multiple successes as the 1970s gave way to the 1980s. Those who spun on the matting wickets then used, after the masterly seam bowlers had had their say, included Zulfiqar Ahmed, who varied his off-breaks with the odd well-disguised leg-break, and took 64 wickets on the inaugural tour of England in 1954, though only one of them in the Tests. A year later he took 5 for 37 and 6 for 42 against New Zealand on the Karachi mat, bringing his eager young country another welcome Test victory. Shuja-ud-Din, a soldier, was a successful left-arm slow bowler who did well on that first England tour, though he will be best remembered for an innings of 45 against Australia which stretched agonisingly beyond six hours. Abdul Hafeez Kardar, who played for both India and Pakistan, as well as Oxford and Warwickshire, before progressing to 'chief commandant' of Pakistan cricket in his retirement as a player, was an assertive left-hand batsman and tight left-arm slow-medium bowler who took 344 first-class wickets and led Pakistan with honour through her first 23 Tests. Haseeb Ahsan picked up 27 wickets in 12 Tests with off-breaks that emanated from a suspect action, his best show coming in the Tests that matter most to Pakistan — against India.

Of all the oddities of Pakistan cricket, perhaps none is greater than that they fielded, within a few months of each other, one of the youngest Test players and one of the oldest. When Khalid Hassan stepped onto the field at Trent Bridge in 1954 for his only Test match, his age was 16 years 352 days. He bowled 21 overs of brisk leg-spin, took a bit of a pounding, but came away with England's two top-scorers: Compton for 278 and Simpson for 101. At Lahore that winter off-spinner Miran Bux, aged 47 years 284 days, played against India in his first season of first-class cricket and took 2 for 82 off 48 overs, 20 of which were maidens. Only Southerton, 78 years earlier, had been older on Test debut. Miran Bux was still to be seen in 1982, when, now aged 75, as groundsman at the beautiful Rawalpindi ground, he prepared the pitch for the match against the touring Australians. His army of assistants had to fetch water in mushks since the local well had long since run dry.

England, Australia, West Indies and South Africa may well have been replete in slow bowling, but no country had more such talent than India. The tall, studious, balding Ghulam Ahmed from Hyderabad, India's first Test off-spinner, was a success in England in 1952, when he adjusted to damp conditions. Four years later he took 7 for 49 against Australia at Calcutta in a match in which spin was king. He took 68 wickets in his 22 Tests, in the last few of which it was clear that, at 36, his powers were waning. He later became secretary of the Indian Cricket Board and a Test selector, having given his country, in league with Mankad, its first truly top-flight spin partnership. Jasu Patel, a jerky, big-spinning off-break bowler from Gujerat, shattered Australia in the 1959-60 series by taking 9 for 69 and 5 for 55 at Kanpur on a fresh pitch to steer India to their first victory over Australia. The best figures ever for India in Test cricket, they put some eminent batsmen to extremes of discomfort, and when it was all over the jubilant Indians, 35-year-old Patel as well, with his faint limp and greying hair, did a lap of honour. The tourists would not have been altogether unhappy when Patel had to pull out of the next Test through illness, though they kept him at bay in the last two contests.

The outspoken Lala Amarnath, a pre-war power, was still around in the early 1950s to back up his exciting batting with slow-medium inswingers and leg-cutters; and Muddiah (off-spin) and Ghorpade (leg-spin) were tried in Tests without success. The two who showed from the start that they were world-class — in their contrasting ways — were Subhash Gupte and 'Bapu' Nadkarni. Gupte was a supreme leg-spinner whose record in Tests could have been even better had not so many catches been spilt and had his captains not been tempted to use him in such long, wearing spells. Nadkarni, a left-armer with an easy, casual approach to the stumps, thrived on marathon stints in which he concentrated on denying the batsman any chance of scoring. His most notorious success came against England at Madras in 1963-64 when his 32 overs in the first innings consisted of 27 maidens, the other five overs being worth a solitary run apiece, figures, like Laker's, that seemed to be misprints. One hundred and thirty-one consecutive balls in 114 minutes escaped punishment. Yet India woke up, rather late in the piece, to the fact that it was all serving no purpose. They needed English wickets, with several of the opposition recovering from illness. Time was their enemy. Chandu Borde, a fine, defensive batsman, who took 52 expensive Test wickets from an action which began with a 'birdflap' of both arms, was at least cutting away at the

England order, taking 5 for 88 off 67.4 overs.

This kind of bowling — Nadkarni took 9 for 278 off *213 overs* in the series — did cricket no good whatsoever. Even more tedious had been the spectacle of Nadkarni's bowling against Pakistan at Delhi three years previously, when he floated down 84.4 overs in the match to take 5 for 67 — a rate of 0.79 runs per over! In his Test career, which netted him 88 wickets at 29 each, he conceded 1.67 runs per six-ball over, which suggests that some of the opposing batsmen came away from the crease with their sanity intact. Indian spectators, of course, will put up with anything.

'Fergie' Gupte was a splendid artist who finished with 149 wickets (29.54) in his 36 Tests against five countries. He tormented the 1955-56 New Zealanders to the tune of eight wickets in each of three of the Tests and nine in the last, totalling 34 wickets in all, as many as all his colleagues together. The peak of his international achievement came at Kanpur in December 1958, when he took 9 for 102 in West Indies' first innings on the jute matting, his vision of emulating Laker ending when Gibbs was bowled by Ranjane, the ninth wicket to fall. Gupte received a tiger skin for his effort, and taunted Rohan Kanhai with 'Hello, rabbit' when he saw him in the tea-room, having bowled him all over the place for nought to claim his 100th Test wicket. When Kanhai slaughtered the Indians in the next Test, at Calcutta, he was presented with a tiger's head. 'Mastering Gupte was my real prize,' said the proud batsman. Disciplinary measures prevented Gupte from touring the Caribbean in 1961-62, but he married a West Indian girl and settled in Trinidad.

Gupte's length was invariably immaculate under fire. Laker rated him as the 'best of modern leg-spinners' alongside Dooland. Sobers said he was the best spinner he faced; Benaud was the most accurate. This was the ultimate praise, not that right-arm leg-spin against a left-hand batsman is as devoid of hope and possibility as many may think. Gupte, in 1954-55, became the first Indian to take all ten wickets in a first-class innings when he worked his way clean through the Pakistan Services & Bahawalpur side at Bombay for a personal cost of 78. With his moustache, high forehead, and intent eyes surmounted by thick brows, slight of physique though he was, he was one of that rare company of spin bowlers who could induce genuine fear into batsmen, his wrist action nothing less than vicious and his range bewildering.

India's best all-rounder, until challenged for that title by Kapil Dev, was 'Vinoo' Mankad, whose prolific bat made over 2000 Test runs, and whose left-arm slow bowling trapped 162 batsmen in 44 Tests. Born in Jamnagar, home of Ranji, he had already made a reputation for himself before the war, but after doing the double on the 1946 tour of England, he had a major hand in setting up India's joyous first victory over England. It happened at Madras in 1952, and Mankad spun out eight batsmen for 55 in the first innings, four of them stumped by Sen, who added another stumping in the second innings, when Mankad took four more. Four months later, called in from the Lancashire League, he embarked on one of the greatest all-round efforts in Test history, making 72 (including an early hit off Jenkins clean over the sightscreen) and 184 against England in the Lord's Test, and backing the runs with 97 overs, 73 of them in the first innings — when his own big innings was still to come — for figures of 5 for 196. Analyses of 8 for 52 and 5 for 79 against Pakistan at Delhi later that year took him to the verge of what was the fastest-ever Test double of 1000 runs and 100 wickets (23 Tests), until Botham beat it in a match against India in 1979.

Mankad raced through an over: a few quick steps and a brisk spin of a low left arm. His coach, Bert Wensley from Sussex, had talked him out of wrist-spin when he was young, and his stock ball was the leg-break, varied by the quicker delivery. Even on a hard, fast pitch, he had the best batsmen straining in vain to get after him. His long spells with the ball would have persuaded many a man that batting around No.7 would suffice. But Mankad usually opened the batting, and in 1955-56, against New Zealand, he did what only a handful of batsmen have done: scored two double-centuries in a series, the second, at Madras, in a world record Test match first-wicket partnership of 413, with Pankaj Roy. Not surprisingly, throughout most of his career Mankad would have been in most folks' World XI.

Laker, Lock, Wardle, Benaud, Gupte, Mankad, Ramadhin, Valentine — the 1980s, for all the crowds and big money, seem so barren by comparison.

16.   Offies — and 'Deadly'

Fred Titmus — Ray Illingworth — David Allen —
Norman Gifford — Derek Underwood — Robin Hobbs —
Johnny Gleeson — Peter Philpott — Tom Veivers —
Lance Gibbs — Intikhab Alam

Cricket's lawmakers continued to puff their way in chase of the game's evolution, endeavouring to cauterize corruption as it took hold. The 1935 amendment to the lbw law, whereby a batsman could now be out to a ball pitching outside off stump, had encouraged the off-spin/inswing breed. Naturally. But the ball had to strike between wicket and wicket; so therefore batsmen poked their front pads outside the line, making for much negative play. Thirty-five years on, this evil was tackled by introducing a rider that a batsman could be out lbw even if his pad was struck outside the line — so long as he was offering no stroke, and, of course, so long as the ball would have hit the wicket. At first this law change incorporated the stupid escape clause that the batsman was not out, even when hit plumb in front, so long as he was attempting a stroke. The error of this was swiftly acknowledged and rectified.

Meanwhile, having helped slow bowlers by raising the new-ball entitlement from 65 overs (1949) to 200 runs (1954) or 75 overs (1956), the lawmakers raised it further to 85 overs in 1961. Twenty years later the need, for the salvation of slow bowling, was for the limit to be raised still further, to 100 overs, or better still, that the second new ball be abolished altogether, even though some spinners in a marathon innings welcome a fresh, hard ball.

Offsetting the benefits to off-spinners of the law penalising batsmen who deliberately padded away had come the restrictions upon leg-side fielders to no more than five overall and no more than two behind square leg. This had the effect of reducing the effectiveness of the leg-trap, for there could be no real cover now against the offensive strokes. At the same time, batsmen were beginning to appreciate that playing well forward to off-spin led them inevitably, on turning pitches, to pop one into short leg's hands. Coaches began to advocate playing with pad well forward of bat ... and now batsmen were being caught on the other side, by silly point. In the late 1970s came the evil of fielders' helmets, which, even allowing that injury might be reduced, enabled fielders to crouch even nearer to the bat, increasing the ugliness of intimidation and causing play at times to be utterly stultified. Not every slow bowler felt like giving the ball some air while so many of his team-mates crouched in danger positions. Cricket's hopes here lay in a swelling of the lobby for restrictive circles to keep the close-in fieldsmen at a reasonable distance. No pedigree slow bowler will flight the ball as boldly as he should so long as men huddle within killing distance of the bat. Many a spinner's flattened arc has been caused as much by this fear as by the necessity to reduce the scoring rate.

England was rich in shrewd and skilful off-spinners in the 1960s — so much so that, far from believing, as before, that such bowling had no hope in Australia, the selectors sent three in 1962-63 and two in 1965-66. Fred Titmus utilised the breeze in both Sydney Tests on the first tour and took 7 for 79 in the first, which was lost, and 5 for 103 in the second, which was drawn. David Allen bowled 73 eight-ball overs in the three first-class matches preceding the first Test match and failed to take a wicket while 254 runs were scored off him. Ray Illingworth picked up only 17 wickets in 12 first-class matches in Australia and New Zealand. But he was to return successfully in 1970-71.

These three finished with a combined total of 397 Test wickets, 122 each to Allen and Illingworth, 153 to Titmus, all at a cost of 30 or just above. They spun and schemed and toiled in their separate ways, and two of them had the legs — and, more importantly, the wisdom and strength of finger — to be playing in top company at the age of 50. Titmus wandered into the Middlesex dressing-room for a social visit one morning in 1982 and found himself pressed into service. He took 3 for 43 in Surrey's second innings and helped Mike Brearley's side to get closer to the Championship. Titmus had first played for Middlesex at the age of 16, back in 1949, when his 1982 skipper was a seven-year-old in short pants. Illingworth, having carved out a second career for himself with Leicestershire (which brought him the England captaincy) after 18 years with Yorkshire, returned to his native county as manager, and, in one of their recurring crises, took over the captaincy at 50. This, at least, seemed to be an area where the slow bowlers had it over the quicks.

Born in North London, Fred Titmus retained a boyishness only ever slightly diminished by weight increase and a slight loss of mobility after the loss of some toes, taken by the propeller of a boat while he was swimming during the 1968 Test tour of West Indies. His twinkling brown eyes would regard a batsman unemotionally as he set his field, twiddling the ball in eager fingers, an uneven smile crossing his mouth as a cheerful aside emerged. He had magical control of the floating ball, which never seemed in a hurry to reach the batsman. Nor was he ever over-keen to impart his secrets. Middlesex keeper John Murray worked with him as an anaesthetist teams with a surgeon, flicking off the bails as a helpless batsman stretched forward, or pouching the thin edge as the out-curve held its course. 'JT' knew his Titmus. Eight times Titmus did the season's double, and his tally at the end of the 1982 season was 2830 wickets. Four of them came in one over in the Test against New Zealand at Headingley in 1965. Twice he took nine in an innings for Middlesex. He was still worthily regarded in 1974, when he was sent to Australia with Denness's side at 42, and weathered some blitzing bowling by Lillee and Thomson. Had he been used early in Adelaide at the other end to Underwood, who was in the course of taking seven wickets, Australia might never have recovered to make 304. But it is with Lord's ground that Titmus will always be associated, in the same fashion as Hearne and Hendren, Compton and Edrich. With the pavilion behind him, the little dark-haired fellow would bob in all afternoon, wheeling down every conceivable variety of the off-spun ball with a haunting, disciplined slowness. The boundary hit never ruffled him. The desperate sweep shot pleased him — and won him scores of lbws. As he short-stepped from the field in the evening shadows, it always seemed that the small boy had got away with it again against the big men.

There was never much that was boyish about Ray Illingworth. With the years came a sense of command — unostentatious, but still clearly there. He crept and shuffled rather than bobbed up to the bowling crease, ball held sinisterly, as if it were a grenade he was about to lob into an enemy trench. Here was wisdom of the hard Northern kind. Nothing given away, traps being sprung several balls ahead. Exploitation of the crease, a studied trajectory, fine control of the degree of turn. It was said of 'Illy' that, most of all, as captain he knew when and when not to bowl himself. As England captain he was often accused of not using himself enough. One morning in Sydney, when Australia needed only 100 to win with five wickets left, he placed himself right into the breach, and deceived Greg Chappell with an away-drifter. Alan Knott completed the execution. That ball as good as won the Ashes.

Like Hutton, whose birthplace, Pudsey, and whose quiet toughness he shared, Illingworth pulled off the hardest task in cricket, winning the Ashes in Australia. He also brought to Leicestershire such honours as they had only ever dreamed of. He finished with over 2000 wickets, 10 times reaching the hundred, and made many runs too. He never courted popularity, but read the game so well that all inside it respected him greatly. Like Grimmett, who spun the other way, his arm was low. And again like 'the Gnome', Illingworth was padding in and causing gentle destruction long after younger men had left the game, either worn out or worried about their futures.

David Allen played 39 times for England, and might have secured a more lasting reputation had he not turned to club cricket when still some years short of 40. Despite his creditable England record, he goes down essentially as a *Gloucestershire* bowler. More than that, he was part of a renowned duo, John Mortimore sharing the off-spin attack through summer after summer. Allen, whose black hair, pointed nose and long legs gave him an air of Pinocchio, took a short run, jacking himself into position with a wide cradling motion of the arms and a springy step. He spun the ball a lot from wiry fingers, and had a positive attitude about his every movement. He took over 1200 wickets, but never bettered five in a Test innings. Quite unfairly, he is remembered for an over at Old Trafford — in

'Benaud's match' in 1961 — when Davidson belted 20 off him, persuading May to take him off when he seemed certain to collect his fifth wicket any time. Davidson and McKenzie put on 98 for the last wicket. England's eventual margin of defeat was 54. Or perhaps Allen is remembered for his coolness at the end of the thrilling 1963 Lord's Test, when he played out the final over from West Indies fast bowler Hall while Cowdrey cut a pathetic figure at the non-striker's end, his arm in plaster. Those who played with David Allen, especially in the East, will recall with admiration the long spells of perseverance under a scorching sun, when he would stride off with two or three good wickets to his name, never having been collared.

Mortimore played only nine times for England, though many thought him the better bowler. This lantern-jawed accountant used the air more, like Titmus, though his action was less smooth. Like a puppet being jerked, he drew his slim figure to its full height and released the ball through a maze of forearms and elbows. His career actually spanned a quarter of a century, his call to arms coming from Gloucestershire in 1950, when, at a tender 17, he took 3 for 62 against the powerful West Indian side. In the winter of '58-59 he was flown to Australia as a reinforcement to May's England team. After failing to land a ball in his first bowl at the nets in the rarified air of Sydney, and unbalanced by jet-lag, he was chosen for the final Test, at Melbourne, and made a gritty 44 not out. He had his moments in India in 1963-64, scoring 73 not out in the Madras Test and sending down 71 overs for only 67 runs in the Kanpur Test, doing a 'Nadkarni' in a match in which the parsimonious Indian himself scored 52 not out and 122 not out.

'Mort' took 1807 first-class wickets, and played well into the age of television coverage in colour. Thus, his four wickets in five balls against Lancashire at Cheltenham in 1962 is forgotten while his suffering in the Gillette Cup semi-final against the same county in 1971 is recalled vividly, even by those who were almost too young to lift a bat. Then, on a dark, dark evening at Old Trafford, David Hughes savaged 24 runs off a Mortimore over to set up a victory which had seemed unlikely when Mike Procter had been steaming in from the other end.

Brian Langford was another West Country prodigy, blooded by Somerset in 1953 when he was 17, and taking 14 for 156 at Bath in his second match. He topped his county's averages that year, and after National Service he continued to impress, especially on helpful wickets, such as that at Weston in 1958, when he took 9 for 26 and 6 for 28 against Lancashire (for whom Tattersall took five in each innings). Langford must have vowed to take his holidays in Weston for ever more after mustering 35 wickets in the three matches there in 1958. Sadly, though, he came to be used as a stock bowler, needful of the denying length. A little of his 'nip' disappeared, and the responsibilities of captaincy did not exactly enhance his prospects of representing England. One performance of his did enter the book, however, and is unlikely to be emulated too often: all his eight overs were maidens in the John Player League match against Essex at

Yeovil in 1969. The lads from the east coast may have forgotten it was Sunday.

John Savage was a good, steady, workaday off-spinner for Leicestershire, taking just over 800 wickets in 14 years before moving to Lancashire for a couple more seasons. He had a hat-trick to his credit, and twice took eight wickets in an innings in county cricket. He coached Lancashire through their years of glory in limited-overs cricket in the 1970s. Peter Parfitt was a useful off-spinner too, though the pastime was always subordinate to his prolific batting. With his slightly extravagant action and special line in patter, he picked up 277 first-class wickets, a dozen in Tests.

Alan Dixon, Kent's bespectacled dual-purpose bowler, took over 900 wickets for the county in an intermittent career which included a 7 for 15 against Surrey at The Oval, a record for Gillette Cup cricket. Then, though, he was bowling medium-pace.

English leg-spinners were now ominously beginning to thin in numbers. One of the best of them was Ken Barrington, whose opportunities were severely limited in home matches by the need to keep him fresh for yet another long innings and by the existent bowling attack, which was based uncompromisingly on pace, off-spin and left-arm spin. Barrington had to find a sunny afternoon in Kimberley, South Africa in 1965 before utilising the scope to register career-best figures of 7 for 40 against Griqualand West. From the briefest of approaches and a whirl of his muscular arm, 'The Colonel' could whip down a leg-break, a googly, a top-spinner, even a flipper; but it is reasonable to suppose that for every extra over this 'give-it-everything' bulldog might have sent down, his admirable aggregate of 31,000 runs might have been reduced. Even at the age of 50, he was still a testing proposition for England's top batsmen as he bowled to them hour after hour in the nets while serving on the tour management.

Bob Barber promised much, though his 42 Test wickets, taken from a deliberate, rather stiff but pronouncedly wristy action, were expensive, and he never managed more than four wickets in a Test innings. His swashbuckling batting illuminated some dull Test series, and his 185 against Australia at Sydney remains one of the most distinguished innings in Ashes history. But just as he had converted himself from dull left-hand plodder to batting maestro, so his right-arm leg-spin, in the needs of the county game, gave way, in the end, to medium-pace — part of the big sellout to the 'high-efficiency syndrome'. Soon he was gone altogether, another who could not continue playing cricket when there was a business to attend to.

Barber began with Lancashire and finished with Warwickshire. One who began and finished in all too lamentably a short time was Warwick Tidy, a highly promising leg-spinner, a pleasant young man, who was tried at 17 and took some good wickets in 1970. But his was not to be a long career. He had a beautifully apt surname and his father had named him after that steadiest of leg-spinners, Warwick Armstrong. He had, too, the benefit of coaching by Hollies, and sympathetic handling. And he was brave. But in the tough 1970s this was not enough.

The left-armers, some of them, flourished with their somewhat less difficult art. Doug Slade, of Worcestershire and later Shropshire, took 502 first-class wickets at economic cost, and bowled well in Worcestershire's Championship years of 1964 and 1965, often opposite either Martin Horton, the off-spinner, or Norman Gifford, fellow left-armer. Gifford was a stayer. Lancashire-born, he joined the West Midlands county in 1958, and must have wondered what county cricket was all about when Worcestershire (25 and 61) were beaten in a day by Kent on a disgraceful, crusty, drying pitch at Tunbridge Wells in 1960 in his debut match. Broad-chested and broad-beamed even then, though with a shortlived thatch of hair, he trod heavily to the crease and released a cunningly loaded ball, usually through a flattish trajectory which served him and his side well in many a limited-overs match. The England selectors turned to him on 15 occasions, and he did take four wickets in each innings against India at Lord's in 1971. Having been at the hot end of a sizzling Rod Marsh onslaught in the 1972 Manchester Test (3-0-29-0), Gifford retained, and justified, the selectors' faith on the winter tour to India, where he finished many an afternoon's work crimson-faced, soaked in perspiration, but having brought the same sort of credit to his side as did the regimental sergeant-majors at Balaklava and Rorke's Drift. He could be cantankerous. He could moan. He could be cheerful in a peculiarly English way. He could ping down a bouncer. He could have bouts of confusion in his run-up, which was stuttering at the best of times. As captain of Worcestershire he once declared only to find himself being asked to follow on. Again, the florid face. But he was a much-liked competitor, and rated highly enough by the establishment to earn an MBE and to be offered England tour management posts. It came as a surprise in 1983 when this pipesmoker put behind him 23 seasons at Worcester, with over 1700 first-class wickets (best 8 for 28 v Yorkshire, 1968), to take up, at 43, an appointment with neighbouring Warwickshire. He took 100 wickets that season.

In a different category was the tall, lean Don Wilson from Yorkshire, who flighted the ball with impressive patience for one so inclined to hyper-activity. His Test caps were few, which would have disappointed him and all in his county who could look back on the grand line of succession: Peate, Peel, Rhodes, Verity, Wardle. But the age of flight was disappearing over the horizon. It would not pay to pretend that Wilson was in quite the same class as those Yorkshire predecessors; but he did take over 1100 wickets for the county, with three hat-tricks, and a 7 for 19 against MCC at Scarborough, and an amazing spell of 15 successive maidens against Lancashire at Sheffield in 1969. He also made several major tours, and took 8 for 36 for MCC against Ceylon at Colombo. His hitting reached a peak in 1966 with 30 off an over from Robin Hobbs, with four sixes, again in the Yorkshire v MCC match at Scarborough, and his involvement in the game stretched most usefully beyond retirement when he became head coach for MCC at Lord's.

The man who kept Wilson out of the England side, and Gifford too, was the phenomenal Derek Underwood, whose speed through the air was such that many might be tempted to classify him as a medium-pacer. He cut rather than spun the ball, though the wrist played a big part, and on the uncovered pitches offered to him in the seasons before it was considered best to pamper the batsman by covering them, he frequently turned into a killer. The ball would veer through the air and knife through an angled, upward plane. The run-up was splay-footed but co-ordinated, the arm swinging, his high forehead bucking then radiating towards the keeper and slips, who waited expectantly. On dry wickets he nagged incessantly at middle and leg, driving batsmen to desperate risks. Knott, behind the stumps, was his fully-informed co-assassin. Captains regarded Underwood as an 'umbrella' bowler: i.e. you carried him around in case of rain.

'Deadly' Underwood was yet another to burst upon the scene when barely out of the schoolroom. Tony Lock recommended him to Kent as a batsman after a coaching session in a department store. Underwood had already seen Lock in action as England won the Ashes at The Oval in 1953. Fifteen years after that, Underwood himself was an 'Ashes hero' when his 7 for 50 rolled Australia over on that same ground for a minutes-to-spare victory.

A sensation in his first season, 1963, when he became the youngest ever to take 100 wickets in his debut summer, he took a nasty bouncer in the teeth from Charlie Griffith in his Test debut at Trent Bridge three years later, and before his 26th birthday he had snared his 1000th first-class wicket. Only Rhodes and Lohmann had been younger. Ten years later, Underwood was taking his 2000th wicket. Surprisingly for one of his penetration, there was only one hat-trick in all this. But he took 9 for 28 at Hastings and 9 for 32 at The Oval in county matches, and 8 for 51 against Pakistan in 1974 on a difficult Lord's pitch, his 5 for 20 in the first innings having been assisted by a stupendous leaping one-handed catch by Tony Greig just in front of the sightscreen to dismiss Wasim Raja. This was the match in which the pitch-covers let rainwater through during the night, and the Pakistanis had something to say about it — as if conditions were always perfect in their homeland. Underwood's efforts were, in a manner of speaking, in vain, for time ran out before victory could be rammed home.

Advice was never in short supply, and Underwood worked on his action. But he always came to the same conclusion. He was getting results with his brisk pace, and to have developed a more looping, slower deliver would have meant dismantling his technique, missing some cricket, and returning to who knew what sort of achievement. The sudden withdrawal of rain-affected pitches had vastly more influence on him than upon any other bowler. But he was skilled enough to go on taking wickets, if not quite at the same rate. Late in the 1970s he struggled to hold his Test place, and when he came back after the tense competition of Packer World Series cricket in Australia, it was only for a brief time. In 1982 he was one of those banned from Tests for three years because he toured South Africa with an unauthorised English team. He was then approaching his 37th birthday, and had a tantalising 297 wickets (Ian Chappell 10 times, Greg 13) in 87 Test appearances. The wise words of Kent coach Claude Lewis had helped him immensely. 'For every wicket on which you play,' he said, 'there is a pace to bowl.' Underwood may have spun his stock ball at a tidy pace, but the held-back ball was the one which needed picking early. Shrewdly, Underwood recognised that with pitches getting slower with every passing season, his margin for error grew wider if he did not accelerate the speed with which the ball met — or passed — the bat. Efforts to adapt to bowling over rather than round the wicket were not successful. Underwood was cast for life: and a most successful cricketing life it had been, financially as well as statistically. Those who were consumed by envy at his three rich pickings — a huge benefit, a Packer pay-packet, and South African gold — tended to forget his service to county and country: and not only as a bowler, for many a time England's captain asked him to weather the evening bouncers as a nightwatchman.

Underwood's dominance left steady performers like Peter Sainsbury and Roger Harman nowhere. Harman shone for Surrey in 1964, taking 120 Championship wickets at just under 20, having taken a quality hat-trick against Kent at Blackheath the previous season. Steady for two further seasons, he was never to touch such heights again. That 1964 effort brought the bespectacled Harman 8 for 12 at Trent Bridge and 8 for 32, again against Kent, at The Oval, where it was thought that Lock's successor had arrived. Flight and gentle spin were not enough. The county grapevine caught up with him. Word went round, and batsmen were able to handle him. His nerve as well as his figures suffered. Sainsbury's career with Hampshire was anything but short-lived. He curled his first spinner down for them in 1954 and twirled his last in 1976, when he was an ageless 42. In that time he was accorded only one tour, with England 'B' to Pakistan in 1955-56. Loyal, tireless, a brilliant close fielder, 'Sains' regularly pouched 40 or so catches in a season, and finished with over 1200 wickets for the county of his birth.

The bothersome spectre of throwing appeared at Bath in 1960 when the promising young Eric Bryant was called by umpire Yarnold for five deliveries as he bowled slow left-arm for Somerset against Gloucestershire. Colin McCool thought it tragic that a known 'jerker' should have been submitted to this experience, having been called in an earlier Second XI match. 'He was given a glimpse of a bright future,' wrote the Australian, 'and then thrown out. Such a system is cruel.' He felt the club should have worked on his action, which was known to have been suspect. It brought back memories of Tyler, similarly no-balled 60 years before.

If one bowler stands out as evolutionary, in the saddest possible sense, it is Robin Hobbs of Essex. Here, had it been but realised in the 1960s, was the last of the English leg-spinners — *pro tem* at any rate. With Hobbs's retirement from the first-class game, only the odd part-time leg-spinner was left, and those were in danger of being converted into something more 'businesslike'. With sleeves rolled well above the elbow, Hobbs crouched and advanced upon the crease to whip over a wrist-spun ball that buzzed and was liable to turn either way. With the lived-in kind of face presented by actor Peter O'Toole, he could smile away the big hit in the grandest tradition. He could also flatten a stump with a fast throw from cover point. England chose him a mere seven times between 1967, when he played in four Tests, and 1971. England did not take the field at Karachi in 1969, so he operated in six Tests, taking 12 wickets at 40 each. This was hardly an inspiring set of figures for selectors or young lads watching. Yet he piled up over 700 wickets for his county before seeking a second coming at Glamorgan — by which time the only Hobbs to crop up in selectors' wistful conversations was the immortal Jack, whose services would have been so useful to England's batting in modern times. In 1970 only three bowlers took 100 or more wickets. Don Shepherd was top with 106; Norman Gifford took 105; and Hobbs (R.N.S.) took 102 at 21.40. Here was the golden chance to exploit him on a tour of Australia. But Don Wilson was taken instead, having taken 59 wickets at 26.13 in 1970. The thinking would have been that Australians eat leg-spin for breakfast; yet Hobbs might just have induced a little indigestion. Perhaps the failure of the statistically-supreme legger, Freeman, still haunted memory.

Overseas, spin flourished in the 1960s. In the wake of Benaud's retirement there came, if no-one of comparable stature, a beguiling array of left- and right-arm bowlers, one of them a 'mystery' man who gave the sports columns good speculative material just as Iverson had done. His name was John Gleeson, known as 'Cho' because his disappearance at the close of play during tours branded him Cricket Hours Only. He came from the lovely New England country of NSW, and was 28 before the State selectors chose him. In the meantime he had toured the world with the Emus, a collection of bush cricketers, for whom he kept wicket. Like so many, he had been fascinated by Iverson's bent-finger methods; like so very few, he could copy Iverson to some effect. He was not as large a man, and lessened still further the loop on the ball by bending at the knees as he delivered it. Coming to the crease in what was nothing more glamorous than a slow, long-striding prowl, Gleeson turned the ball a little but enough, the ball fitting nicely between a long middle finger and crooked thumb. Practising against a gum-tree, and with fingers strengthened by cow-milking, he grooved himself into near-mechanical accuracy, and when he entered first-class cricket he immediately topped the Shield averages. That earned him a trip to New Zealand, in Iverson's footsteps, and in the following season he became a Test player. Not for him the spectacular debut series of Iverson, but he earned a tour of England, which is more than 'Big Jake' did. There Gleeson topped the tour averages, though his effectiveness in the Tests was only moderate. He took five or six wickets against Somerset, Sussex and Kent, and seldom came away without a wicket or two: no Ramadhin, but a sound asset to Lawry's team, even if that captain seemed not always alert to the best time to bring Gleeson into the attack.

He had some good returns against the 1968-69 West Indians and in India a year later, where the batsmen seemed suspicious of him. More catches held and more sympathetic umpiring could have seen his figures soar on that tour. On they went to South Africa — where he was later to play some Currie Cup cricket — and in a highly embarrassing series for Australia, Gleeson carried a fair share of the bowling in the four Tests and came away with 19 wickets. Further Tests against England, home and away, in the early 1970s saw his powers fading. His either-way turn was played with relative safety off the pitch as he relied more on cut than spin, there being little danger of deceit in his flight. He finished with 93 Test wickets at 36 apiece, and had brought tons of character to the game, this laconic postal technician with ears like cabbage-leaves, his green cap perched on his head like a pancake as he plodded out to bat like a right-handed Ken Mackay. In first-class cricket he pulled in an estimable 430 wickets at just under 25 each — and gave a little bit more to cricket later on when his counsel (voluntary) came in useful to World Series Cricket in its formative days.

Gleeson was blatantly unorthodox. Peter Philpott, the small, golden-haired leg-spinner from Sydney, was a thinking cricketer who did it by the book and became an eminent coach. Only 20 when first chosen by NSW, having played first-grade for Manly at 15 (and incredibly topping the Sydney averages at 16), he was to cover almost as many miles as any Australian cricketer, playing and coaching for several seasons in England, South Africa, Asia and New Zealand. A centurymaking batsman, he was chosen by his country for his virile leg-spin/googly bowling. He tossed the ball up from his 5ft 7ins, like a Freeman, but made it spin a good deal further than the Kent man. He, like Gleeson, was much taken by the Iverson method, but whereas Gleeson adopted it, Philpott damaged his finger badly while experimenting with the bent middle finger, and actually retired in 1963. He came back, continued to work excruciatingly hard at his game, and found himself on the aircraft to West Indies in 1965, and getting through a lot of work to finish with 49 wickets on the tour. A year later he marked his debut in Ashes Tests with 5 for 90 at Brisbane, only to bowl 30 overs unrewarded in the next Test, when England (558) took 133 runs off his crazily-spinning offerings. John Edrich's patent discomfort was matched only by his gutsy determination to hang on against something he little understood. Philpott eventually caught up with him (literally: it was a caught-and-bowled) in the next Test, when Edrich had made another century; but this was the last of Philpott's 26 Test wickets. He took 245 in all matches, and it was deduced in 1980, when he had open-heart surgery, that all his career he had carried a weak heart, the legacy of rheumatic fever in childhood. None would have credited it while watching him drive the fast bowlers, pluck screaming slip catches out of the air, and bob in, with a mischievous grin, for his 15th consecutive over, still making the ball 'talk'.

Rex Sellers, born in India, was a promising leg-spinner for Australia, and toured England in 1964, playing his only Test on the way home, ironically in India, without success. He had had a marvellous 1963-64 season, culminating in his Australian citizenship, but he had to have a cyst removed from his spinning finger during the English tour, and it never recovered fully. The only other leg-spin to be seen in Australia's cause in the 1960s came from Bob Simpson, who, having found the tap that turned on vast gushes of runs when he finally made a Test century (311) at Manchester in 1964, proceeded to show that he was no second-rater with the ball. His 71 Test wickets at 42 makes expensive reading, and yet so many top-class leg-spinners have aspired to nowhere near that wicket aggregate. Simpson, as good a slip fieldsman as ever stood by the wicketkeeper, played first-grade in Sydney at only 15 years of age and entered first-class cricket at 16. His career blossomed when he went to Western Australia, later to return to his home State. As a bowler, he waltzed in and mixed a telegraphed googly with his leg-spin and then, if the batsman felt he had him, there came the well-disguised googly. Twice he took five wickets in a Test innings. Remarkably, he came back to Tests 10 years after retirement to help Australia in their hour of need when World Series Cricket was played in opposition to Test cricket. Now approaching 42, he made runs — and was still capable of nipping in for the occasional wicket.

An off-spinner emerged in the early 1960s who seemed to have the makings of a long-term asset. Tom Veivers was no stylist. A burly chap, he bustled in and whisked over a brisk arm, his aim so often seeming to be total denial. One flighted ball at Melbourne — not in a Test match — was picked up so beautifully on the drive by Ted Dexter that oldtimers felt it was the best hit ever seen there. Veivers survived this mauling and three fairly fruitless Tests against South Africa to make the 1964 UK tour, on which he impressed, never more than at Old Trafford, where he bowled 95.1 overs to take 3 for 155 in England's innings of 611. Here Dexter abandoned all idea of knocking spectators' heads off as he ground out 174, while Barrington scored 256. Veivers bowled 36 maiden overs and took the record for most balls bowled by an Australian in a Test. Fleetwood-Smith had sent down 522 at The Oval in 1938, 49 fewer than Veivers. Another three overs would have seen the Queenslander pass Ramadhin's world Test record. In the next match Veivers took eight wickets in 56 overs against Glamorgan, to show what 'Bananabenders' are made of; unfortunately for the Australians, the men of the Daffodil county were victorious, Don Shepherd taking nine in the match. Veivers, a hard-hitting left-hand bat, retired at only 30, just when he had seemed a possible Test captain. Had he risen to that eminence, one wonders if he would *ever* have taken himself off. In 1983 he presented the Old Trafford ball as an inspiration to fellow Labour Party politician Keith Wright, 'to help us keep in mind the task in front of us — to send the Government into a spin, to bowl them over at the elections, their stumps spreadeagled'.

Off-spin was dispensed by the elegant Bob Cowper, who picked up 36 wickets for Australia, 183 in all first-class cricket. His batting distinctly overshadowed his bowling, and his 307 against England at Melbourne in 1966 set a new record for his country in a home Test match. Nevertheless, the hold he exerted on English batsmen during some of the 1968 Tests, bowling tidy off-spin, had the colonels spluttering into their gin-and-tonics. John Inverarity was another irregular spinner — another ambidextrous, bowling, in his case, left-arm. At Headingley in 1972 he actually took 3 for 26 off 33 overs, a performance not as impertinent as it seemed, for 'Invers' was a scholarly man who knew that line and length and a bit of movement on a responsive pitch would place demands on even the best batsman.

Among the 'legitimate' left-arm spinners, Johnny Martin, a cheerful little NSW country player, rose to the Test team by dint of extraordinary enthusiasm (he would travel from Burrell Creek on the night train to play in Sydney, returning that night) and clever wrist-spin allied to devastating hitting. He transferred to Adelaide, but was back in Sydney by the time the Test selectors favoured him. Then, at Melbourne, New Year 1961, he took the wickets of Kanhai, Sobers and Worrell in four balls. No man could have wished for a richer haul in such a short span. Martin had also whacked 55 in his first innings. He never touched such heights in his remaining seven Tests. He missed the 1961 England tour and played in Lancashire instead, reaping an expectedly handsome reward with his mainly googly attack, compelling batsmen to swing hopelessly from the crease or dance out to a dipping ball which often eluded the downward swish of the bat. He did tour with the 1964 Australians, but could not find a place in the Tests. In South Africa two years later he took 7 for 30 against Griqualand West, who must still have been recoiling from Barrington's wristy performance two years earlier. Like Barrington, Martin was to suffer a heart attack. It happened soon after his retirement, but he bounced back with typical smiling resolve. Benaud described him as a 'happy-go-lucky little bowler', a big spinner of the ball, who could never remember his figures but could tell you how many sixes he had hit. And they were numerous.

A curious choice for an England tour, in retrospect, was Ian Quick, a Victorian left-armer who had some fine figures behind him, and indeed took 50 wickets on the 1961 tour (as did seven others). But he never looked like making the Test side and upon his return to Melbourne he was even dropped from his district's first team, a sad decline for a shy and likeable cricketer. The Australian selectors may have thought they were on to something when they chose Bob Bitmead of Victoria to tour New Zealand with a 'B' team in 1967. He headed the bowling with 15 wickets at 14.80, despite a mid-tour return to Australia because of a bereavement. Tall and fair-haired, left-armer Bitmead had been second in the Sheffield Shield averages to Gleeson, both of them in their first year. It seemed an exciting prospect, but Bitmead, who bowled 'off the wrong foot', left foot coming forward before the arm came over, faded from the game.

The need for a good left-arm spinner was there because the earlier 'hopeful', David Sincock from Adelaide, had moved to Sydney and concurrently lost his form and his place in interstate cricket. At 18 he had caught the eye of the West Indians when he bowled to them at the nets. The red-headed youngster bothered Kanhai and Nurse and Solomon, while Frank Worrell looked on in amazement, proclaiming him the best left-arm bosie merchant in Australia. None of the touring batsmen could 'pick' him. Soon none of the NSW batsmen was picking him as he burst on the first-class scene with 6 for 52, helping his State to a rare win over the mighty NSW. Then came dental studies; and when Sincock — now predictably known as 'Stumps' — returned, he worked his way into the Test side, having broadened his experience in Lancashire league cricket. Sadly for Test cricket's entertainment value, he played in only three Tests, sharing a Test debut with Ian Chappell against Pakistan in Melbourne, touring West Indies (one Test), and facing England at Sydney, when he ran into Barber and Boycott, and then Edrich, in full cry: result — 20-1-98-0. Another terror had evaporated from batsmen's nightmares.

No batsman would have thought of Lance Gibbs as a 'terror'. The tall, painfully thin Guyanese off-spinner slipped quietly into Test cricket during West Indies' home series against Pakistan early in 1958. In the last of his 79 Test matches, at Melbourne 18 years later, when he was 41, he passed Fred Trueman's world Test record of 307 wickets, finishing with 309 at 29.09 off an unapproached total of 27115 balls. Dennis Lillee later passed the record 309 — like Trueman, in fewer matches and off fewer deliveries.

Gibbs was to win the unwavering support of the selectors in the aftermath of the decline of Ramadhin and Valentine, and during the 1960-61 tour of Australia, shirt billowing as he thrust his slender body into the breeze, he came close to a hat-trick in the Sydney Test, getting Mackay, Martin and Grout in four balls. He made amends in the very next match, at Adelaide, beating Mackay, Grout and Misson with successive balls, though the match is remembered for the stubborn saving tenth-wicket partnership of Mackay and Kline, when Gibbs spun but remained wicket-less. A year later he returned his best Test figures, 8 for 38 against India at Bridgetown, his wickets all coming in the final session of the match off 15.3 overs — 14 of which were maidens — for six runs: final figures 53.3-37-38-8. He next showed England what he was worth, taking 11 wickets at Old Trafford in the opening Test of the 1963 series. Bulbous but dreamy eyes, close-cropped hair and the loosest of gaits gave Gibbs the appearance of a New Orleans trombonist; but his patience as a spin bowler was immense, his accuracy torturesome. He secured his victims by means of deceptive flight and sharp bite from any helpful pitch, the short-leg fieldsman, usually Sobers, waiting by the batsman's hip to complete the execution. Just a few high-kneed strides, a quick arm action just ahead of the torso-twist, and the problem was delivered. He floored Australia at Georgetown in 1965 with 9 for 80 in the match, and showed, in contrast, his durability in the next Test, at Bridgetown, by sending down 73 overs in the first innings — in which Lawry and Simpson made double-centuries — to finish with 2 for 168. Back at Old Trafford in '66, he took five in each innings, and was now verily the gentle menace behind the fire of Hall and Griffith and the skills of Sobers. The West Indies attack was not only one of the most effective of all time, but it consisted of a pleasing balance, soon to be lost in the obsession for speed.

Gibbs toiled away predominantly as a stock bowler through series after series, bearing the wear on his knuckle, tying batsmen down for hours without necessarily reaping great harvests, and stoutly refusing to up-grade his comical batsmanship at No.10 or 11. A return of 7 for 98 in the first Test to be played at Bombay's Wankhede Stadium showed him still to be a force at 40, but a theory persisted, especially among some English sources, that he was being sustained as far as the world record. Eventually he equalled Trueman's 307 in the fifth Test at Adelaide in 1975-76, and pushed two ahead in the sixth Test. Then came honourable retirement and pursuit of business interests in the USA.

There had been no lasting challenge to Gibbs as an off-spinner among West Indians during his time; but several had risen to Test ranks as leg-spinners, the tall David Holford, Sobers's cousin, taking 51 expensive wickets but writing a few golden lines for himself by scoring a matchsaving century at Lord's, alongside his cousin, in 1966, in only his second Test. Willie Rodriguez, a talented Trinidad all-rounder, played in five scattered Tests without achieving anything of note. And Basil Butcher, a valuable middle-order batsman, was sometimes entrusted with the ball, and surprised a lot of people by taking 5 for 34 against an embarrassed England at Port-of-Spain in 1968, getting rid of Cowdrey (148) and the tail for 15 runs in 10 overs.

India, on the threshold of a spin revolution, used players like Salim Durani (75 wickets in 29 Tests), a graceful left-handed all-rounder whose bowling had much in common with Nadkarni's. His team-mates called him 'Uncle', and he relished punishing opposing slow bowlers, a reprisal opportunity denied tailend spinners like Gibbs. A lively, humorous cricketer, quite unselfish, Durani was 'a genius', according to Gavaskar, 'whom the authorities have never bothered to understand'. He earned 23 well-priced wickets against England in 1961-62, 18 of them in the last two Tests, and in West Indies straight afterwards he and Nadkarni (pitching monotonously just outside off stump) headed the production for an Indian bowling line-up consisting almost entirely of all-rounders. In time, this popular cricketer, who entered big cricket while still at school and who came close to becoming a film star, gave way to Bedi in the national team. Kripal Singh made 100 not out against New Zealand in his Test debut, but managed only 10 wickets with seam and off-spin in 14 Tests spread over nine years; while V.V. Kumar began promisingly, taking 5 for 64 with leg-spin at Delhi against Pakistan in 1961. He played only one more Test, the competition being too stiff. Venkat Subramanyam toured England in 1967 and Australia that winter as batsman and wristy leg-spin bowler, but was another to fail to cement a place: for a worldbeating Indian spin quartet was gradually assembling itself to take India to unprecedented power in the 1970s.

Spin had served the other countries well in the 1960s. Lancashire-born Vic Pollard, New Zealand's youthful all-rounder, bowled a persistent if somewhat guileless off-break to some effect, while Bryan Yuile, the fair, bespectacled left-armer, endured such extremes as bowling to John Edrich when he made 310 not out in the Headingley Test of 1965 and taking 9 for 100 in an innings for Central Districts against Canterbury a few months later. In 17 Tests he pounded away without ever taking more than four wickets in an innings. Narotam Puna, born in India, had great success in Plunket Shield matches with probing off-spin in 1965-66, but failed to make an impression in the three Test matches against the touring England team. New Zealand were doomed to a few more years on the outside looking in before dogged batting and determined pace bowling were to raise them to the reality of their most optimistic dreams.

Slow bowling did little to help South Africa to their last sweet triumphs before political banishment after the 1969-70 series against Australia. For them, power batting and blitzing fast bowling were the winning factors against Australia in the seven victories achieved in nine Tests in '66-67 and '69-70. The 1960s had heralded a bright new hope in Glen Hall, who took 9 for 122 in his first-class debut innings; but his one Test, against England in 1964-65, was disheartening — one of a number of nails in leg-spin's coffin. Graeme Pollock sometimes filled his time between batting masterpieces by bowling leg-spin, with the occasional googly, as when he trapped England captain M.J.K. Smith lbw in the Trent Bridge victory of 1965, which won the series. As Pollock had already contributed a famous innings of 125, he and his team-mates could be excused for prancing around the old ground that evening in celebration, their attire amounting to nothing more than underpants.

Genuine spin was supplied to the Springboks by bowlers like 'Kelly' Seymour, a doctor who, at Test level, was seldom able to progress beyond examination to operation. Harry Bromfield, an upstanding, military figure from Western Province, peered through his glasses, moustache bristling, in nine Test matches, in one of which he excelled: at Cape Town in 1965, when he took 5 for 88 off 57.2 overs, 26 of which were strangulated maidens. David Pithey, a Rhodes scholar at Oxford who foxed Benaud's 1961 Australians to the tune of 7 for 47, played in Tests for South Africa, like his brother Tony, and took 12 wickets with off-spin against New Zealand at the end of the 1963-64 tour. But his career was short-lived too. Atholl McKinnon, the burly and cheeky left-arm bowler from Eastern Province, never did more than a containing job during his eight Tests, though he did win a place on two tours of England. McKinnon's favourite self-introduction, provocative to a degree in his particular homeland, has been (in Afrikaans): 'My father was white and my mother was white and they were married before I was born.' It was not only fierce and blunt fast bowlers like Peter Heine who rendered life uncomfortable for 'foreign' batsmen.

One spinner to progress in that final summer of Test cricket for South Africa was Grahame Chevalier, 32, who struck with his fifth ball in his sole Test appearance, getting Sheahan caught and taking four other wickets with left-arm spin, including the last, to win the match at Cape Town. Another South African (Rhodesian to be specific) spinner to miss out on further Test honours was Jackie du Preez, an all-round record-holder for his country, who took three wickets cheaply with leg-spin in his two Tests against the 1966-67 Australians. And, poignantly, came the last to be capped by South Africa before isolation was sealed. John Traicos, born in Alexandria, Egypt, and a student at Natal University before representing Rhodesia, was encouraged and tipped for big things by Xenophon Balaskas and Athol Rowan. Beatle-mopped Traicos, always touching the turf with two fingers before staring to bowl his off-spinners, did nothing sensational in his three Tests against Lawry's Australians, but popped up in England a dozen years later with the victorious Zimbabwe (formerly Rhodesia) ICC Trophy 'mini-World Cup' team. Four for 21 he took against Israel while the South African Cricket Union officials were being rebuffed yet again by the International Cricket Conference at Lord's.

The rising power, Pakistan, had been launched by patient batting and Bedser-class seam bowling from Fazal Mahmood and Khan Mohammad. Then, gradually, spin came to play a part, Nasim-ul-Ghani, Mushtaq Mohammad and Intikhab Alam all proving to be world-class, while others like the slow-medium off-spinner Saeed Ahmed, nipped in for an occasional wicket or two. Nasim was the youngest Test player ever at 16 years 248 days — or so the story goes. Then along came cuddly little Mushtaq at 15 years 124 days, too tender in years to appreciate that the fate of the world depended on the result of a Test match, that one was supposed to be consumed with nervous tension. He was a member of Pakistan cricket's 'royal family', brother Hanif having broken batting records galore, brother Wazir playing in 20 Tests, and brother Sadiq — also a useful leg-spinner — soon to win Test honours. 'Mushy', who modelled his action on Benaud's, bounced up to the crease with a bustling run-up, all Oriental ceriphs and curves. He laughed a lot — if not always with sincere feeling, at least with commendable frequency. His was the original joy of fooling a batsman. If the googly popped over the leg stump he laughed. If a catch went down he chattered away without malice even if sometimes the language was unintelligible. Mushtaq gathered in 79 wickets at just under 30 in 57 Tests, usually supplementing his flow of wristy runs with something worthwhile with the ball.

Young Nasim, orthodox slow left-arm, earned a privileged key role in Pakistan's first win over West Indies when he took 6 for 67 at Port-of-Spain in 1958 to ram home his side's big first-innings advantage and secure an innings victory. How many 16-year-olds, pundits mused, could walk onto a Test field and spin out Sobers, Hunte, Walcott and Collie Smith? Oddly, in a Test career that stretched to the early 1970s, Nasim never touched such figures again, though he did make a century in a Test match at Lord's which, when coupled with his Port-of-Spain bowling performance, could have proved intimidating to many of his opponents in his years of English league and Minor County cricket.

Intikhab Alam, 'Inti', the massive, gentle leg-spin craftsman, looked deceptively like one of Capone's bodyguards, especially when his black hair thinned away to nothing. He was the first Pakistan bowler to take 1000 first-class wickets, and began his Test career, when a few days short of 18, by bowling Australia's Colin McDonald with his first delivery. He harvested over 1500 wickets, over 600 of them for Surrey, where he earned a living between Test tours, as Mushtaq did with Northants. Intikhab, who learnt about Northern conditions as a professional in Scotland, was a master spinner. His approach was fast and businesslike, the ball massaged threateningly as he headed for the bowling crease. An immaculate side-on action fired the ball on an unerring length, and only the most educated eye could detect its imminent course. His range included the problematic 'flipper'. And he was tireless. His hefty bat brought him fast, exhilarating runs, and his diplomacy and calm won him the Test captaincy. In 1974 his side was unbeaten on a short tour of England. His career figures of 125 Test wickets included some large hauls against New Zealand (7 for 52 at Dunedin the best); but so often he was up against it in that conditions favoured fast bowlers or the pitch was too slow to enable him to beat batsmen completely. Spin bowling was already in need of a protection society, and big, popular 'Inti' was one of the last regular practitioners to be seen and enjoyed on the county grounds of England, plying his trade in the classical manner.

17. Modern Torchbearers

Pat Pocock — John Emburey — Geoff Miller —
Phil Edmonds — Eddie Hemmings — Bishan Bedi —
Prasanna, Venkat and Chandra — Dilip Doshi —
Jim Higgs — Ashley Mallett — Bruce Yardley —
Abdul Qadir

'The fault I find with many bowlers of the present day,' wrote David Buchanan, 'is that the ball comes from their hands too often like a bit of lead. It ought to come as if it had a fiend inside it, which works the mischief immediately it touches the ground. My wrist sometimes used to crack when imparting spin to the ball.'

The old Scot was commenting at the turn of the century, but he might just as well have been passing judgment on the 'spinners' of the 1970s, many of whom gave in to the needs of the frenetic one-day cricket by whisking the ball in at the batsman's ankles, with flight and heavy spin the province of what they considered to be naive altruists, unrealistic dabblers in old-time fantasy.

And yet those who did best in that revolutionary decade knew how to exploit the air, could actually deceive with pure slowness. On some of the sluggish pitches they were given to operate upon, there was little alternative.

Surrey's Welsh-born Pat Pocock, a county player at 17, won his first England cap at 21, and bowled crisp off-breaks with a confidence that sometimes troubled his captains, so certain was 'Percy' Pocock of his field setting and his 'line'. He typified those who were faced with half a summer devoted to the crash-bang of limited-overs cricket. Wishing to stay aboard, he flattened his arc, bowling not so much to tempt as to deny — though usually keener than Titmus or Illingworth to keep on experimenting. Intikhab, loyal to his art, often found himself sitting in civvies in the Surrey dressing-room during one-day games. Pocock's promise flickered as he was accepted by the national selectors and then put aside. He bowled not all that well against Australia at Old Trafford in 1968 but came away with good figures. That has happened before; and it has persuaded selectors to hold onto a player. Not in Pocock's case. Even 10 years afterwards his case was not proven. England had not, after all, found another Laker, even though he did well on foreign pitches, especially in the Caribbean. A spell in Surrey's match against a bat-swinging Sussex at Eastbourne in 1972 made history too. In 11 balls Pocock took seven wickets for four runs, finishing with an unexceptional 7 for 67 which contained world record sequences of six wickets in nine balls and the final seven in 11 (Sussex's Indian off-spinner Joshi was run out off the next ball). It made Percy Fender's seven wickets in 19 balls against Middlesex in 1927 seem a trifle humdrum.

Off-spin became all the rage — where spin was fostered and tolerated — in the 1970s. Players such as Jack Simmons of Lancashire (and Tasmania) bowled it at middle-and-leg with marked absence of loop ('Flat Jack' they called him) and markedly regular success — the ultimate dividend in the case of this huge, auburn-haired and popular cricketer taking the shape of a staggering £128,000 benefit in 1980. Jack Birkenshaw, the slightly-built Yorkshireman who was coached by Johnny Lawrence, a neighbour of his, made progress with Leicestershire, and bagged over 1000 first-class wickets before donning the umpire's coat, having played five times for England — and pluckily — in India, Pakistan and West Indies (where part-time off-spinner John Jameson scored a morale-boosting point for the slower men by bowling Clive Lloyd in the Kingston Test). Birkenshaw's left-hand batting and smart catching also helped Leicestershire, for whom Illingworth headed a strong spin assortment which included Chris Balderstone and John Steele. Birkenshaw went through several style-changes, but was at his best when flighting the ball. Bob White served Middlesex and then Notts with distinction as an 'offie' without ever seriously entering Test selectors' discussions, while Geoff Cope, of the monstrous goosestep delivery, and who caused anxiety among certain umpires and players who felt he threw, climaxed 11 years of county cricket by winning Test caps on England's 1977-78 Pakistan tour. There, at Lahore, he had the dispiriting experience not only of bowling (39-6-102-3) against Mudassar Nazar as that batsman made the slowest century of all time (557 minutes) but Cope's maiden Test brought him a 'hat-trick' — which was cancelled within seconds as catcher Brearley indicated that he was not certain of the cleanness of the 'catch'.

There are those who believe that almost every off-spinner transgresses the law which insists that the bowling arm should not be straightened 'during that part of the delivery swing which directly precedes the ball leaving the hand'. Some actions, however, seem less pure than others, and Cope's worried the authorities in England to such an extent in 1972 that he was suspended halfway through the season: only to be cleared after filming of his action next summer. Johnny Wardle helped reshape Cope's action, but in 1978 — his career-best of 8 for 73 at Bristol intervening — he was suspended again, and drifted, heartbroken, into Minor County cricket.

No such problems befell Peter Willey of Northants. He had difficulties of another kind to overcome before rising to international ranks. He began as a fast-bowling all-rounder, but knee trouble forced him to slow down, and to his rugged batsmanship he added a crisp off-spinner bowled with a muscular arm after a short, unelaborate run-up. But though his brave batting was immensely useful to England, especially against the ferocious West Indian attack, his bowling never seemed likely to win a Test match as he faded from the scene under the politically-inspired ban because he toured South Africa.

That illicit tour took away, for a minimum of three years, England's top spin bowler, John Emburey. Tall, sedate, with a remodelled nose through injury and a leisurely Jack Benny walk, chest out in somewhat matronly fashion, Emburey joined Middlesex in 1972 after rejection by Surrey. He studied under Titmus, and was ready for an England cap in 1978, when his fourth ball in Tests dipped in and had New Zealand's Bruce Edgar caught at short leg in the Lord's match. 'Embers' was already close to being classified as a master of flight, gliding side-on to the crease, bent arm held up near his cheekbone, and wheeling into a beautifully-controlled action ending in a give-away whipping twist of the ball. The ball hung in the air, then dropped and deviated who-knew-how-much? Emburey's conquest of Graham Yallop and Allan Border won the Edgbaston Test of 1981 as much as Botham's 5 for 1 at the end. Agile gully fielding and resolute batting made Emburey a cricketer England could ill-afford to lose through political or any other means in the early 1980s. He was free of ridicule, as only a purist artist would be, when Glamorgan's Mike Llewellyn drove him a seemingly impossible distance into the uppermost guttering of the Lord's pavilion during the 1977 Gillette Cup final.

Because he was not tempted by South African gold, Derbyshire's Geoff Miller was able to continue on his curious course in Test cricket, gaining more and more caps without achieving what many a predecessor had managed in only a handful of appearances. As he broadened out and became as solid an all-rounder for England as Botham was mercurial, 'Dusty' Miller proved to be a reliable off-spinner without satisfying the yearnings of English fans who awaited a matchwinner. Miller contributed much to England's Ashes success in 1978-79, often curling a teasing ball into a breeze from fine leg, as at Brisbane, and befuddling Australia at Sydney, where Titmus had once enjoyed himself. Miller's 5 for 44 and Emburey's 4 for 52 sent Australia tumbling for 143 and nine-wicket defeat. (This was the match in which the umpires incorrectly allowed Australia to start bowling with a used ball in the fourth innings, when England needed only 34: Brearley's protest was overruled). Miller, who had come up through Young England ranks, headed England's bowling in that '78-79 series with 23 wickets at 15.04. Striving, after many close misses, to attain his first century, Miller nonetheless retained genuine classification as an all-rounder, his confidence growing every season.

Anyone lacking confidence ought to have shaken hands with Tony Greig, who, with golden hair and the gigantic, swaying strides of a man of 6ft 7ins, became the most extrovert captain England had known. He was not yet Test skipper of his adopted country when Scots-born Mike Denness used him as an off-spinner in West Indies early in 1974. And it was there, at Queen's Park Oval, Port-of-Spain, that Greig astonished everyone bar himself by spinning and cutting his way to figures of 8 for 86 and 5 for 70 on a helpful pitch. Greig's elongated arms and legs rendered his fast-medium bowling anything but pleasing to the eye; when he reverted to off-spin there was a giraffe-like quality about his action which served as a constant reminder of the country of his origins, South Africa. A major figure in Kerry Packer's revolutionary World Series Cricket, Greig served England well, making 3599 runs (40.43, eight centuries) and taking 141 wickets (32.20) in his 58 Tests. But his extraordinary performance in Trinidad was isolated in its penetration. He completely failed to make the West Indians 'grovel' when they toured England in 1976. Underwood remained unchallengably England's No.1 spinner for years.

During Greig's Test captaincy it seemed that England had found herself a slow left-arm bowler to rank with the best of the line. Phil Edmonds, Zambia-born of a Belgian mother and British father, had shown promise at Cambridge, and when called up, at 24, by England at Headingley in 1975 (the match ruined by vandalism during the final night), he took 5 for 28, including both Chappells, Walters and Ross Edwards. He was anything but accurate, but spectators were thrilled to note how much spin he applied. David Buchanan would have been beside himself with satisfaction. Edmonds, though tall and heavily-built, then had a schoolboy air about him, which added to the delight of seeing him successful on the Test match field. But, like the vast majority, he was not to make his Test place secure or become anything like a fixture in the side. As the 1980s unfolded he seemed on course for 1000 wickets, but eight years after his notable debut his Test caps numbered only 21 (55 wickets: best 7 for 66 at Karachi — the best figures in any Test in Pakistan until 1982). His personality was not blending easily with those around him, and, again reverting to past spirits, Charlie Parker, had he still been around, might profitably have taken Edmonds into a corner and spoken to him.

It was not as if Phillipe Henri Edmonds was not an accomplished all-rounder. On the contrary, he has batted forcefully and well, and is an adept if garrulous short-leg fielder, usually wearing a sunhat shaped like a chamberpot. His use to England could have been — and still might be — boundless. Had the captaincy come his way, there might even have been an anachronistic return to amateur, i.e. daring, attitudes. By not playing safe on his Test debut, he bowled some long-hops, full-tosses and fizzing leg-spinners to finish with five cheap wickets, lazily wiping his spinning fingers in the dirt before each delivery.

The virtues of 'line and length' had been demonstrated in brief spells in that same 1975 series by grey-haired, bespectacled David Steele, who was in the England XI for his determined batting. This was the canny professional who made certain of a long career by serving the needs of a struggling county (Northants, with three seasons with Derbyshire) with dour batsmanship and tidy-to-the-point-of-meanness left-arm spin which was good enough in 1966 to bring him 8 for 29 against Lancashire. Ray East of Essex came closer than Steele ever would have done to consideration of a Test place as a left-arm spinner. Yet East, one of the funniest men ever to tread a first-class field, almost certainly did himself a disservice by not leaving his clowning in the dressing-room. A former village cricketer, he could never be made to see that the pros — and the selectors — had a deep distrust of frivolity. It was always in the mind, even when watching him take 8 for 30 against Notts, or a tailend hat-trick in the 1973 Test trial at Hove. Eric Hollies may have been the first to ride a bicycle across the field in order to reach his farflung fielding position but most of East's pranks and vaudeville displays, including banging his head until sawdust apparently came out of his ear, outWardled Wardle. East's very features spelt comedy. Flickering, egg-like eyes, unkept hair, the wide, expressive mouth of a ventriloquist's dummy; disjointed walk, a bowling action that suggested persistent electric shocks running through his body. Test cricket would have been enhanced beyond belief as an entertaining spectacle if East had been a slightly better bowler — and the selectors slightly more game in their attitude.

There were steadier English slow left-armers around who served their counties well but never quite aspired to Test cricket. Phil Carrick bore the Yorkshire heritage bravely without managing to extend it with his own name. David Graveney, of the distinguished cricket family, used his great height and his stiff action to defeat over 500 batsmen for Gloucestershire. David Hughes and David Lloyd had some memorable afternoons at the bowling crease for Lancashire. Dennis Breakwell, another amusing cricketer, served Northants and Somerset faithfully and well. Apart from the left-arm bowlers, there were a few batsmen who trotted up to bowl leg-spin from time to time, though this, in modern times, is customarily greeted with guffaws tantamount to scoffing the dead, for leg-spin in England is now a foreigners' pastime. John Hampshire has bowled it well, though a high proportion of his career aggregate came in one innings in 1963, when he took 7 for 52 for Yorkshire against Glamorgan at Cardiff. Keith Fletcher actually spun out two batsmen — Lawry and Vengsarkar — in Tests. In the hard Test match cricket of day, leg-spin just isn't the thing done by Englishmen.

Even 'Harry' Latchman, the gleeful, pint-sized Middlesex and Notts leg-spinner, was born elsewhere — in Jamaica. He claimed almost 500 wickets with cultured leg-spin which befuddled many a top name. Spin as the 1980s unwound over Trent Bridge came from the other direction, from Eddie Hemmings, the comfortably-built, asthmatic off-spinner whose years with Warwickshire were filled with mediocrity and low confidence. Moving to Nottinghamshire at the age of 30, he was 'reborn', taking 90 wickets in helping his new county to the 1981 Championship, and working his way into the England Test team a year later. Even unlikelier, he scored 95 in a Sydney Test match after going in as nightwatchman, having not so long ago become the first to take all ten wickets in an innings in a first-class match in West Indies. He kept going into his 50th over to return 10 for 175 for an International XI against a West Indies XI in Jamaica. When Bill O'Reilly saw Hemmings bowl in Sydney he instantly detected him to be a man of intense purpose as he placed and adjusted his field and showed hints of aggression which always characterised the 'Tiger' himself. Unfortunately for England, in the Ashes-deciding final Test at the same ground, neither Hemmings nor Miller bowled well enough to win the match on the vital fourth day. Not for the first time during the 1982-83 series, English fans and journalists lamented the absence of Emburey.

When the team was chosen, with its odd combination of three off-spinners (Somerset's little bearded Vic Marks, the 'air' bowler, was the third), there was outcry at Edmonds' absence, while many thought that the steady John Barclay's off-spin might have been valuable — even though he had never proved either more penetrative or economical than Marks — with his batsmanship and captaincy potential also in mind. Had he not, in the rhythm of things, had a poor year, little Richard Williams of Northants might have come into the reckoning. Tough and well-rounded, he could toss up a big-spinning off-break from his 5ft 4ins height that had a loop not dissimilar to Tich Freeman's so long ago. Alternatively, if Edmonds' omission from the Australian tour could have been justified, then John Childs or Nick Cook might profitably have been considered. Childs, Gloucestershire's Plymouth-born left-arm spinner, recorded the best figures of the 1981 season, 9 for 56 against Somerset at Bristol. Moreover, he shamed those who believe the place for slow bowlers during one-day matches is serving the drinks by taking 1 for 4 off 11 overs in a Benson & Hedges Cup match against Notts. If Childs had anything else in his favour, it was that, like Clarrie Grimmett, he was a qualified signwriter. The other prospect, Nick Cook, had experience of Australian conditions through playing club cricket in Perth. When Edmonds damaged his back in 1983, Cook was plucked out of Leicestershire's match and took nine wickets against New Zealand on his Test debut. Cook and Childs remained hopeful. For slow bowlers the age of 30 is nothing to be afraid of.

And one promising English leg-spinner waited patiently for his fate to be decided: Kim Barnett of Derbyshire. Yet so limited were his opportunities that he began to dabble in uninspired medium-pace at the nets. His fine batsmanship stood him in good stead, as it had Graham Johnson of Kent, whose off-spin would seldom have been seen had he needed to command a place in the team for it alone. David Acfield of Essex, an Olympic fencer, piled up over 750 first-class wickets while averaging under nine with the bat, a specialisation which paid the price in repeated exclusion from limited-overs matches. The one-day game has bulked up the financial area, but has cost cricket unimaginable art.

Against this background of bias towards faster bowling, with its alleged economy and its known denial and occasional brutality, the Indian game has grown in attraction, for strength in slow bowling was nowhere more pronounced than when the great foursome of Bedi, Prasanna, Venkat and

Chandra began to win Test series. Until Kapil Dev began to leap up the tables of Test wicket-takers, India's top six were all spinners, and these four contemporaries accounted for 842 wickets in their combined 224 Tests, 65 per cent of the wickets which fell in those matches to bowlers. One or more of the quartet played in the 91 Tests between 1961-62 and 1979-80, and India counted herself proud to have won 23 of these contests. Venkat actually came back into the reckoning for the 1982-83 tour of West Indies, though his best was surely behind him.

The four were even less alike than the members of South Africa's googly quartet before the Great War. Bishan Singh Bedi was recognisable from half a mile away by his patka, a supply of which always took up a corner of his bag. He usually changed colours for every session, and rarely revealed his balding head off the field. Bedi cherished the art of slow bowling. So much so that he refused to sell out for the one-day county game. Craftily, in the Rhodes tradition, he would clap a batsman as he was hit for six. Countless victims fell trying to repeat the stroke. One will never forget the fury shown by Northants team-mates after Bedi's final flighted over of the 1976 Gillette Cup final at Lord's had been smashed for 26 by Lancashire's David Hughes — much as he had slaughtered Mortimore five years earlier on an important occasion. Bedi had refused to hurl the ball in at leg stump. It was this very strength of will which made him a great slow bowler. It also led him into many a *contretemps*, such as when he objected noisily to the vaseline allegedly used by England fast bowler John Lever in the Madras Test of 1976, the vehemence of which protest Bedi felt eventually cost him his contract with Northants. A year earlier he had made headlines by calling India's second innings off with five down for 97 after his men had taken a battering from the short-pitching West Indian fast bowlers. He abhorred brutality.

Bedi played his first Test, in 1966, at the age of 20, and collected 266 wickets (28.71) in his 67 Tests. Along the way, his expansive turban gave way to the patka while his slim figure thickened comfortably, rendering him a jogger after the ball on the long-leg boundary. The finger-power of this Delhi Sikh was immense, his range wide, much of it based upon varying points of release. The ball could hurry on, or spit away to slip, or hang in the air, dropping a foot or two short of expectation. The off-side field was on constant alert when 'Bish' was bowling, and the wicketkeeper's job was a delight.

Just as teasing was Erapalli Prasanna, from Karnataka, who was no more athletic than the bearded Bedi, no better equipped with the bat. His approach to the bowling crease was more urgent, but less convincing in its lack of polish. The message was in the ball's tempting curve and unpredictable antics upon pitching. He spun his off-break sharply, but did much damage through the air. He could have been forgiven for losing confidence, since the national selectors did not exactly show consistent faith in him in the earlier years. Prasanna was blooded at 21 against England at Madras in 1961-62 and was still serving his country 17 years later, taking his tally to 189 wickets in 49 Tests, average 30.38. But an early West Indies tour, as in so many cases, did him no good. Later he was to cast a spell over New Zealand and Australian batsmen, taking 10 wickets against Australia at Madras and 11 in a Test at Auckland. Time and again he and his fellow-spinners were at work only minutes into an innings, genuine or token new-ball bowlers having taken a little of the gloss off the ball with a few preliminary overs before the real business began. Eventually his subtlety was not enough: his fitness and form sagged when he was in sight of 1000 first-class wickets.

Srinivas Venkataraghavan, the typesetter's dream, was urbane, slender and languid, and outlasted his rival Prasanna. He was only 18 when first capped by India, against New Zealand early in 1965. A man of charm, 'Venkat', like Bedi, was honoured with Test captaincy, a job he tackled with more obvious diplomacy. With a toss of his flopping black hair, he put away his flashing smile under a neat moustache as he moved purposefully to the crease and dispatched a ball loaded with off-spin but no lavish flight. Though the Test selectors swayed in their opinion of him, he showed early that he had the makings, having taken 8 for 72 in New Zealand's first innings at Delhi in his fourth Test match, the best figures by any of the four in all Tests. Like Bedi, he played county cricket, serving Derbyshire for three seasons, and his Test haul up to his recall in 1983 was 145 wickets (34.09) in 50 Tests. The man from Tamil Nadu, in addition to his other merits, was a stayer.

The fourth member of India's glorious squad of four amazed everybody by playing top-class cricket at all, for Bhagwat Chandrasekhar carried a withered bowling arm, legacy of childhood poliomyelitis. His arms were never exposed to the sun on a cricket field, for his sleeves were perpetually buttoned at the wrists. Nor did batsmen ever, for long, feel free of his threat, for, like Doug Wright, he bowled a ball loaded heavily with top-spin and at such a brisk pace that the task of his wicketkeepers, from Kunderan and Indrajitsinhji to Engineer and Kirmani, has been among the most onerous in sport. The comparison with Wright is inevitable. On off-days they were pulverised. And their luck, by the very nature of their specialty, was often atrocious. But they were matchwinners in the most dramatic sense, Chandra usually inspired to the point of ecstasy by the strains of his favourite music beforehand.

Chandra's performance at The Oval in 1971 brought India their first Test win on English soil. England, with a first-innings lead of 61, went in again without any particular worries; but 45 overs later they were all back in the pavilion for 101, Chandrasekhar 6 for 38. This alone would have guaranteed him immortality, but just under seven years later he took 6 for 52 in each innings to bring India their first victory in Australia and net his own 200th Test wicket. The Melbourne pitch tended to keep low, but was no spinner's paradise. Chandra did it with bounce, with scurrying top-spinners — and the occasional full-toss — against a side weakened by the absence of Packer players. Suitably, he contributed 0 and 0 with the bat, for he was a top candidate for the title of worst batsman ever seen in Test cricket.

On his form in that series, as in others before his powers plainly began to wane, partly through the fatigue of over-use, Chandrasekhar ranked with the best in history. Visiting batsmen who faced him and the others on receptive Indian pitches, with hordes of voluble close fieldsmen, led by Solkar or Yajurvindra, and panicky umpires in range, were left with nightmare visions for years afterwards. The latterly-bearded Chandra's run-up, starting with the ball held before his face, as if he were a tenpin bowler, was a loose, loping affair. Then the withered arm whirled over like a speeded-up windmill. (He threw left-handed in the field.) He bowled a higher proportion than Wright of balls which went straight on or came in as wrong'uns, and in the 1972-73 series he took what was then a record of 35 English wickets. He returned, too, the best first-class figures of any of the famous quartet, 9 for 72 for Mysore v Kerala in 1969-70. Only Venkat of the others had taken nine, and that was against Hampshire in 1971. The waif-like Chandra topped 1000 wickets too, though falling short of Bedi's 1500-plus. And his Test total of 242 wickets placed him next to Bedi, his striking rate of 4.17 per Test being best of them all. He would never have aspired to the kind of figures Bedi produced at Delhi in the first Test of that 1972-73 series: 47-23-59-2 and 39-20-50-3. But the pair of them, with one of the off-spinners in support, proved a formidable force that thrilled the thousands up on the terraces, some of them youngsters whose imagination will have been captured forever, to the benefit of the game in India. Bedi, enchanted by the guile of Mankad and Gupte, made his first-class debut at only 15, and when he left Test cricket he was considered to have been the best of Indian left-arm bowlers — except by some loyal to Mankad, and those whose memories stretched back to the gifted Jamshedji, from Bombay, who played his only Test in 1933-34, when he was already 41, an age well in the future when Bedi played his last for India. Wilfred Rhodes said, with Jamshedji in mind, that if he had had the Indian's power of spin, no batting side would ever have reached 100. Further back, in India's — not Yorkshire's — line of left-armers, was Palwankar Baloo, a gentle 'Untouchable' who broke through the social barriers to play alongside superior castes, and took over 100 wickets on the 1911 tour of England, spinning the ball from leg and from off. Baloo had no Test match cricket to measure himself by. The wondrous four of the 1960s and 1970s climbed to the top and successfully challenged England, Australia, New Zealand and Pakistan. Their successors are prejudged, which is their inevitable misfortune.

Bedi's rivals among left-arm slow bowlers included Shivalkar and Goel, who were actually a little older, and Rajinder Singh Hans, of the flowing WG beard, who took 9 for 152 for Uttar Pradesh in the Ranji Trophy final of 1977-78; but missed the higher call which brings national idolatry and a little wealth. The man entrusted to carry on Bedi's good work — it being thoroughly understood that no-one would ever take the place of

Chandrasekhar — was Dilip Doshi, the cultured little Bengali whose patience was rewarded in 1979 when he won his first Test cap against Australia. Bobbing enthusiastically up to the crease, emphatically side-on, he peered through his horn-rims, gave the ball a businesslike twist, with plenty of left shoulder and downswing of the arm, and proceeded to share Grimmett's record of taking 100 Test wickets after having made a Test debut when past the age of 30 (Mailey took 99). Doshi flighted and spun well, and took 101 wickets for Warwickshire in 1980 before a setback in the following season. His Test career was not so smooth either. Friction with captains, selectors and journalists led to his taking up a defensive position, and, though he seemed still to have years of prosperity ahead, he was overlooked for the 1983 Caribbean tour. Favoured for the left-arm spin spots were Ravi Shastri and Maninder Singh, with the teenaged Sivaramakrishnan a tender leg-spin hope. Shastri was an obvious prospect as he dominated youth internationals, and when he was flown to New Zealand early in 1981 as a reinforcement, he instantly impressed with his confidence — he was not yet 19 — by taking command of his field placings and taking 4 for 54 and 3 for 9. Tall and sleek in appearance, Shastri made advances as a batsman, giving rise to hopes that another Mankad might be in the offing. Dangerous hopes. Maninder, who had a rough time in Pakistan on his first tour (when a petrol bomb fell near him during the Karachi riot) was variously regarded as the best of prospects ... or just lucky to receive the selectors' early support. Certainly, at 17 years 193 days, he was the youngest Indian to play in a Test, Sivaramakrishnan shortly relieving him of that record. The only other thing of which one could have been certain was that the supply of spin bowlers in India was practically never-ending, the game the more beautiful for it.

Not that all was lost elsewhere in the wide world of cricket, even if no population could compare with India's. During the 1970s, Australia boasted several quality spinners in every State. New South Wales had the tall Kerry O'Keeffe, whose arrival excited the ever-hopeful Bill O'Reilly, from whose old club, St George, he sprang. O'Keeffe, whose love of French cooking caused weight problems never entirely solved by road-running, had a peculiar action which threatened to give the umpire a thick ear. But he grooved himself to fair accuracy, and gradually came to rely upon an almost endless stream of overspun incutters, with a fearless short-leg fieldsman his major ally. He played in 24 Tests but managed only 53 wickets. Nor did a spell with Somerset advance his cause. Left out of the side for limited-overs matches, he became understandably morose.

O'Keeffe's style differed enormously from that of Terry Jenner, whose outgoing nature showed in his almost absurd trajectory. High into the air went the ball, spinning like a top, and the batsman did the rest. If he waited, he often perished. If he went to the pitch of it — or, better still, intercepted it before it pitched, as Garry Sobers so often did during his 254 for a World XI in Melbourne, 'TJ' was catsmeat, as he would have put it. He was shrewder than many gave him credit for, and widely-travelled. He was honoured by his country only nine times, but he did have some successes in West Indies, including a 5 for 90 in the fifth Test at Port-of-Spain in 1973. His fate was infinitely more agreeable than that of John Watkins, NSW's self-taught leg-spinner who was ready for the psychiatrist's couch after a 'meteoric' international career involving one Test, against Pakistan at Sydney in 1973, when, after years of consistency, he could not land the ball on a length for the life of him. As the sounds of mockery rose around him, he froze into a hopeless state. His analysis, which read a merciful 6-1-21-0, hid four wides and numerous long-hops and full-tosses. Poor 'Wok' did at least help Bob Massie put on a crucial 83 for Australia's ninth wicket in the second innings. Then, far from sparing him further suffering, the selectors packed him off on the Caribbean tour which followed immediately. With only 10 first-class wickets behind him at a cost of 39 each, Watkins had meagre prospects. And so it turned out. He took 10 wickets for 336 on the tour and played in no further Tests, returning to his job as a carrier of fruit and veg, a tale to laugh or cry over, but probably one which did leg-spin's cause untold harm.

There were other leg-spinners around in Australia who could claim high ranking. Bob Paulsen of Queensland and WA did well against several touring teams, and was as unlucky as Sri Lanka-born Malcolm Francke, a confident little operator who reckoned on a repertoire of seven types of delivery: only Queensland and Derrick Robins' XI — and Cornwall — were destined to benefit from them. Tony Mann of WA, son of an underarm spin bowler, learned to bowl leg-breaks on the verandah of their home, and went on to play through two decades for his State. He played four times for Australia against India in 1977-78, hitting a century from the nightwatchman position; but he found wickets hard to come by. Still, his love of cricket took him to the Lancashire League and Minor County success with Shropshire between Australian seasons, during which he often gave satisfaction by spinning out clusters of Test batsmen, home and foreign, despite being dropped by his State what he considered a record number of times.

On his day, Ian Chappell was a testing proposition for Test batsmen, letting loose wristy leg-breaks and wrong'uns from a strong action, though never with the success of Bob Simpson, another useful support bowler. Greg Chappell, too, began as a capable leg-spinner, but the calculating mind — during a spell of county cricket with Somerset — persuaded him to revert to seamers. The Chappell boys were destined to carve enormous niches for themselves as batsmen in cricket's Hall of Fame, even if they had never bowled a ball or touched a slip catch. The player who looked the genuine replacement for Benaud — following the years of the unorthodox Gleeson — was a young Victorian whose methods were as pure and copybook as Benaud's, Jim Higgs. His drooping eyelids suggested an unflappability and his long legs lifted him confidently to the stumps. The arm was beautifully high, the cocked wrist well controlled, and through several dreamy afternoons in the 1978-79 Ashes series the decades were rolled back as the Victorian bowled tidily for hour upon hour against Randall and Boycott and Brearley and Gooch. The dead pitches made his task more difficult, and his captain was not always aware of the best time to use him, but his economy (2.38 runs per eight-ball over) was admirable, his results (19 wickets at 24.63) highly satisfactory in support of the penetrative fast man Rodney Hogg. Besides which, Hogg and Higgs had a distinctive ring about it as a bowling duo. A year later Higgs spun Victoria to victory in the Sheffield Shield by taking 6 for 57 against SA on the final day, stopping Ian Chappell and company in their tracks. That was the season, 1979-80, when he took his Test-best, 7 for 143, at Madras. But the hopes of a steady Test career were dashed as the going got harder. Groundsmen were as much to blame as the selectors. Higgs, like any skilled leg-spinner, needed a surface with pace and bounce in it. At least he had posted himself in the Marriott/Chandrasekhar class by going through a tour (England 1975) without making the slightest impression as a batsman. He faced only one ball throughout — and was bowled by it.

One spin bowler spanned the 1970s for Australia with a reliability and potency that persuaded Greg Chappell to the opinion that he was the best spinner he faced. This was Ashley Mallett, a Sydney-born Western Australian emigre to Adelaide who became the best off-spinner produced by his country. He trapped Cowdrey lbw with his fourth ball in Test cricket, at The Oval in 1968, when Gleeson had tied up Dexter and bowled him with a googly. Australian spin could hold its head high. Mallett — 'Rowdy' for his sparse conversation — made a comeback or two during his lengthy career, resuming Test cricket after a few good paydays with World Series Cricket. Tall and facially not at all dissimilar to Benaud, he used his height to effect, bowled a nagging length and gave the ball a sharp tweak that drew response from even the deadest wicket, his pace then a good deal brisker. When he formed the perfect adjunct to the Lillee/Thomson blitz-krieg, while waiting for the fast men to tire and the ball to become rough from the impact upon pitch, bat and ribs, he would pick up gully catches that were even more astounding when it was realised that he wore contact lenses, and was also about the most clumsy person ever to have played Test cricket. If he wasn't treading on the ball and spraining his ankle, he was spiking his own fingers, or tripping over the stumps. He once swallowed sleeping pills instead of salt tablets, and batted with unaccustomed dreariness. And he was a nervous air traveller, smoking non-stop, setting fire to his newspapers, downing Scotch — and spilling it accidentally, thus putting out the imminent conflagration. A professional journalist, Mallett dazzled his colleagues with a tartan sports-coat during the Melbourne Centenary Test match, when it was thought that his Test days were behind him. But he went on again, and took his tally for Australia to 132, at just under 30, in 38 Tests. For South Australia, he earned over 340 Shield wickets, placing himself above Tony Lock's 302 into second place behind Clarrie Grimmett (513), who coached him so beneficially in his early days.

From the assortment of spinners playing in Australia as Mallett's career drew to a close, another off-spinner, Bruce Yardley, emerged as the big surprise of 1981-82, when his 51 Test wickets in 14 innings against Pakistan, West Indies and in New Zealand made him the International Cricketer of the Year despite all the batting and fast-bowling competition around him. Originally a fast-medium bowler, 'Roo' Yardley (nicknamed after the lean kangaroo dog) was encouraged to switch to off-spin by Keith Slater, who had done the same in the late 1950s. Gradually lengthening his run, Yardley developed a capacity to extract sharp bounce, and his odd grip, in which the spin was applied by the long middle finger rather than the index finger, lent itself to a good faster ball as well as an outswinger, a relic of his baseball days. It took him a dozen seasons of cricket for Western Australia to graduate into the Test team, and the 1978-79 English side were not generally impressed with his bowling. He missed the 1981 tour of England, but in the Australian season that followed, advised by wicket-keeper Rod Marsh to slow down and develop more loop, Yardley suddenly showed as an off-spinner with command of all that mattered — with perhaps only a modicum of accuracy still lacking. The drift, wide spin and control brought him riches in that unforgettable 1981-82 summer, when he twice took seven wickets in a Test innings. Australia lost one of those matches, to Pakistan, by an innings, and drew the other, against West Indies. But a year later his contribution towards England's defeat was substantial, his long spells tying up batsmen who would have liked to have celebrated their release from the grip of the pace men. To the relief of all Australia, there seemed no suspicion of any irregularity in his action such as caused umpire Sang Hue to call him for throwing in Jamaica during the 1977-78 tour. Predictably, though, there was no room for Yardley in the international one-day tournament following the '82-83 Tests. Like Higgs, he was regarded as a five-day player. Those who shaped such policies could not get it into their heads that high-quality spin is more difficult than fast-medium bowling to hit without risk.

The signs were that slow bowling was not yet quite in the intensive-care unit in Australia, even though Victoria's Ray Bright had forsaken classical methods in favour of a flatter trajectory. The fault lay less with the player than with the selectors, who had shown less than complete confidence in him. A tempestuous nature argued against the ideal slow bowler's approach, yet 'Candles' Bright was a State player at only 18. Success on tours of New Zealand and England suggested a long tenure, but after participation in World Series Cricket, where the opposition was stiff, and a tour of Pakistan, where he took 7 for 87 in the Karachi Test and 5 for 172 from a marathon 56 overs at Lahore, something seemed to drain from his game. Once more, though, the spinner's aims and ambitions can be spread over a playing lifetime at least twice as long as that of a fast bowler; and patience is usually inbuilt. Bright became Victoria's captain in 1983.

Graeme Beard's promise as an unusual off-spinner was cut short by early retirement, while David Hourn, the swarthy little NSW left-armer, proved to be no more than an anachronistic shadow of Fleetwood-Smith, even though he could make batsmen and wicketkeepers look utterly stupid with his googlies and top-spinners. Constant accuracy was needed, and was never remotely likely to be forthcoming. Murray Bennett, an orthodox left-arm bowler with a teasing parabola, quickly gained recognition during the 1982-83 season, and a cluster of hopeful leg-spinners practised their wares in several States. Trevor Hohns of Queensland had some field-days; Peter 'Sounda' Sleep, though blooded too early by Australia, seemed a good bet in that his batting warranted at least a middle-order place, giving scope for leg-spin as and when required (Rex Sellers made him a side-on bowler and talked him out of forsaking leg-spin); Stuart Saunders bowls with a challenging natural loop, and was Tasmania's 1981 Esso scholar in England; Bob 'Dutchy' Holland, though in his mid-thirties, is one of the finest players to come out of Newcastle, NSW, and could yet join the list of leg-spinners and others who have been capped by their countries at an age when others are reverting to their gardens at weekends. The Queensland selectors fanned the flames in 1980-81 by recalling Dennis Lillie, a 9 stone (57 kg) 5ft 5ins (165 cm) leg-spinner who had last played for the State — without success — 15 years before, when he was only 20. And young Greg Matthews, NSW off-spinner, rose swiftly during the 1982-83 season to merit an Esso scholarship to England. And while Allan Border, not without a certain self-consciousness, tossed guileless left-armers down as would-be partnership-breakers in Test matches, a young man in Adelaide appealed to Ashley Mallett as the most exciting spin prospect he had ever seen. This was Malcolm Dolman, a dapper little figure who impressed with the Australian Under-19s in England in 1977, and made his Shield debut in 1981-82, when his left-arm off-breaks, googlies and top-spinners were not seen at their best. As with Fleetwood-Smith and so many others, more accuracy would have led to the severest challenge to even the highest class of batsman. Tom Hogan, the bearded Western Australian, took five Sri Lankan wickets in the second innings of his maiden Test and bowled meanly in his 1983 World Cup appearances, suggesting regular employment in the years ahead, even if the life of a slow bowler in international cricket was now seldom secure.

Australia's administrators were not doing much to 'save the spinner', though the abandonment of bonus points and the minimum ration of overs per day did something to help, even if there was no immediate rash of stumpings and outfield catches off slow bowlers. Oldfield stumped 28 batsmen off Grimmett in Tests, Grout 11 off Benaud. Marsh standing up at the stumps looks as natural as Nelson standing among the lions at the foot of his column.

The South Africans, during the early years of their period in the wilderness, produced a fine leg-spinner in Denys Hobson, whose greatest day was when he took 14 wickets between breakfast and supper for Western Province against Natal in 1975-76. The Springboks naturally thought him good enough to take his place in any World XI, just as Transvaal's Alan Kourie was considered a world-class slow left-arm bowler. West Indian

Lawrence Rowe, during the historic and tremor-making tour of South Africa in January 1983, remarked that Kourie did not spin the ball a great deal, but made it dip and come in awkwardly. 'Big Al', who facially is a fleshier Bruce Yardley, lets the ball go from behind his head, which, as with Jeff Thomson's hidden right hand, makes for late reading of the path of the ball. One of the most unlikely analyses to be reported in the early 1970s was 9 for 71 by Mike Procter, for Rhodesia v Transvaal at Bulawayo. It would not have been unlikely if 'Procky' had been bowling his usual terrifying fast stuff: but on this occasion he was dispensing off-spin — a medium that was to come in useful as his knees began to crack under the strain of his long sprint and punishing action.

Pakistan has continued to produce a stream of spinners, some full-time, some all-rounders who dabble only occasionally. Wasim Raja showed promise as a purveyor of mainly top-spinners and googlies, while Maazullah Khan was sent to England in 1974, billed as 'lethal' and 'unreadable'. The county players must have worked him out, for his end-of-tour figures were 68-16-183-1. Mohammad Nazir junior, an off-spinner, had some good times against New Zealand in 1969-70 (7 for 99, six of them bowled, in the Karachi Test) before spending a wicketless Test against England at Hyderabad: another 'mystery' man undone by the Holmeses and Watsons in pads. Majid Khan, initially a pace bowler, was a deceptively good off-spinner. His apparently innocuous offerings brought the downfall of Boycott, Gower and Botham in a World Cup quarter-final at Headingley in 1979. Javed Miandad, who has never lacked confidence, looked to be a highly promising leg-spinner until his own booming batsmanship and a pool of regular bowlers crowded him out. Pervez Sajjad, a left-arm spinner with a cramped and rather musclebound action, toured England twice and also plagued New Zealand home and away. Being a graduate in psychology would not have harmed his cause. Next in line was Iqbal Qasim, a quiet, round-faced, moustachioed left-armer from Karachi who stealthily crept up the table of Pakistan's Test wicket-takers, bagging his 100th wicket at Faisalabad against Sri Lanka. Qasim is anything but a colourful cricketer, and will tend to be remembered more for having his mouth horribly lacerated by a Willis bouncer at Edgbaston in 1978, or for the punishment he had to take from Botham's weighty bat in a one-day international at Old Trafford four years later, than for his 7 for 49 in the Karachi Test against Australia in 1980, the same match in which little Tauseef Ahmed entered Test cricket — and the peculiar politics of Pakistan cricket — with 4 for 64 and 3 for 62 with brave off-spin. It was a source of concern for Australian radio and TV commentators when off-spinning all-rounder Ejaz Faqih was chosen for the '81-82 tour of Australia, and a source of relief when form restricted him to only one Test, when he ran into a full-blast double-century from Greg Chappell at Brisbane.

The Pakistanis left probably their best spinner at home for that tour. Yet Abdul Qadir, the bouncy little preacher's son from Lahore, was soon to emerge as a torchbearer for leg-spin, an operator who bemused dozens of county batsmen in the best Freeman tradition, and whose concealment of several varieties of top-spinner and googly was to baffle the best England had — including some eminent men in the television box who attempted to call the ball in flight. Sadly, the old problem of lifeless pitches denied Qadir full reward, though on one notorious occasion he seemed to be doing his best to improve conditions for himself as he jumped up and down on a length, frantically appealing to the umpire to change his mind about an lbw appeal after Botham had been struck on the pad by a full-toss. Those who had toured Pakistan in 1977-78 had not forgotten the powers of 'Bau' after he had bemused them with 6 for 44 in the Hyderabad Test, which was then the best-ever by a Pakistan bowler against England. A year earlier he had taken 66 wickets in 11 matches for Habib Bank, and his examination in top company was eagerly awaited. Almost inevitably, he did not become a fixture in the Test team, but he was lucky in having a captain, Imran Khan, who believed in him to the point of insisting on his selection. With his indispensable prayer mat in his bag, Qadir marched off to face the Australians after his successful English tour, putting them on the rack with 5 for 76 at Karachi and 11 for 218 in the Faisalabad Test. But against India a few weeks later his figures suffered as he tried for too much variety. 'He tried to be very smart,' said his skipper, not without a certain compassion. Qadir's case strengthened when, in 1982-83, he became the first bowler to take 100 wickets in a Pakistan season.

Abdul Qadir thus bore the responsibility of holding a life in his hands, for true leg-spin, delivered from a compact, even cocky, approach and with all the mystique of a dozen different wrist-angles allied to strength of finger and pinpoint length, really belonged to another age. Was this the last example? Was he the Truganina of the race? Or would youngsters discern from his methods that pace and economy were not all? That leg-spin could be fun as well as matchwinning?

Already New Zealand seemed to be following the other countries in viewing speed and containment as the keys to success. Hedley Howarth had been a master of languid left-arm spin, gathering 86 wickets in 30 Tests between 1969 and 1977. Among other left-armers, David O'Sullivan, though his action seemed borderline to some, played 11 times for New Zealand, holding an end down, and actually insinuating his way to 5 for 148 in an Adelaide Test, having taken a few wickets in three seasons with Hampshire. After 'Daffy' came Stephen Boock from Canterbury, tall and steady, a New Zealand domestic record-holder with 66 wickets, but almost a non-playing member of the New Zealand team on his historic debut, when his country won their first-ever Test against England, at Wellington. It was a sign of the times when Boock requested a return home during the 1980-81 tour of Australia because he was getting no cricket midst all the Test matches and one-day internationals. It left motor mechanic Peter Petherick's performance at Lahore in 1976 as a glowing museum piece: an off-spinner, in his maiden Test at the age of 34, taking a high-class hat-trick (Miandad, Wasim Raja and Intikhab). A year earlier, in his first season,

Petherick had taken 9 for 93 for Otago against Northern Districts, and hopes rose. The Pakistanis put an end to that. After their Lahore aberrations they took him for 158 runs in the next Test, and the Indians did not exactly dislike his flighty off-spin.

Nowhere, though, was slow bowling in such a poorly state in the eighth decade of the 20th Century as in the West Indies territories, where there has never been any noticeable predilection for subtleties. There may be deeply-rooted reasons for the obsession with fast bowling: man's own condition — a universal increase in civil violence coupled with a deep, ingrained anxiety regarding the threat of extinction without warning should the super-powers start pressing nuclear buttons. This, though, seems nowhere a more remote possibility than in the idyllic Caribbean islands. It is there that the boys play cricket on the beaches, in the small, dusty streets, and wherever they can find some flat ground. They play with all kinds of makeshift equipment, and with very few exceptions they want to bowl fast, like Holding and Roberts and Croft and Marshall and Garner. They have no Ramadhins and Valentines to copy. The fault, then, lies with those who manipulate first-class cricket. And it is hard to argue against the logic of picking your *best* bowlers, and if they happen all to be fast men, so what? Selectors, captains and players imbued with the need to win prizemoney and national — even religious or racial — 'honour' care little for aesthetic balance. The spectacle, though, can be killingly boring. It would be so if nothing but slow bowling was on display all day, even though more overs would be bowled.

West Indians may argue that slow bowling has won them few victories in recent memory. Even Jack Noreiga's 9 for 95 against India at Port-of-Spain in 1971 — the first-ever 'nine-for' for West Indies — was not enough to win the match. To which the retort might be: 17 West Indies wickets were secured by India's spin bowlers.

Noreiga's was a romantic tale. A Trinidad stationmaster's son, he used to practise his off-breaks against the wall of the railway station every night until it was too dark to continue. He had begun as a batsman, but his pride was so badly bruised when a local off-spinner repeatedly bowled him out at the nets that he 'borrowed' his grip and began sending them down himself. A tall, jovial man, Noreiga seemed to have missed high honours, until Wes Hall urged his selection once more at the age of 34. He took 12 wickets against Barbados, won his first Test cap at Kingston, and, within the fortnight, was working his way through the Indian first innings at Port-of-Spain — Gavaskar, Durani, Wadekar, and after the rest day, Solkar, centurymaker Sardesai, and down through the tail: 9 for 95 off 49.4 overs. Grayson Shillingford, who took the first wicket, said to him as they trudged up the pavilion steps: 'We was real unplayable. We wreck them.' One wicket at Georgetown, dropped for the Bridgetown Test, and 5 for 129 back on his home track in the final innings of the series, and that was the end of Noreiga's Test career. Inter-island rivalry, suspicion of his age, or whatever it was, the selectors thereafter ignored the bowler who had surpassed the eight-in-an-innings by Valentine and by Gibbs.

Inshan Ali promised more than his eventual 34 wickets in a dozen Tests, a boyish little left-arm over-the-wrist bowler who confused and dismissed Sobers several times. The young man from Trinidad became one of the select few to top 100 wickets in Shell Shield cricket, and England's batsmen were usually relieved when he was removed from the attack, even if his figures were seldom flattering — and Frank Hayes hit him out of The Oval during his debut Test century in 1973. Raphick Jumadeen, also from Trinidad, gave West Indies sound if unspectacular service as an orthodox left-arm spinner in 12 Tests, and formed a testing duo with Inshan. Jumadeen's 130 Shell Shield wickets constituted a record which pleased all who love the slow bowler's art. He could tie up batsmen in limited-overs matches and once held Combined Islands at bay when they needed a mere four runs off the final over. 'Jummas' would have played more frequently in Tests had the obsession for speed not already begun to take root. Fortunately for him, his captain, Joey Carew, knew how to handle him in inter-island games. This same Carew, essentially an opening batsman, had himself had an incredible spell in a Test against England at Port-of-Spain in 1968 when he bowled 90 successive 'off-spinners' from which no run was taken. It was a dreadful day's cricket, with Boycott, Edrich and Cowdrey almost strokeless, and Rodriguez having started with what Jock Barker described as 'the most horrible over ever bowled in a first-class match': a no-ball, a wide, two full-tosses and three long-hops. It was a maiden. Spin, we salute you!

Arthur Barrett had shown class as a leg-spinning all-rounder, becoming the first to score a century and take 10 wickets in the same match for Jamaica. He had the necessary qualities of personality to make him a winner — lighthearted and ever ready to smile — and though he turned not lavishly, the ball could spin either way or go bouncily straight on. A new left-arm spin wizard seemed to have emerged in 1973 when the dreamy-eyed Elquemedo Willett was chosen for the tour of England at the age of barely 20. Before his brief (five Tests) international career was over he had perplexed some eminent batsmen with his stealthy methods, boxing in the Australians as he took 2 for 124 off 65 overs in Bridgetown on his Test debut, and 3 for 33 off 28 overs in the next Test, on the receptive Port-of-Spain pitch. Though he failed to make the Test team during the UK tour, he went quietly about his business, and had field days at Swansea, where he took 8 for 73 against Glamorgan, and when he took 5 for 35 against a star-studded Gloucestershire line-up. Many thought Leeward Islands' first-ever Test player would return with the next West Indian team, but by 1976 the transition to almost undiluted pace was nearly complete. Albert Padmore, the Barbados off-spinner with almost an exact Lance Gibbs look-alike action — the short, knees-up approach and brisk arm-over — was given two Test chances, the first of which hardly helped his cause as India scored a sensational victory, making 406 for 4 at Port-of-Spain in the fourth innings, Padmore 0 for 98 off 47 overs. At Old Trafford a few months later his figures were 3-2-1-0, but by then everyone was still talking about the wicked onslaught on Edrich and Close by the fast bowlers.

Padmore did at least pick up some big money for his skills, managing the renegade West Indian tour of South Africa early in 1983. Derick Parry, a Leeward Islands off-spinner with an unsightly action, had in his turn collected a large pay-packet from participation in Packer cricket in Australia, having distinguished himself in a Test against Australia at Port-of-Spain in 1978 with a return of 5 for 15, even if all bar Yallop were tailenders. This man from the speck of an island called Nevis began his short Test career (he, like Padmore, was banned for life for touring South Africa) with a first-ball duck and a wide when it was time to test his big-turning off-breaks. He did, though, take 9 for 76 in a Jamaican innings at Kingston in 1980, and was unquestionably a force. It was just that he, like so many other spinners, did not fit into the West Indian scheme of things. Nor did Ranjie Nanan, the hefty Trinidad policeman who broke Inshan Ali's Shell Shield record with 32 wickets in five matches in 1982 (the record went to a pace man a year later when Winston Davis took 33). Nanan managed to scrape a Test appearance in Pakistan when Joel Garner was injured, taking a couple of wickets in each innings, and finishing top of the tour bowling.

Still Trinidad continued to serve up spinners of talent. Harold Joseph was heralded as another Ramadhin, bowling a mixture from a hand action difficult to decipher. Known as 'Joe', he took to cricket late for a West Indian. Born in Carapo Village in 1956 during the Test match in faraway Leeds, when Laker took 11 wickets as a warm-up for his Old Trafford *tour de force* (for the delectation of those who believe in the powers of the zodiac), Joseph was 18 before he decided to share his commitment to horse-racing. He took a hat-trick in his first official club match, developed the Ramadhin grip after discussions with an old club member, and was soon in the Trinidad side. Against the 1981 English side the diminutive civil servant took 5 for 116 in 51 overs, forcing the bemused batsmen to play him off the pitch, so hard was it to comprehend what he was doing to the ball as it left the front of his hand. Nor did the darkish background of the pavilion help matters. Boycott so completely misread him that he was bowled round his legs by a leg-break while thinking it was a harmless leg-side off-break. In an inter-island match Viv Richards, no less, confessed to having been flummoxed throughout by Joseph, though characteristically he put a century together. Perhaps as window-dressing, Harold Joseph was taken to Australia with the 1981-82 West Indian team. He hardly featured; but a year later he was back to play club cricket in Sydney, where wickets proved rather harder to come by. Still, when Chris Cowdrey found himself keeping wicket to Joseph's bowling, 24 byes accrued — a mild case of 'Ramadhin's revenge' when it is recalled what Cowdrey's father did to Joseph's inspiration at Edgbaston in 1957.

The highly promising Roger Harper, the tall off-spinner from Guyana, and Donovan Malcolm, orthodox left-arm from Jamaica, keep hope alive, but while West Indies use part-time spinners such as Viv Richards and Larry Gomes, just as the innocuous Alvin Kallicharran was known to toss down a few overs of off-spin, there is little to enthuse lads in the Caribbean whose natural disposition might be to deceive by flight and spin. For all the frightful apprehension concerning a possible dissolution of the Caribbean territories in their inevitable inability to reach unanimity in matters political, there would be one benefit only in the event of a split, and that is that Trinidad, if it were to take its place as an independent Test match nation, would restore the glory of spin. The reddish soil of that cosmopolitan island has bred so many fine spinners. Of late, they have blushed almost unseen, the international game the poorer for it.

The presence of a balanced and polished spin attack was an underlying reason for the welcome proffered by many to the new Test nation of Sri Lanka, who had the swift leg-spin/googly/top-spin of D.S. de Silva, the left-arm spin of Ajith de Silva and the off-spin of Kaluperuma to harry England in their inaugural Test match at Colombo in February 1982. The tension of the occasion reduced the Sri Lankans' effectiveness, and indeed Ajith de Silva, who teased Ian Botham with a sequence of widish leg-side deliveries, was to suffer a nervous breakdown during the disapproved Sri Lankan tour of South Africa later that year: a sure sign that Sri Lanka had left their condescended-upon backwater existence far behind them. Sri Lanka's spinners, in support of fast bowler de Mel and backed by several good innings, placed the island unexpectedly in a winning position against England by the fourth morning, and with Botham and Willis making little impression in the second innings, Sri Lanka were poised at 167 for 3, 162 runs ahead, with the pitch threatening to break up. Eight runs later they were all out. Bob Willis, the vice-captain, had whipped the England players into a fresh state of mental initiative during the interval, and with alert fielding and clever bowling, panic was inflicted on the Test newcomers. And the glory of it all was that, far from battering them into submission with rounds of heavy artillery, England had spun the match their way — Emburey lazily easing his way to Test-best figures of 6 for 33, Underwood finishing with 3 for 67 in 38 vice-like overs, a dashing six over long-on by Duleep Mendis having added to the entertainment. This was no sudden return to any 'golden days of yore'. It was 1982: this was apparent by the unsavoury sight of a close fieldsman in a helmet, and by the occasional yells of 'Catch it!' — cricket's vocalized ensign of corruption and mental retardation — when a ball popped up off the pad. But it was fast bowling followed by slow bowling, an all-round test of batting skills. The pupils were found wanting, but the youngsters watching at least had something to attempt to emulate.

Slow bowling — the hardest of cricket specialties to perfect. As the game becomes less intellectual in its growing obsession with one-day matches, with the consequent shrinkage in the role of the spinner, those who treasure the art of the slow bowler grasp at any straw. No fast bowler, they will say, could ever hope to match the feat of stamina of Indian leg-spinner C.S.

Nayudu who, in 1944, for Holkar against Bombay, had figures of 64.5-10-153-6 and 88-15-275-5 — 917 balls. Today's fast men buckle at the knees after 88 balls, let alone 88 overs. Ask Alec Bedser! The former chairman of Test selectors has been a regular and plaintive spokesman for those who feel that most young bowlers, fast or slow, are not prepared to put in the time and effort necessary to reach even a moderate grasp of the skills and strength necessary. Frank Allan developed his wrist while possum-hunting; Hugh Trumble had his feather target on the practice pitch; Albert Trott had a kerosene tin representing the obdurate Giffen; Clarrie Grimmett had his faithful dog to collect the ball; Wilfred Rhodes practised through the cold winter in a barn. In all probability every bowler who has ever devoted untold hours at solo practice has shared one quality: an undisciplined love for the game. That *cannot* be taught.

Which spin bowler has had the most profound influence on the game? The traditional answer is Bosanquet, whose 'wrong'un' turned the coaching manual inside-out. A facetious answer could be another of Huguenot descent, Benaud, by his important consultancy role during the Packer revolution — which ironically accelerated cricket's headlong dash into an age of media-bred brutality.

Nor, in pursuance of the traditional choice, Bosanquet, is the googly necessarily the last technical innovation, for the 'flipper', so much more difficult to bowl, came several decades later, and the Iverson/Gleeson middle-finger delivery after that. What is next? The off-break wrong'un, producing a leg-spinner from a hyper-cocked wrist? A back-spun 'hanger' which drops late? The scientist will say all this — and more — is possible. Batsmanship can hardly advance in technique. In fact, it has lost some of its features — the delayed late cut, the draw, the 'dog stroke'. The backhand ('reverse') sweep is no new thing. Mushtaq, Hughes, Botham are only continuing the line of Lockyer, E.M. Grace, Hornby, O'Brien, Fender, etc. Batting ingenuity has necessarily become directed towards survival against spoiling and persistent short-pitched fast bowling. How much more fascinating it has been to watch a world-class batsman wrestle with the complexities of dealing with an accurate and devious spinner.

Moves are afoot to 'rescue' slow bowling. In England, pitches are covered. Long ago, nothing was covered, which meant that after rain the spin bowler had a feast: not only was the wet pitch his to exploit, but there was no competition from the faster bowlers, since they couldn't stand up on the slippery turf. Then came covered run-ups, and the slower bowler — unless he was an Underwood — dropped behind the medium-pacer in the pecking order. Modern covered pitches, with the added instructions to make them reasonably turnable in the later stages of a match, are intended to bring the slow bowler back into the picture. Further, the 100-overs limitation on first innings in the County Championship, which again played into the hands of the faster bowlers, was scrapped. Next came the move to extend Championship matches to four days each. If boundaries were extended, no second new balls were permitted, and outfields were made less lush, the spinner could come back into his own. The know-all professional should be reminded that fine spin bowlers like Eric Hollies did not have to wait for the third day of a match before being of any use.

Limit run-ups if necessary — only two bowlers per innings being allowed to cover more than seven yards. Maybe the wicketkeeper should be compelled to stand up at the stumps for all bar the said two bowlers. Perhaps, if things don't work out and future spectators are denied the pleasure of watching a Mailey or a Laker, there will have to be two distinct forms of cricket, just as there are two kinds of rugby. The one-day match can have its excesses of pace bowling and ever-increasing violence. Let the highlights be shown on television late at night, graded X for over-18s only. And the three-, four- or five-day match can be played on a scale familiar to the ranks of old, where balance and beauty are paramount. Already it is becoming more than some batsmen can grasp that it is actually possible to feel relief at the return of fast bowlers to the attack.

Index

Gunn, G. 113
Gunn, W. 44
Gupte, S.P. 146-8, 174
Gwynn, Nell 14

Hewett, H.T. 47
Higgs, J.D. 176-8
Hill, C. 37, 50, 54, 61, 62, 65, 67, 68, 71, 80, 86
Hill, G. 117
Hill, J.C. 139
Hilton, M.J. 133
Hird, S.F. 127
Hirst, G.H. 32, 46, 53, 54, 66, 81, 95, 99
Haigh, S. 95
Hall, G.G. 163
Hall, H. 14
Hall, W.W. 152, 162, 182
Hallows, J. 74
Hamlet 11
Hammond, J. 14
Hammond, W.R. 96, 97, 105-8, 110, 114, 115, 120
Hampshire, J.H. 170
Hanif Mohammad 164
Hanley, M.A. 126
Hans, R.S. 174
Hardstaff, J. snr 65
Harenc, C. 19
Hargreave, S. 73
Harlow, Jean 92
Harman, R. 156
Harper, R.A. 184
Harris, D. 14
Harris, Lord 30, 40
Hartkopf, A.E.V. 102
Harvey, R.N. 129, 144
Haseeb Ahsan 145
Hassett, A.L. 85, 88, 107, 121, 125
Hawke, Lord 30, 40, 41, 46, 51, 60, 94
Hayes, F.C. 183
Haygarth, A. 15
Hayward, T. 30
Hayward, T.W. 44, 65, 66, 82
Hazell, H.L. 121
Hazlitt, G.R. 78, 83, 84
Headley, G.A. 92
Heap, J.S. 74
Hearne, A. 49-51
Hearne, J.T. 35, 46
Hearne, J.W. 84, 92, 98, 151
Heine, P.S. 164
Hemmings, E.E. 101, 171
Hempleman, Mr 106

Hendren, E.H. 92, 98, 107, 151
Hendry, H.S.T.L. 97
Hercules 70
Hitch, J.W. 56
Hitler, Adolf 92, 116, 118
Hobbs, J.B. 40, 52, 59, 67, 68, 70, 71, 76, 82, 84, 86, 87, 97, 101, 102, 157
Hobbs, R.N.S. 154, 156, 157
Hobson, D.L. 179
Hodgson, I. 30
Hogan, T.G. 179
Hogg, R.M. 177
Hohns, T.V. 179
Holding, M.A. 142, 182
Hole, G.B. 139
Holford, D.A.J. 162
Holland, R.G. 179
Hollies, W.E. 112, 119, 154, 170, 187
Holmes, E.R.T. 110
Holmes, Sherlock 180
Hopkins, A.J.Y. 61, 82
Horan, T.P. 33, 60
Hordern, H.V. 61, 64, 68, 70-2
Hornby, A.N. 186
Hornibrook, P.M. 109
Horton, M.J. 136, 154
Hourn, D.W. 108, 178
Howarth, H.J. 181
Howell, W.P. 33, 34
Howorth, R. 121, 122
Huddleston, W. 74
Hughes, D.P. 152, 170, 172
Hughes, K.J. 186
Huish, F.H. 79
Humphreys, E. 80
Humphreys, W.A. 55, 56
Hunt, W.A. 109
Hunte, C.C. 164
Hurwood, A. 109
Hutton, L. 107, 108, 122, 125, 134, 137, 139, 151
Huxley, Aldous 92

Iddison, R. 26
Iddon, J. 96
Ikin, J.T. 121
Illingworth, R. 16, 18, 150, 151, 166, 167
Imran Khan 181
Indrajitsinhji, K.S. 173
Inshan Ali 183, 184
Insole, D.J. 131, 144
Intikhab Alam 164-6, 181
Inverarity, R.J. 160
Iqbal Qasim 180

A 200-year cavalcade of speed bowlers

THE
FAST
MEN

DAVID FRITH